Events Exposed

EVENTS
Exposed

MANAGING &
DESIGNING
SPECIAL EVENTS

Lena Malouf

CSEP, AIFD

WILEY

JOHN WILEY & SONS, INC.

Copyright © 2012 by Lena Malouf. All rights reserved

Published by John Wiley & Sons, Inc., Hoboken, New Jersey

Published simultaneously in Canada

For general information on our other products and services or for technical support, please contact our Customer Care Department within the United States at (800) 762-2974, outside the United States at (317) 572-3993 or fax (317) 572-4002.

Wiley also publishes its books in a variety of electronic formats. Some content that appears in print may not be available in electronic books. For more information about Wiley products, visit our web site at www.wiley.com.

Library of Congress Cataloging-in-Publication Data

Malouf, Lena.
    Events exposed : managing & designing special events / Lena Malouf.
      p.   cm.
    Includes index.
    ISBN 978-0-470-90408-4 (cloth); ISBN 978-1-118-11036-2 (ebk);
    ISBN 978-1-118-11037-9 (ebk); ISBN 978-1-118-11038-6 (ebk)
      1. Special events industry.   2. Special events—Management.   3. Special events—Planning.   I. Title.
GT3405.M34   2011
394.2068—dc22   2011011527

Printed in the United States of America

10 9 8 7 6 5 4 3 2 1

Life dealt me a blow in January 2006, when I was diagnosed with peritoneal spread of colon cancer, which is colon cancer that had spread into the abdomen. It was in a life-threatening stage, but due to one surgeon's unparalleled knowledge and skill, I came out of a groundbreaking ten-hour operation with flying colors. I am now, six years later, a cancer survivor.

I wake every morning and thank God and this surgeon. This exceptional man has given me many more years with my kids, Shaz, Gregory, and Brett, and their respective families. How could I ask for more?

Therefore, I dedicate this book to
Professor David L. Morris and his medical team.

David L. Morris, MB, ChB, FRCS, MD, PhD, FRACS
Professor of Surgery
Head of Department of Surgery
St. George Hospital
Kogarah NSW 2217
Sydney, Australia

Contents

PART ONE: All About BUSINESS

PART TWO: All About DESIGN

Many special events professionals are proud of the passion they have for this business. But very few are able to combine that passion with professionalism. And fewer still are able to turn their passion into a business that turns a profit. Lena Malouf is one of those select few. I have known Lena for more than a decade, and I have always been impressed by her unique combination of design creativity and business sense. If you pay attention to her advice in this wonderful book, you just might find the same success she has achieved.

Events Exposed provides a blueprint for success in the events industry based on Lena's years of experience. And in addition to sharing her own expertise, she has also recruited some of the top talents in events today to share their approaches to the best in event design and production. For example, turn to Point 2 for a rich array of mission statements from the leading event producers today. If you've ever wondered how the top event professionals in our business stay at the top, you can find their road maps here.

This book is also a treasure trove of insider's tools of the trade. Did you know that your crew's parking fees can scuttle your profits if you let them? Learn more in Point 6, where you will also find insider tips on how to invoice clients. Later chapters include information on the key elements to include in a proposal, an invaluable list of which team members should handle which tasks, and much more. Read on to learn what to check for in the ballroom directly before guests arrive, the dangers of mixing puce pink and orange, and why you should study *ikebana*.

Besides offering all these specifics for event design and production, this book gives you solid management techniques for any business. I often hear event professionals stress their passion for this industry. But without strong management skills, passion might not lead to profits.

If you didn't already know, Lena has won the *Special Events Magazine* Gala Award for Lifetime Achievement in recognition of her venerable event resume, her leadership in the industry, and her generosity in sharing her expertise. In light of how many event "stars" seem to flame out in a couple of years, a career as long as hers and at the level of hers is worth watching.

Watch—and learn!

—Lisa Hurley

Editor

Special Events Magazine

Preface

I write about a field I love and have been successful in: the business and design of special events. Writing also provides me with an opportunity to expand and share my knowledge of this ever-changing and innovative industry. I have indeed been very fortunate, as I have experienced a journey that has given me a spectacular career.

As I reflect on how this career of mine started, it seems that I was groomed from an early age for a life in business. I spent my childhood in the big general store run by my parents in a small country town called Canowindra in New South Wales, Australia. I often reminisce about this humble and uncomplicated upbringing. Without fully realizing it then, my loving parents, Nicholas and Rose, passed on pearls of wisdom through everyday conversations.

But it was only after I reached maturity that I truly understood their words and made their valuable life philosophy a road map to live by. I recall clearly Dad's words, "Always show respect; it will bring respect," and "Gather people in your life; they will be your richest asset." From Mum I would hear, "Do what is right; protect your reputation." The message my parents sent was clear: it is important to maintain a sense of goodness through life.

As a young bride, I moved from the country to the regional city of Wollongong, 50 miles from Sydney. During those next few years, I was blessed with three wonderful children. But soon it became obvious that I would be left to bring up my daughter, Shaz, and two sons, Gregory and Brett, on my own as a single mum.

In the late 1950s, while they were still small, I opened the Academy of Floral Design to conduct floral design classes in my home studio. It worked with the help of a nanny/housekeeper. But I also needed to learn more, so I began studying the art of ikebana under a Japanese master and continued to do so for about eight years.

In the mid-1960s I followed in the family retail tradition and opened a flower shop. My main competitor at that time had her flower store at the "top" end of town. She was always seen with huge pink rollers in her hair, pink fluffy slippers, and a pink gingham apron. It seemed to be the company uniform, but without a doubt, she had the funeral trade.

My retail studio was positioned at the lower end of town. I purchased and renovated a bank building, and it became a showpiece. In regard to customers, I clearly wanted clients with more longevity than my competitor's, so I vigorously went after the wedding and party market. I learned on my feet and knew no fear. But then, that is the joy of youth.

The business grew and my work multiplied. Soon I was invited to teach commercial floristry courses at the Sydney Institute TAFE NSW. I made the decision to move to Sydney with my teenage kids. They shared the highs and the lows of their working mum even through their college years, and I believe that through this exposure they learned how to overcome any obstacle.

What followed were two years in television with the Australian celebrity chef Bernard King. My segment, "The Feminine Touch," was part of his show and it featured creative floral designs for the homemaker. By then I was ready for the larger aspects of the events business in Sydney. Shaz joined me around that time and we swung into specialization by servicing only five-star hotels and high-profile clients, planning corporate events, weddings, and parties.

We experienced the excesses of the 1980s, when "events" was the buzz word. As organizers, we programmed lavish spectacles with beautiful settings designed to leave both client and guest breathless.

In 1982 I was accepted into the prestigious American Institute of Floral Designers (AIFD), which marked the beginning of my international travels to demonstrate and present at conferences and industry symposiums. In 1988 I was introduced to the International Special Events Society, which led to an introduction to The Special Event (TSE) organization (Penton Media).

From the warmth extended to me in the United States and from the spirit of my American peers, I learned three very important lessons: that education and growth are a lifelong commitment, that competition can be replaced by cooperation, and finally, that sharing knowledge and skills with the upcoming generation will secure the future of this strong and respected industry. Because of my involvement with the United States, I was determined to make Sydney a part of the international scene rather than let it remain an isolated entity.

I was invited to start the first overseas chapter of the International Special Events Society. With strong support from a handful of Australian professionals—Glen Lehman, Merri Took, Ken Airth, Perry Snodgrass, Robert Johnson, Trevor O'Connell, Wayne Elstub, Tim Kennard, and the late Clifford Wallace—the Sydney Chapter was chartered in 1992.

Throughout the 1990s, I continued to deliver stage presentations at The American Institute of Floral Designers and The Special Event conferences, along with training programs for a range of industry organizations and academic institutions, including the International Special Events Society (ISES); the Meeting Industry Association of Australia (MIAA); the University of Technology Sydney (UTS); Macleay College, Sydney; George Washington University, Washington, D.C.; and the University of Nevada, Las Vegas.

I served as founding president of the Australian chapter of the International Special Events Society for four years, and then I was invited to join the international executive, where I served another four years before being elected international president. It was an exciting and fulfilling term. I focused my energy and efforts on membership growth, financial stability, and promoting and encouraging industry accreditation.

As I complete the manuscript for *Events Exposed*, I reflect on the challenges that event professionals have had to overcome in the economic downturn of the past few years. It has been tough; there is no other way to describe it. But although we don't have the budgets of the 1980s to work with, I think that the future of our industry looks strong. Because of this difficult climate, as business owners, we have learned to streamline our operations: we do not overcommit with staffing; we adapt to working with tight budgets; we regularly evaluate the efficiency of our companies; and we search for innovative ways to bring more value to our clients. As a result of our adaptation to adversity, we have become better businesspeople applying best business practices.

My career has brought many awards and accolades over the years, but in 2010 I was privileged to receive the very prestigious Life Achievement Award from The Special Event organization in New Orleans. Truly a highlight from the culmination of my involvement in special events.

Finally, I have loved centering my life around my work, and now whatever I do for the industry is for the love of the craft and the sincere friendships that will stay with me forever.

Enjoy the read!

Lena

Acknowledgments

I wish to express my sincere thanks to the following people and event associates, who have supported me in the publication of *Events Exposed*. See pages 225–227 for contact information for these generous contributors.

Olivia Edwards Bellevue Hill, of Sydney, for the strong assistance she has provided to me personally with the secretarial aspects of writing this book. Liv's sparkling personality has made our many hours working together fun.

Ava Zhan, book editor based in Tucson, Arizona, for working closely with me in the latter stages of editing this book. She has the artistic gift of reshaping a sentence or paragraph that makes reading a pleasure.

Michael Gebicki of Wordplay, Rick Williams of Platform XXIV, Maryrose Heffernan of MRH Solutions, Sydney, for assistance in editing the manuscript.

I am especially grateful to the American event companies that have strongly supported and sponsored my presentations at the annual Special Event conferences for years and in particular the following individuals:

Bill Pry of BBJ Linen in Skokie, Illinois. Bill is a very close friend. His beautiful tablecloths, seat covers, and table accessories are a pleasure to show. For a case study contributed by Bill, see pages 129–130. To view samples of BBJ's lavish linen collection, see color plates, Figures 4–14.

Craig Ferre, photographer of CFPStudio, Culver City, California. His photographic expertise has assisted me with this publication.

Laura Ferre of Get it Done!, Culver City, California. Laura's outstanding approach to conference logistics and coordination is complemented by her professional attitude.

Kelly Mace of Smithers-Oasis, Kent, Ohio. Kelly has given me strong sponsorship support for many years. Her attention to detail is to be admired.

Peter Van Antwerpen of Virgin Farms, Miami, Florida. The roses that Peter supplies for my presentations are stunning. Whether they are one-foot or five-foot in stem length, it is a sheer delight working with them.

Stephen Hamel of Fancy Faces, Covington, Louisiana. The range of high-style table lamps this company supplies complements any table setting.

Bob Kocher Jr. of Fortune Products, Inc., Lake Stevens, Washington. Bob's products are the answer when looking for innovative lighting accessories for any application.

Jack Weiner of Kool Party Rentals, Phoenix, Arizona. Jack is a valuable asset to the events industry due to his active sponsorship at The Special Event conferences.

Randy Rice of Lion Ribbon, Dallas and Atlanta. Any table or room design is enhanced by the use of Lion Ribbon with event decor.

Margaret Hofland of Accent Décor, Inc., Norcross, Georgia, and Dallas, Texas. Margaret supplies beautiful products and accessories for events and parties.

I thank my event associates of many years who have contributed case studies and other materials that will surely interest and benefit those in this industry.

Paul Venables, creative director of Venables Creating Entertainment, Drummoyne, Sydney, for providing the artistic drawings on the following pages, which illustrate Paul's artistic ability with the pen.

Fredrik Campioni of San Antonio, Texas, for the conceptual art on page 182.

Glen Lehman, CSEP, of Lehman and Associates, Ultimo, Sydney, for the case studies on pages 150 and 180.

Trevor O'Sullivan of DTS International, Darlinghurst, Sydney, for his contribution on pages 213–221 in the Appendix.

Jeremy Koch of Innovative Production Services, Botany, Sydney, for the case study on page 198.

Andrew Cameron-Smith of Wonderment, Brisbane, Queensland, for the case study on page 17.

Kellie Mathas of USA Hosts in New Orleans, Louisiana, for the CAD plans on page 69 for the TSE gala event 2010.

Meri Took of Staging Rentals and Construction Services, Alexandria, Sydney, for the stage photograph in the color plates, Figure 26.

Andrea Michaels of Extraordinary Events in Sherman Oaks, California, for the innovative CAD plans on pages 65–67.

Tim Lundy, CSEP, of Distinctive Design Events in Atlanta, Georgia, for the case study on pages 210–211 and accompanying photograph (see color plates, Figure 15).

Sean DeFreitas of Designs by Sean, Dania, Florida, for the case study on pages 202–203 and accompanying photographs (see color plates, Figures 38 and 39).

Cheryl Fish of Cheryl Fish and Associates, Las Vegas, Nevada, for the case study on page 154.

Joe Jeff Goldblatt, FRSA, professor and executive director at the International Centre for the Study of Planned Events at Queen Margaret University in Edinburgh, Scotland, for his contribution on page 37.

Robert Sivek, CSEP, and Deborah Borsum, CSEP, of the Meeting House Companies, Elmhurst, Illinois, for the company mission statement and event facility information on pages 12 and 24.

Wayne Elstub of VenueCAD, Dural, Sydney, for the event floor layouts on pages 59–60.

George Merkouris, Catering Sales Manager at the Four Seasons Hotel, Sydney, for the CAD plans on pages 56, 57, and 58.

Andrew Roberts, Business Development Manager at Sydney Showground/ Sydney Olympic Park, for the CAD plan on page 62.

Paul Davison, Audio Visual Services Manager, Sydney Convention and Exhibition Centre, for the CAD plans on pages 63 and 64.

Greg Pullen, Business Development Manager at Playbill Venue Management (Hordern Pavilion), for the CAD plan on page 68.

Refer to the Industry Contacts section on page 225 for further information.

I extend thanks to Christine McKnight, associate editor at John Wiley & Sons, Inc., in Hoboken, New Jersey, for guiding the editing and production of this publication.

I would like to thank Lisa Hurley, editor of *Special Events Magazine*; Kim Romano, special events manager; and Tara Melingonis, conference manager of Penton Media Organization, USA, for the invitation to present to thousands of event professionals over the past 10-plus years. These presentations have allowed me to promote the industry to the industry and also enabled me to act as a mentor to the young upcoming professionals who are the future of our business.

Personal Acknowledgments

Many people ask me about my children. Well, like any mother, I am totally biased. They are great adults, and I am proud to see that they instill the philosophy of their grandparents, Nicholas and Rose, into the lives of their children. My beautiful daughter, Shaz, is absolutely my best friend and from 2007 on, she has been a presenter at the International Special Events Conference in the United States. She has continued the family tradition of creative flair with practical ability, and she has outstanding design skills. We talk to each other as mother and daughter every day, and then, during the planning of events or major projects, we talk as one designer to another. I value this precious mother-daughter relationship.

I equally value the strong and loving bond I have with my two gorgeous sons, Gregory and Brett; both are dynamic businessmen and marvelous fathers who further enrich my life. We all get together for family breakfasts and dinners quite often, and it is always a ton of fun with loads of laughs.

I also wish to lovingly acknowledge my brother, Doug Malouf, who is indeed a man of honor. He has always been there for me, but more importantly, he has been a valued male role model for my three kids.

All About
BUSINESS

In today's business world, it is extremely important to have a plan to succeed in the special events industry. You need to learn and master a range of skills to build a successful company and to develop an ability to turn the mundane into magic.

Part One of this book focuses on the essential side of the events industry—that is, the business side. While some might consider the business aspect boring, it is an extremely important element. The following chapters offer advice on building your own events business based on my professional experiences. Whether you are just beginning or have been in this business for a while, you will find this advice useful. For those of you who are more seasoned, the pointers and case studies included will serve as a springboard for further development and a refresher for best business practices.

You and the Events Business

THE ROAD TO OWNING AN EVENTS COMPANY IS RARELY straightforward. Some are born into a family business, some are born with the need to make their mark, and others simply get tired of working for someone else. But wanting to be a business owner and actually achieving success in this field are two different things. There are many factors that can cause the failure of your operation no matter what your level of expertise and passion. It could be from lack of the basic organizational and business skills, poor money management, or failing to understand the needs of your clients. I offer the following advice to the inexperienced and experienced.

What Is Event Planning?

A professional event planner is a specialist who gets hired by organizations or individuals to plan and execute special events from conferences, parties, fundraisers, galas, company product launches and staff seminars to weddings, bar/bat mitzvahs, and anniversaries. That specialist planner is supported by their team of employees and usually outside contractors.

Such events are commonly referred to in the industry as "special events" because they are unique, special occasions to which guests are invited for educational, celebratory, or other reasons—as opposed to routine, everyday events in the life of a company or individual. Planning such events, particularly ones for hundreds or thousands of attendees, is typically a process that takes the professional from weeks, several months, a year, to sometimes longer to plan, coordinate, and organize. Throughout this book, I refer to parties and special events interchangeably, but always meaning the kind of events that professional organizers are hired to pull together.

The special events industry has evolved into a sophisticated field that today often requires professional credentials on top of organizational and creative talents, practical industry experience, and the passion and drive to succeed in the business.

According to Professor Joe Jeff Goldblatt, FRSA, executive director at the International Centre for the Study of Planned Events at Queen Margaret University in Edinburgh, Scotland, a bachelor's degree is a qualification for working within the modern event management industry. My take is that, in a perfect world, Goldblatt is correct.

However, the special events industry organizations now offer professional certifications that will benefit individuals who wish to come into this industry without a bachelor's degree, or even planners who have been in the industry for years. Accreditation status is always a plus and considered an essential advantage.

There are many individuals now that hold the Certified Meeting Professional (CMP) designation. Another new credential, the Certified Event Management Professional (CEMP), has been developed recently by the Canadian Human Resource Tourism Council. Both organizations bring very prestigious accreditation.

A certification, one very close to my heart, is the Certified Special Events Professional (CSEP), an accreditation that is growing through the International Special Events Society. According to the ISES Web site (www.ises.com), "The CSEP designation is the hallmark of professional achievement in the special events industry. It is earned through education, performance, experience, and service to the industry, and reflects a commitment to professional conduct and ethics." Moreover, an accreditation designation can make you more attractive to potential clients and employers.

Aside from professional degrees and certificates, I recommend that aspiring event organizers closely study a specific aspect of the event business. Formal classes at universities or colleges offer courses in production, technical light, sound, vision, set dressing, floral design, food and beverages, event marketing, and event management. This study coupled with practical work experience at an established events company is ideal.

Event planners who have decided to start their own events company will also need to educate themselves in the basics of running a business. This involves creating a business plan, being informed of the legal entity, and establishing an accounting system and a company identity. With a start up plan such as this, be advised by a business specialist and financial planner.

When just entering the field, you may be dazzled by the number of subfields, which include corporate events, public events, sporting events, weddings, fundraisers, and incentive programs. Beginners are best advised to choose one specific area at first and strive to become the best they can be in it before moving on to other specialties.

Allow me to share the reasons that I love working in this exciting profession:

1. The event planner gets to work independently with a talented and reliable team that he or she has personally assembled, and every event offers an opportunity to meet new people.

2. The event planner never experiences boredom as the range of events is broad and includes themed corporate events, press breakfasts, gala dinners, fundraising balls, weddings, staff programs, Christmas celebrations, theater nights, and sporting events.

3. The event planner has the opportunity to travel to other countries and interact with colleagues from around the world. This provides another perspective in regard to event planning and contributes to lifelong education.

4. He or she also has the opportunity to attend industry trade shows and conferences to keep abreast of current trends and the newest products on the market.

5. The interesting people the event planner meets and works with can also become his or her closest friends. This is due to the obvious dedication and passion of the people involved and the constant communication that is needed in planning an event.

Loving the work and the industry is not enough. Be aware of the more challenging aspects of running the business and organizing special events:

1. The long hours involved when there is a crack-of-dawn start and a midnight finish on event days

2. The administrative demands of mile-high paperwork regarding coordination, production, and management of events

3. The meticulous detail work pertaining to every facet of an event, from creating the proposal, developing the concept, and coordinating staff and contractors to the finalizing of financial details

4. The constant need to control the budget to ensure profit rather than loss

5. The necessity to be understanding of clients' needs at all times

Tips for Success as a Business Owner in the Events Industry

You may be motivated by the desire for more money, more independence, and more prestige, or simply crave the peace of mind that being your own boss affords: the comfort of knowing that you will not wake up the next day and find you no longer have a job. On the other hand, I know of some who have gone into business with the simple intention of buying themselves a job. The latter is the wrong approach and a short-lived dream because individuals who jump into the business for the wrong reasons may not have considered the real issues involved in building a company or understood the challenges that event professionals face each day.

Those with little or no experience often fall into the trap of believing that the grass is greener with ownership, and, admittedly, the events business looks great from the outside. When people ask me, "What do you do for a living?" and I respond, "Well, I am an event planner," I sense their excitement and desire to hear more. Their interest is evident and possibly they hold a deep-down desire to be just that. In fact, I rarely meet a person who does not want to be an event planner! Part of the reason for this is the movies, which have initiated a boost for the industry because they dwell on the glamour, the fun, and the fantasy. But remember that the movies and even the TV reality programs fail to show the blood, sweat, and tears that accompany this business.

Here are a few guiding principles that will help you succeed and avoid unnecessary hard lessons, discouragement, or failure.

> *Make Each Event Your Best Yet.* The industry is forever evolving with the times and current demands. There is a saying that "you are only as good as your last event." If you put on a great show last week, the clients expect you to put on an even greater show next time. Success is the key to repeat business, and it is important that your clients become your raving fans. You cannot beat word-of-mouth recommendations. Attracting lucrative jobs through referrals will bring growth and profit.

> *Always Be Profit Focused.* Any business principal must remain profit conscious. It is also necessary for all people in the business to play their part in being accountable and to exercise diligent oversight of financial resources. The business that keeps asking itself questions and that takes the necessary actions to improve is well on its way to becoming truly dynamic. There should always be a level of healthy discontent, so that you know you can perform at a higher level.

Watch Your Cash Flow. I am sure some of you have heard of businesses that have closed their doors because they have run out of money over a period of time. A cash-flow crisis can happen for a variety of reasons, but in most cases, with proper planning or sound advice, it can be avoided. The idea here is to always have cash reserves and money steadily coming in every month for both regular and unexpected expenses. Implement a system in which you get paid for every project in a timely manner (refer to Point 6, "Manage the Money," page 71). Then manage your spending wisely so your cash doesn't get trapped in items you don't need or won't use for a long while.

Have a Plan. If you are in this field without a plan, with low business expectations, or with only a hazy view of where you want to be, then absolutely nothing will happen. Your vision must be clear and your goals in sight.

What is it that sets some companies above the rest? How did they get there? And what are they doing that is so right? It is no secret. They achieve success through effective management, impressive leadership, driven determination, and consistent performance. This is the kind of enterprise you should aspire to build.

Top 10 Tips for Entrepreneurial Success

1. Be passionate about what you do; otherwise, you will not lift your level of competence and skill.

2. As the principal, you must be the one who takes responsibility for the company's success or failure.

3. It is your money being invested, so watch where it is going. Rumor has it that Oprah still signs her own checks.

4. Strive to continually learn from others. Find your mentors and observe their performance whenever possible.

5. Be willing to adjust your expenses and, if needed, seek advice from a professional financial adviser or accountant.

6. Market yourself and constantly look for new business opportunities.

7. Understand your clients' needs and learn about their corporate history and culture. Strive for frequent face-to-face communication with your clients.

8. Do not make the same mistake twice.

9. Live by the philosophy that "near enough is not good enough."

10. "Walk the talk." Do what you say you are going to do.

Develop Your Strategy

BUSINESS OWNERS SHOULD HAVE A TEMPLATE OR WORKING model for their business that can be implemented easily. Such a document involves the client, the team, and the contractors. From the smallest company to the largest corporation, every organization must have a vision, or reason for being, and also needs a well-prepared, well-thought-out tactical plan that becomes law within its place of business, from top management down.

One thing to remember: beware of a false sense of security. When your business is booming and the jobs are rolling in, you feel as though success is here to stay. When times are good, you may be tempted to take your eye off the finances, but this can and will be fatal.

I suggest that you follow these four overriding strategies when creating a detailed road map for your business:

1. *Bulletproof your business against failure.* Ensure that with every job, you have a plan for a profit. If you do not know the profit on any single event you undertake before starting the job, do not do it. It is a surefire way to show a loss. Some events business professionals might say, "Well, it is just a small job so the loss will be small, and I will make up for it with this bigger job coming up," but I advise that you always focus on the job at hand and never put your faith in future jobs that you don't have yet. The continuity of even small profits makes for a very healthy enterprise.

2. *Step up performance standards for yourself and your team.* Some event organizers think that their many years in the business give them the right to assume they know it all. They tend to neglect to check their own

performance or review their level of competence periodically. I believe that the only way I can improve my performance is to step back after every single job or presentation and ask myself, "How could I have done this better?" Question your abilities and realize that there is no end to learning. Regardless of our number of years in the business and our level of experience, we must strive to improve. Importantly, it is what we learn after we think we know it all that counts.

3. *Walk the talk.* If you lead the way by displaying positive attitude and skillful leadership, this professional behavior will flow down to your staff. As a result, their level of competence will keep improving because of the leader's example.

4. *Take full responsibility for the services you provide.* Some business owners blame someone else or a circumstance if their company is not doing well. But as they say, success comes from the top, and I believe so does failure. Accept responsibility for your company as the principal player.

The Mission Statement

A mission statement is a road map for any company, large or small, established or new. This statement, written in short, clear, and precise language, should express the company's purpose in a way that inspires the principal, employees, and anyone connected to the business. Every member of the staff needs to read and understand it. Your team members will be connected, committed, and powerful because they are clear on the aims and objectives of the company they are working for.

A mission statement provides a pathway to success. It enables a business to set standards; it says whom it will serve, what products it sells, or what services it will provide. It defines clearly the plan to meet the needs of its customers and bring about growth.

Start the process of crafting your mission statement by asking yourself or your team, if you already have one, to list proactive words or phrases that may generate ideas in relation to the following four areas.

1. *Purpose.* What is the unique purpose of your event's venture/business?

   The purpose is clear: you go into business to bring about financial security and to provide a comfortable livelihood. The purpose establishes the guidelines for what you intend to do for your clients and clarifies how you will provide the very best in event management services. You also need to identify opportunities and take advantage of the growth that they bring.

2. *Culture.* What key words would accurately describe the general aura of your company?

The culture of your business is the atmospheric environment in which it operates. This working environment is about you, the company image, and what you want to be identified with. For example, Chanel's culture is one of elegance, refinement, and class. Disney's is one of fun and bringing happiness to the family through entertainment. Culture, to me, is about atmosphere. When I walk into Nordstrom's in the United States, a salesperson approaches immediately and guides me through my shopping requests as well as offering fashion options. The company extends care, comfort, and a sincere sense of commitment to me when providing service. Why is culture so important to you as an events business owner? It is necessary to strive for a wonderful atmosphere in the workplace, not only for yourself and your staff, but also for your clients. You want your staff to say "I love working here," and as a result your clients will say, "I love being here."

3. *Value System.* What is the value system that guides your work and your vision?

If your value system is "artistry above all else," then the client who wants quality, creativity, and originality regardless of cost will be drawn to you. If your value system is "quality service at an affordable price," creativity might be a lower priority, subject to budgetary constraints or preferences to save money. In order to supply the best service or product possible, your attention to detail must be impeccable. When every single element comes together in meticulous order, the result is outstanding and unparalleled.

4. *Business Strategy.* What is the tactical plan that will ensure that you remain in business and profit by providing for your clients and staff?

Strategy refers to the direction your company will take, and it also dictates how you plan to achieve business success. Determine exactly what you want to do for the business and act on those issues to bring about success. It is necessary to create an appropriate process that gives you the plan to perform the work in logical sequence.

The following list includes examples of mission statements of a few established event businesses. You might note the variation of statements, but the objectives remain constant.

Extraordinary Events, Sherman Oaks, California
(Courtesy of Andrea Michaels)

Our name is our commitment.

Our purpose: To project your message and solidify your brand by providing creative solutions to your marketing challenges.

Our passion: Creating and producing your business communications and events with innovation and style.

Our plan: To listen to your needs and achieve your goals with your expectations exceeded and your budget respected.

Extraordinary Events: Our name, your expectation, stunning results!

Lehman and Associates, Sydney
(Courtesy of Glen Lehman, CSEP)

To create and execute distinctive, versatile concepts for the successful promotion of conferences, exhibitions, launches, and spectaculars by delivering a high standard of professional service to our clients, developing a strong working relationship throughout the process and into the future, with no event being too large or too small.

USA Hosts, New Orleans, Louisiana
(Courtesy of Kellie Mathas)

To provide the best possible services and to exceed client expectations each and every time, and as a result to be the destination management company by which all others are measured.

The Meetinghouse Companies, Elmhurst, Illinois
(Courtesy of Robert Sivek, CSEP, and Deborah Borsum, CSEP, past international presidents of ISES)

This company does not use a standard mission statement but instead, rallies their team around what they call the "5-Star Quality Statement: Quality, Professionalism, Service, Attitude, Teamwork." Each of these qualities is then broken down into specific subareas.

The quality statement was developed by this company to keep their team on the same page.

Malouf Consultancy & Design, Sydney

- To provide stunning event fashion through décor and florals.

- To develop a desirable culture for both the client and the team.

- To offer professional, uncompromising service and value.

International Special Events Society (ISES), Chicago, Illinois

The mission of ISES is to educate, advance, and promote the special events industry and its network of professionals along with related industries. To that end, we strive to:

- Uphold the integrity of the special events profession to the general public through our "Principles of Professional Conduct and Ethics."

- Acquire and disseminate useful business information.

- Foster a spirit of cooperation among its members and other special events professionals.

- Cultivate high standards of business practices.

And here follow the ISES Principles of Professional Conduct and Ethics:

- Promote and encourage the highest level of ethics within the profession of the special events industry while maintaining the highest standards of professional conduct.

- Strive for excellence in all aspects of our profession by performing consistently at or above acceptable industry standards.

- Use only legal and ethical means in all industry negotiations and activities.

- Protect the public against fraud and unfair practices, and promote all practices, which bring respect and credit to the profession.

- Provide truthful and accurate information with respect to all performance of duties. Use a written contract clearly stating all charges, services, products, performance expectations, and other essential information.

- Maintain industry-accepted standards of safety and sanitation.

- Maintain adequate and appropriate insurance coverage for all business activities.

- Commit to increase professional growth and knowledge, to attend educational programs, and to personally contribute expertise to meetings and journals.

- Strive to cooperate with colleagues, suppliers, employees, employers, and all persons supervised in order to provide the highest quality service at every level.

- Subscribe to the ISES Principles of Professional Conduct and Ethics, and abide by the ISES bylaws and policies.

Meet the Client

How important is your corporate image? And to whom? In other words, who do you most want to impress? I say your clients should be at the top of your list. They are certainly at the top of mine. Without clients there is no business. The bottom line aside, clients, along with staff, are the ones worthy of your focus.

Winning Your First Clients

Event planners who are just setting up their own companies must be in a position to establish their standing in the events industry. This standing must be based on their past or current work experience and training, in order for their ventures to succeed. For example, they may have decided to become event business owners because they have previously worked for a catering house, a four- to five-star hotel, a floral design studio or a production house.

They have most likely attended classes in the course of their choice to obtain a professional degree or certification. Such experience may provide these entrepreneurs with a network of initial contacts in the business.

But winning that first client is easier said than done. The best advice I can give is to take small but progressive steps to build a new venture.

New business owners are advised to utilize the power of networking to connect with industry contacts. Another important source of contacts for new businesses is to advertise their services by creating an information-rich, professional Web site and by looking into search engine optimization (SEO). The range of tools presented throughout the rest of this chapter will also aid new and experienced business owners in establishing a client data base.

Caring for Your Clientele

Most companies know that their clients like to feel appreciated. They arrange for periodical displays of gratitude toward regular customers in the form of a luncheon by the water, a dinner at a renowned restaurant, or perhaps a theater evening followed by a supper party. Such occasions carry an expectation on the part of the client as never before, and tossing something together at the last minute is not appreciated. It will read as paying lip service without a backup of sincerity.

Care is an emotion that is disappearing from our corporate strategies, yet it is the very thing our clients crave. Feeling cared for is the client's safety net. If the company can show it cares, clients can relax because they know that their important event is in very competent hands.

It is worth remembering that gone are the days when events were produced for pure entertainment as in the 1980s. Today, we talk about ROI, return on investment. If client companies are outlaying $100,000 or more on a special event, they want to be sure that they get a measurable positive impact on their business from that investment. One way for the event planner to show care for customers is by working with them to meet their desired business objectives.

Caring Retains Clients

When first-time clients have a need for an event to be organized, you want them to immediately think of you. How do you make this happen? By making your philosophy of client care a sincere experience. Do not allow technology to be the primary communicator. Have face-to-face meetings and present proposals in person at every opportunity.

When sitting with the client, the care you show will be evident. Be prepared to go the extra mile with a smile on your face and remember that your attitude and organized manner can be your secret weapon. Most important, establish two-way communication with your clients and remember to listen, not just talk.

Be responsive in regards to their needs by showing flexibility and demonstrate willingness to adapt to meet any request. Make your clients feel valued at every turn by showing respect for what they say, feel, and think because this kind of attitude will ensure that your professional relationships have a solid foundation. The result of this style of communication will bring the reward of repeat and referred business. Perform well and let your clients sing your praises to other potential clients.

Another way in which your company imprints itself on the mind of your client is the actual event you have organized. If the event shows organizational know-how everyone involved will be impressed, from the guests and the client to the contractors and your staff. If the impression is one of amazement, excitement, and confidence in

Launching "The Best Job in the World" Campaign: A Case Study

WONDERMENT

A. K. Cameron-Smith, Principal
Event Production: Concept & Management

The following case study has been provided courtesy of Andrew K. Cameron-Smith, principal at Wonderment, an event company based in Queensland, Australia.

In January 2009, Tourism Queensland launched the now internationally renowned "The Best Job in the World" marketing campaign: a contest to select a caretaker of Australia's Great Barrier Reef Islands for six months.

As a culmination of the highly publicized applicant-selection process (34,684 candidates from 197 countries applied), a live, several-day event was held on Hamilton Island in early May of 2009 to which 16 of the top candidates as well as representatives of the world's media were invited, for a total of 150 guests.

Wonderment was engaged a year prior to the event to serve as production consultant to Tourism Queensland's Marketing and Events team and as the event's producer. Andrew K. Cameron-Smith also served as the facilitator on the live event.

The client stated in a brief that it wanted a live event that would feel vital and energetic. The client requested an event representative of the region and its tourism product; the event was to be environmentally responsible, enormously appealing to a growing in-

ternational audience, safe, and cost-effective. Meeting numerous domestic and international media deadlines was a critical priority.

Wonderment partnered with contractors that specialized in feeding live events to the world's media in order to achieve the goal of meeting tight daily media deadlines. A dual-path HD satellite access and significant FTP capabilities were also secured.

Various components of the event were decided on in the first few months of production, including four inclement-weather contingency plans. Then, in February and March, only two months before the event, the plan had to be restructured six times to accommodate media representatives from additional countries. Effectively, the event expanded by 40 percent during this time period.

To illustrate the degree of involvement of the event planner in an event of such high media visibility and high stakes, Cameron-Smith and his key crew conducted four site inspections during the planning months. Cameron-Smith also conducted extensive meetings and briefings with all operators, inspected tide reports and transfer times, and personally flew all the routes anyone involved would be taking, whether by seaplane or helicopter.

The event turned out to be an outstanding worldwide publicity success. Every media deadline was met, the media representatives and the client were satisfied, and the event was produced under budget.

your skill, talent, and expertise, it will translate into new business through word-of-mouth referrals. The caring approach will bring long-term business to your company.

Another point to bear in mind is that if you organize 50 top-class events for a client, and if your 51st has not been successful because of a series of mishaps, it is the last one they'll remember. The previous 50 will be forgotten. That is why I repeat the industry cliché "you are only as good as your last event."

Client care always brings a positive result.

Fighting Complacency

One important question you have to ask yourself is, "Do I make it difficult for my clients to do business with me?" Also ask yourself, "Do I show intolerance when clients phone to inquire about something?" Put yourself in flashback mode and recall how you acted toward your early customers when you first opened your business. You would bend over backwards to meet the client's expectations; in fact, you would do anything to exceed them. Nothing was too much trouble, and the slightest hint of customer unhappiness or discontent would have you begging for forgiveness.

Over time, though, we can become client familiar, and as the business grows we take them for granted. We may find that we spend less time dealing with them face-to-face and when the client complains or airs a problem, we begin to dislike them. They become a source of aggravation. Clearly we will have problems holding existing clients if we are not in a positive, customer-service-focused state of mind.

If we send out the wrong message—the signs that silently say, "What a bother, I'm too busy for this," or "I don't need this at 4:00 p.m.," or "Ring me back, I'm on a job"—little by little, our business will be affected. We can't expect to keep clients only on our own terms. If your business relationship is based on arrogance and assumes that the clients will tolerate poor service, rest assured, they will vote with their feet; your competitor is there ready to serve.

As the business owner, learn to become the business barometer. There is the need to constantly audit the client relationship because the bottom line is this: if you wish to expand your client base and increase your business, it is essential to hold on to existing clients.

The Difficult Customer

Human beings get emotional, and very few things make them more emotional than parting with money. Arousing the right emotions can be a big help to you. On the other hand, stirring up the wrong emotions can have a very damaging effect on not only your reputation but on repeat and referred business.

There will always be some clients who you will find very difficult to handle. Don't get disheartened. No matter how good you are at your job, it is bound to happen. If a client starts to get heated, handle it like a professional. Don't get angry; empathize with the client and take action to solve the problem. Most important, don't give any potential argument a chance to develop. If you sense that tension with a client is likely to develop because of a personality clash, encourage the client to sit down with you so you can amicably resolve the complaint. Here are some top tips for dealing with a difficult client. Refer also to the appendix on behavioral styles on page 213 in regard to these points.

1. Remain positive and listen carefully to the complaint and rephrase the response to show you understand.

2. Once you know what the client does not want, you are one step closer to finding the solution.

3. If the objection is legitimate, work out with the client what you can actually do to satisfy him or her. One sure way to lose a client is to display indifference or boredom, or to aggressively argue your point of view. In short, clients' objections are clues to what they want.

Another tool for avoiding difficult clients is creating an atmosphere of trust as you work together. You can achieve this by making sure you follow up on promises, moving immediately to find the information the client has requested or the product they require. A top tip to avoid problems is "do what you say you are going to do." This is the best possible advice I can give because the basic goal when handling a customer complaint is to show empathy and help the client by providing what is right for him or her.

Build the Business

EVERY EVENT PLANNER I KNOW WANTS TO EXPAND HIS OR her business by servicing new clients. The foremost point to remember here is that gaining a new customer and losing an existing one equals no advance in business growth. The existing customers cannot be overlooked in the expansion process, as they represent repeat and referral business.

Keeping Existing Customers

The first thing to keep in mind is that communication with your existing clients must remain consistent. It takes directed effort to maintain and strengthen client loyalty (for more on issues of client care, see Point 3, "Meet the Client," page 15). Do not underestimate the aggressive competitor pursuing your clients in an attempt to secure their business. You want your client to say, "Thank you for calling, but we are very satisfied with the company that is looking after us."

While developing business growth, introduce a specific plan for the existing customers to monitor the service your company is giving this group; you can keep them happy by knowing what they want, while you also try to get more business from them. Sweat the small stuff with meticulous planning for each event to the best of your ability. Those $2,000 jobs can turn into a $20,000 windfall. If your clients are really happy with your work, they will surely tell 10 of their associates. If they are dissatisfied, they will surely tell 100.

Take the following steps:

1. Concentrate on high service through "over service." Be keen and willing to help, and do what you say you are going to do.

2. Implement follow-up phone calls or e-mail questionnaires for post-event client feedback.

3. Find new products that differ from those of your competitor and keep your current customers informed about these new offerings. Collect a wide range of new product samples or catalogs from trade shows that you can show the client during the planning process. The regular customer will appreciate your being up-to-date with what is new in technology, lighting, and special effects.

4. Offer the higher-end event as an option.

5. Create a system for informing your existing customers about newly added services and products, such as e-mail newsletters or news flashes on your Web site.

If there is any dissatisfaction with your firm through the client's verbal or written feedback, you will be able to detect this. You then have the opportunity to address a symptom before it turns into a problem. Your existing clients will become walking testimonials for your firm if their expectations are met. You will get client referrals from this base of existing customers. People are happy to spread good news, especially when you give them good news to talk about.

The Master Plan to Grow Your Client List

First, a Closer Look at Your Operation

The company image you present is long remembered, and, as they say, there's no second chance at a first impression. Components of this image are you, your place of business, your team, and the visual representations of your company such as your promotional literature, business stationery, and Web site. All must work for you, not against you. The way you professionally present yourself speaks volumes about the value you place on your position in the business. A poor image is self-defeating.

Your Place of Business

Your place of business, whether you own the property or lease the premises, will fall into one of three categories:

1. *The office only facility.* This commercial space is technically equipped to house your employed personnel, with an allocated area for client meetings, and is set up with communications pertaining to handling the business. This type of office area does not have staff working on sets, décor, or florals. This style of professional office based within close proximity to a city ensures easy traveling distance and access.

2. *Commercial office with separate warehouse.* This is an alternate commercial premises and allows the event planner to have an affordable office in the city with a separate warehouse out of town for the prefabrication of event props and floral designing. Ideally the rent for this commercial warehouse space is less expensive, but this depends entirely on the location of both office and warehouse.

3. *A factory/warehouse/office layout.* With this type of space, there is an area designated for administration, a specific boardroom for meetings with clients, and ample workspace for staff to assemble props and floral arrangements. Make sure that the administrative and meeting area is well equipped as a working office and that it is free of disturbances, noise, and interruptions as a result of any fabrications under construction.

An obvious advantage of this last option is that you are paying only one rent and have only one office/studio to go to daily. It may also be an inspiring setting for clients to visit. As they come to attend meetings, they get a feel for the creativity of your company and your team by observing your employees at work on the artistic aspects of events. With this commercial scenario, the clients will love your service if you hire a town car to bring them to your studio/warehouse for the meeting and return them to their place of business at its conclusion. (See the case studies on page 24 for more information on setting up an office space.)

Whichever type of facility you have, take the time now to reassess it in preparation for more clients and more business. Examine the following:

1. *The administrative area.* Evaluate its position and its capacity to accommodate extra calls, foot traffic, and perhaps new employees.

2. *The meeting room.* This room should be furnished with a board table for client and team meetings. Is it big enough, decorated tastefully, and up-to-date? Does it need any technical improvements, such as a screen projector or better wall insulation?

3. *The showroom display.* This allows clients to see and touch product, linens, or similar stock. Should it be revamped in any way?

4. *Event display areas that can showcase formerly used props and other items.* Do these need dusting, repositioning, or rearranging for more appeal?

5. *Decorative wall hangings.* This could include framed pictures of event work, framed accreditation diplomas, award photos, and press clippings for client viewing. Are they up-to-date or should others be selected?

Some may now say, "But I don't have this luxury of space, nor can I afford it." In any place of business, space is usually restricted, so you should work with it and be absolutely organized with inventory, props, and florals. You must be able to put your hand on whatever you need at any given time in an instant. A product that doesn't have its place or is not labeled in a workroom can be costly. You will either waste time looking for that product when you need it or you will waste money when you forget you had that item and need to repurchase it.

You and Your Team

Sight is the dominant sense and overrides all others, and the golden rule here is to avoid extremes. The way you dress does create a powerful impression. It can sug-

Office Spaces That Sell Your Business: Two Case Studies

Two outstanding events businesses jump to mind. Firstly, Theme Travelers Inc. based in San Antonio, headed by Tina Sturchio.

At Theme Travelers Inc., the moment the clients enter the commercial premises, they step into a fully theme-designed, spacious room with lights, sound, and music, and the theme changes on a monthly basis. This striking first impression puts them into a "must have this" mode. Once through the entrance, they walk into the office, which is divided into areas of specific function, including a room for conceptual art, a room for administration, and a studio showcasing event props. At the rear of the office area, there is a factory and workroom, where clients can view the construction of props and the end results. The impression clients get is of a well-organized workroom with casually but smartly dressed artists at work.

Secondly, the Meetinghouse Companies in Chicago, under the ownership of Robert Sivek, CSEP, and Deborah Borsum, CSEP. Both are past presidents of the International Special Events Society.

At the Meetinghouse Companies, the client enters a spacious building and sees smartly uniformed staff at work in the administration area ready to service the client. This area leads into a studio/factory-style space where floral designers and set dressers are at work, creating floral arrangements, painting, or making props. Rows of labeled inventory, from linens to props to glassware, are organized and ready for any party that may be booked. This big workspace extends to the well-run and orderly loading dock area, where trucks load in and load out the required equipment and products.

gest that you are reliable, professional, and efficient or indicate that you look far too casual to be organized. The choice is yours.

Your team represents you and the image of your company. Some event companies are quite happy to have their team members wear jeans with a T-shirt, or even sweat suits for some types of technical employees. Generally these garments are suited to staff handling technical equipment and staging units. However, only you can decide on the best attire for your crew; if you think that an informal look is acceptable for the image you wish to project, then it's your choice. Well-designed uniforms do work for some events businesses; however, the jury is still out on casual attire versus the more tailored look.

When your team members are on the job through the duration of the event it is necessary to give care to what they wear or how they dress. The formality of black is always safe. Black trousers, shirt, and tie with a jacket is a foolproof option for men, while a neutral-colored suit, pants, or skirt and jacket is appropriate for females.

When in doubt about the best professional look for you and your team, consult a wardrobe stylist. Be advised, and dress to impress.

Your Promotional Materials

Let me share an interesting story with you from a very close friend in marketing. This woman saw my company's promotional literature, and she asked, "How long is it since you updated your company collateral?" My response was, "I can't remember, but I love it!" Her next comment was, "It's out of date. You need a 'today' look." I still insisted, "But I think it's great." She advised me to go to the upcoming trade fair and pick up printed company profiles of my competitors. I did exactly that. Then I scattered those 24 company profiles, including mine, on the dining room table and proceeded to pick them up in order of my visual preference. I picked my company profile up at only around number 12! My friend was right; it was time for an update.

Here are some ideas to help you revamp your promotional materials and have collateral with clout:

Company Profile. Write up your company profile and have it printed, so it can be given out to clients. This needs to be a paragraph or two, not a chapter. Two hundred words in total should tell the story. If the profile is too long, the client will not take the time to read it. In addition, post the company profile on your Web site.

Letterheads and Business Cards. Have letterhead stationery, business cards, and company brochures professionally designed. Decide if you wish to have a classic or contemporary look. Ideally a style that is timeless and will not date quickly is best used.

Professional Portfolio. Create an impressively packaged portfolio for display in your office, so clients can view it when they visit. Include the following items in a beautifully bound black leather book to be placed on your studio desk for client viewing:

Press Clippings. Keep a file with all your press clippings for yourself, but show your clients the most important ones. There is no need to include every snippet in your portfolio, as the client will not have time to read it all.

Awards and Accreditation. The portfolio should contain photographs and copies of certificates pertaining to any awards you have received and professional development courses you have participated in. In addition, make sure to display these credentials in your office and on your Web site.

Client Testimonials. Select six impressive testimonials for inclusion in your professional portfolio. It is best to keep these testimonials short and sweet but detailed enough to attract the attention of the client.

Select Photos of Your Work. Feature your most impressive work to arouse the client's interest.

Web Site. You must have a Web site in today's world, and it will serve you best if it is well designed and easy to navigate. Populate your Web site with as much current information about your company as possible, making sure to include a collection of photographs of your work and testimonials.

E-mail Newsletters. You may find it useful to create a monthly or bimonthly newsletter to send to you clients. It could highlight changes in the industry and within your company, and announce new products and services you are offering. Just make sure to create newsletters that are educational and interesting. If your newsletters are not worthy of your clients' time, they will read the first one and then delete all the subsequent ones.

A List of Your Services. It is a good idea to have a concise list of all the services you can offer clients as an event organizer. Have the list printed for inclusion with promotional literature for clients' perusal and also present it on your Web site. The template on page 27 will help you create such a list.

Find the New Clients

It is time to talk about what you really want, and that is new clients.

Where do these new and prospective clients come from? Will they walk through the door? Probably not, because this is not the 1980s, when clients would book an

The following template is a document designed for you to present to the client. Use this as a guideline and detail the services you wish to provide.

The Services We Offer:

Event Management

Coordination of components

Meticulous planning

Detailed schedules for pre-, during, and post-event

Contractor recommendations and source quotations

Event budgets

Production

Professional services for production team coordination

Venues

Location selection

Liaise with venue operator

Contract review, including limitations and restrictions

Advice on stage layout

Mapping of floor and table charts

Food and Beverages

Menu creation

Advice on style, timing, and service

Overseeing back-of-house activity

Technical Services

Visual production

Innovative lighting

Audio and special effects

Entertainment

Unique and exciting options presented

Feature artists, speakers, and music bands

Artists/entertainment requests

Specialty acts and site performers

Décor and Thematic Concepts

Venue transformation

Stunning set dressing

Tabletops of distinction

Floral artistry and balloon artistry if required

Conferences

Registration services

Guest accommodations

Air travel and transfers

Marketing and sponsorship

event and ask the price later. Today, if a client wants an event planner to do a job in Zanzibar, he or she only needs to surf the Web. Will that event planner meet the client's expectations? Who can say? But this I do know: clients will buy from you if they have an absolute trust in you and if they like you.

Recognize the Three Client Streams

There are three groups from which new clients can be sourced:

1. The corporate stream

2. Professional associations, not-for-profit organizations, and educational institutions

3. Events industry associations

The following will explain each of the three client streams in more detail.

TARGET GROUP 1: THE CORPORATE STREAM

- Hotels

- Advertising houses

- Fashion houses

- Cosmetics companies

- Model agencies

- Financial institutions

- IT Companies

- Car companies

- Sports leagues

- Walmart and other supermarket chains

- Wine companies

- Drug companies

- Magazine publishers

- Supermarket chains

Most corporate clients have events to entertain their own clients, as well as potential clients. However, their primary aim is to always get a return on their investment. These corporate clients also hold events to serve as an incentive for staff, especially during the Christmas period or at the end of a financial season. Catering to this group requires the event planner to produce the entire event or to partner with the company's in-house employees.

Let's look at some examples of events this corporate stream needs to organize. Wine companies, for example, always hold events to launch a new wine into the market. Fashion houses launch their range of garments each season, and cosmetic companies such as Dior, Armani, Elizabeth Arden, or Chanel also increase their exposure through event programs.

Supermarkets and other retail stores such as Walmart, Thrifty, Aldi, Dillons, Bottom Dollar, or Home Depot usually hold quarterly training programs for their employees and celebrate Christmas festivities with their staff.

TARGET GROUP 2: PROFESSIONAL ASSOCIATIONS, NOT-FOR-PROFIT ORGANIZATIONS, AND EDUCATIONAL INSTITUTIONS

- Medical foundations

- Universities

- Sports associations

- Convention and visitor bureaus

- Professional charity associations

Professional associations have dinners on a yearly basis and hold their signature fundraising events once, sometimes twice, a year. Associations are volunteer heavy with willing but unskilled people. The event planner often functions as the lead person. He or she organizes the event, delegates tasks, and coordinates the event components including directing and supervising the volunteers. In this case the management fee can be high, making a project profitable to undertake.

If you are a member of the convention and visitor bureau in your city, you have access to the upcoming events listed in its books and such lists could be your starting point to pursue this client stream.

TARGET GROUP 3: EVENTS INDUSTRY ASSOCIATIONS

- International Special Events Society (ISES)

- National Association of Catering Executives (NACE)

- Wedding Industry Professionals Association (WIPA)

- Meeting Professionals International (MPI)

- U.S. Chamber of Commerce

- City Visitor and Convention Bureaus

If you have membership in any of the industry associations, then you have access to the membership lists, either in hard copy or online. Meeting new people or contractors from industry gatherings or conferences is useful only if you follow up and cultivate communication with the contact to eventually establish a potential client.

What usually happens with networking meetings is that we meet, greet, and exchange business cards, and the next day it is work as usual. Those new business cards received from the night before get filed and forgotten. Do not let them drop "out of sight or out of mind."

Learn the Cold-Call Technique

I know cold-calling is a chilling thought. Large companies employ staff to specifically handle this task in order to bring in new clients, with the intention of increasing

The Cold-Call Script: A Template

You: Good morning, this is Lena Malouf from Malouf Consultancy & Design. Can you direct me through to the Special Events Division and may I have the contact name of the person in charge?

Receptionist: Yes, certainly. Her name is Minnie Mouse.

Minnie: Hello, this is Minnie.

You: Good morning, Minnie. This is Lena Malouf. I'm the creative director of Malouf Consultancy. Thank you for taking my call. Tell me, is it convenient to speak now or would you prefer I call back at a later time?

Minnie: What is this in regard to, Lena?

You: Our company has some new and exciting event concepts that you may care to consider for your upcoming events, so, Minnie, can you tell me, do you produce your events in-house or partner with outside professionals?

Minnie: Lena, it can be a bit of both.

You: In that case, may I forward through some information for you to consider for your file?

Minnie: Yes, that would be fine.

You: I realize how busy you are, but perhaps I could call you at the end of the week and arrange an appointment to meet?

Minnie: Yes, call me on Thursday at 4:00 p.m.

The aim with any cold-calling exercise is to leave your footprints in the company's office, and basically you are looking for a yes response to arranging an appointment.

sales. Small companies cannot take on this expense, but by planning carefully and following the step-by-step approach given here, they can cold-call successfully. Consider the following tips before embarking upon cold-calling a company:

- Select a person in your operation with a good voice and pleasant manner and make this person responsible for the project.

- Select a day and time for the calls to be made. Tuesday or Wednesday from 11:00 a.m. to 4:00 p.m. is more suitable than calling companies on Monday or at the end of the week.

- Track calls by having all comments recorded so progress can be measured.

Target Company History: A Checklist

The following checklist will help you gather information about potential clients and their past involvement with events. The checklist is usually sent by mail or e-mail to potential clients with a request to fill it out at their leisure. Of course, if they agree, it could be completed over the phone as well.

Company name: _____

Address: _____

Phone: _____ E-mail: _____

Company contact: _____

1. How many events does your company hold each year?

2. What is your company's business objective?

3. What are the usual number and demographics of invited guests?

4. Does your company usually hold its events in-house, on-site, or off-site?

5. Do you prefer breakfast, lunch, dinner, or cocktail events? Formal, informal, or themed events?

6. Do you organize the overall management of the event with the in-house staff or with a professional event planner?

7. Can you indicate the budgets for your past events?

8. Is there a standard billing practice?

9. Would you consider having our company partner with your team?

10. Can we arrange a time to meet?

- Have the designated employee learn the cold-call script on page 30 and rehearse it.

- Have the employee be prepared for each call and know a little about the targeted companies.

Give this project time, energy, and effort, and you will reap the rewards. And yes, you can expect rejection, but do not be concerned. The worst-case scenario is that the receiver of the call will hang up. Remember, your aim is to get an appointment and go face-to-face for your initial contact. For every 100 calls you make, on average only 1 to 3 percent of companies will respond positively.

Implement the Plan to Expand

Host an Open House

Host open houses for small groups of representatives of companies from your Target Group 1 (see page 28). For each of these by-invitation-only events, select a mix of companies that could include representatives from insurance, banking, cosmetics, car dealerships, or similar industries.

I feel it is an advantage to keep these events small and intimate. If they are too big and unruly, you and your people are not able to network effectively and create a strong and committed impression. Keep it personal. A small group gives you time to communicate.

When deciding whom to invite to the next open house, make lists of companies you would like to attract. Sift through telephone directories, your local newspapers, and online sources for company ideas and contact information.

Ensure that you only invite one or, at a maximum, two representatives from each type of company at one time. For example, if you would like to attract business from three different banking corporations, make sure that only one bank is represented at each soiree. If you invite all three, it could backfire on you, leaving you holding the empty bag, so to speak. They each might resist giving business to a company that is wooing their competition.

Now, it goes without saying that this invitation is not intended for junior employees. While I'm sure they would be very pleasant, they have no buying power. Make sure your invitation gets to the top. Do your research and find the decision makers.

With the potential clients on your turf, you and your team have the opportunity to impress them and get to know them.

Be sure to present your place of business immaculately, with specific areas allocated for food, beverages, and hospitality. Use your display area or floor to showcase some of your spectacular ideas and designs. This is show time, so put your best foot forward. Everything from service to décor to refreshments must be exemplary. As guests arrive, have a registration table at the entrance and provide nametags with each guest's name and company name printed clearly.

No matter how much the guests seem to enjoy themselves, if you put on a loose and disorganized gathering on your own premises, your invitees will not trust you to produce a professional show in which they might potentially be investing thousands of dollars.

An open house is something you can do on a monthly or bi-monthly basis, and I guarantee it will pay off. It doesn't matter if it is breakfast to kick-start the day or an evening gathering for the cocktail hour after work. What matters is that you get it right so that it brings about favorable results.

Entertain Industry Associates

Host an open house similar to the one for clients for your industry peers and contractors on a quarterly basis. These potential clients in Target Group 3 (see page 29) are right under your nose and should be exposed to the services you can provide. For example, if your strength is décor, then catering, technical, production, and other related companies might require your services to bring the artistry of florals and set dressing to their events.

On the other hand, if production is your specialty, then decorators and caterers would consider hiring you to assist with the overall management or coordination of the event. This becomes an added service they can provide for their clients. The least these contractors will be able to do is recommend you to their clients for services they are not providing.

Attend Trade Fairs

A trade show puts your offerings in front of hundreds of potential buyers. Trade show attendees are there specifically to find new companies with fresh conceptual ideas and new products, such as linens, tabletop elements, lighting, stage structures, and special event embellishments.

To maximize your success at a trade show, try the following:

1. Set up an eye-catching booth that showcases your style and products.

2. Staff the booth with confident, well-dressed, and knowledgeable people to represent and sell your company.

3. Carefully prepare your promotional literature to ensure that your message is clear and concise, and reflects your professional image. Have an abundance of such brochures to hand out.

4. If the budget allows, display corporate giveaways such as pens, key rings, and even coffee cups printed with your company name and contact information. Your prospective client will walk away with a company memento.

Trade show involvement costs money, but attendance is a surefire way to communicate with many companies in a short time frame to bring exposure to your company.

Consider a Marketing Guru

Hiring a marketing specialist is not a cheap option, so it will depend on your budget. Discuss this idea with your financial adviser. You would want to find a marketing specialist or company familiar with the events industry and employ this person or firm to build a new marketing plan for your business.

It is wise to have a set figure in mind before you begin discussions. Initially, seek advice on what this marketing company could offer you for the amount you are prepared to spend. You will be able not only to find out what your money can buy you, but also to gauge what this particular marketer can offer in terms of expertise and savvy. Ask the marketing company to provide you with a plan detailing the exposure that it may be able to bring to your company.

Many smaller operations shy away from using outside marketing specialists, fearing the cost will be too high, but it is possible to get some help on a limited budget. Don't reject this option without doing the research. The worst-case scenario is that the marketing company you have approached will tell you it can't offer a package on such a low budget. *C'est la vie!* But I still think it's worth the effort of going through the motions. If the cost of a particular marketing company is prohibitive, there are always others to meet with to negotiate an acceptable fee to assist in this area.

Allocate Some Advertising Dollars

Review your budget and allocate some funds to advertise in trade magazines. I firmly believe that any print advertising should be done in magazines that cater to and are specifically associated with the events industry. I also believe that smaller ads placed on a continuing basis will outweigh a big splashy one-off ad.

Try to negotiate for some free editorial coverage when you commit to an advertising program. You could suggest a profile of yourself or a spotlight on one of your events to be written by the editorial staff.

Better yet, since you are talking with the chosen magazine, offer to write a regular column for free. The magazine might go for your proposal, in part, because it wants to keep your advertising dollars flowing in. It could be a question and answer column where industry problems could be posed by readers and answered by you. Being seen as the professional that other professionals turn to will set you above the rest. A column will achieve exactly that.

Whether you choose one or all of these methods, the idea is to strive to get your name out there. Once you have increased your exposure, new clients will be knocking on your door.

Venue Essentials

CHOOSING A VENUE IS A CRITICAL COMPONENT IN THE event planning process, primarily because its choice affects the myriad of choices that follow. The selected space dictates the options the planner will have when coming up with the detailed creative and technical plan. The client, on the other hand, experiences a big impact on the cost of the event.

With most events, clients will approach the planner without securing the venue on their own upfront—though the client will often have a preferred venue in mind and perhaps even alternate suggestions. An exception here might be weddings, for which the bride and groom may have already chosen the church where they want to have the ceremony, or even have found a candidate for the reception hall.

At the first meeting, the planner will get an idea of the type of venue that should be considered based on information gathered from the client regarding the site preferences—for example, whether it should be outdoor or indoor, conventional or unconventional. The venue will be further determined by the number of guests, type of event, and approximate budget.

Based on this information, the event planner will be able to recommend appropriate venues for the client to inspect, and for faraway or out of city locations, the planner will at least have enough background information to research venue facilities.

Once the prospective venues have been inspected, one is selected and the contract with the venue operator is called for, read, and signed by the client, provided the cost is within budget.

Considerations When Choosing a Venue

Whether the selected venue is an on-site or off-site location (for definitions of on-site and off-site locations, see pages 38 and 46), this rental space has many variables. A savvy planner will make sure to learn the different components of the considered space. In addition to knowing the dimensions of the space—the length, width, depth, and ceiling height—the planner must understand the surface structure; the stress, or weight allowed for ceiling suspension; the finish of interior and exterior walls; the noise abatement; and the available utilities.

Make the venue operator your best friend. It is vital that you share the vision and the business objective of the company with this person. The venue director and his or her engineer will advise and assist you with reference to the building's blueprints, drawings, and technical specifications. Their expertise is an absolute must on very large jobs.

Sight the Venue

Whether you are organizing a gala dinner, cocktail party, wedding, 40th birthday celebration, or another occasion, the facility will determine the style of décor and the amount of equipment that needs to be brought in to produce the event.

It is necessary to visit the venue with every event you do, even if you have previously held events in that location. If for any reason you cannot sight the venue personally, send your assistant or producer. It is only in person that you can get a true feel for the place: its ambience, size, character, and color. No number of phone calls and e-mailed photos taken by someone else can replace a personal impression. And this personal impression is what helps the event planner establish the creative plan and create décor that will best fit the place.

Even if the chosen venue is some distance away and the client has a limited budget, it is still advisable to request that you be able to visit the site and meet with the venue operator in person. If it is an out-of-town location, of course, the expense of the airfare and at minimum, a one-night accommodation should be covered by the client. If clients cannot afford this expense, then, quite frankly, they cannot afford to hold the event. An exception would be a very small event, with a small number of guests and a modest budget—in that case, have a phone interview with the venue operator and request information such as floor plans, measurements, event contract, back-of-house information, and rental costs.

Failing to take time to inspect the interior and exterior of any property is a surefire way to lose money and eat into the profit of the job.

Be mindful of three important points:

1. We love to impress with clever décor and florals, but if most of the budget is allocated toward the creatives, the quality of the food and beverages will

suffer. In this case, the client will be disappointed; the quality of food and beverages served at an event are paramount.

2. You may have booked an area within a restaurant that you have not sighted. You may very well arrive to find that the area designated for your event is positioned within a public area of the restaurant itself. In such a case, it would be essential to phone a rental company to deliver wall panels to give the event a private environment. This unexpected cost would need to be absorbed by you because it was due to lack of planning, and consequently will affect your profits.

3. You might arrive at a venue to find that some of the chairs supplied by the operator are damaged or have unsightly marks on them, and you have not planned for chair covers in the initial budget. In this instance, you would, once again, have to make a last-minute arrangement to rent the chair covers, and you would incur this extra expense.

Venue Evaluation: A Checklist

The following venue inspection checklist has been provided courtesy of Professor Joe Jeff Goldblatt, the distinguished founding president of the International Special Events Society.

- ✓ What is the capacity of the venue?
- ✓ What is the stress weight for items such as lighting and scenic devices that will be suspended?
- ✓ What official permission is required to use open flame or indoor pyrotechnics?
- ✓ What does the fire code require with regard to material composition for scenery or other decoration?
- ✓ What is the policy regarding live trained animals (if applicable)?
- ✓ How are the fire sprinklers controlled?
- ✓ Is a fire marshal or warden required?
- ✓ What is the electrical power capacity of the venue?
- ✓ Is there a working on-site reserve generator in case of power failure?
- ✓ Where are water sources with an off-site venue?
- ✓ Does the venue supply rope, stanchions, dance floor, fabric drape, and standard piping?

Finally, Goldblatt advises that planners carry a retractable tape measure or electronic laser measuring device (for measuring the dimensions of the space, such as the ceiling height), an instant or digital camera, and a notepad and pencil.

On-Site Venues

The definition of an on-site venue is a location that has fully equipped kitchens on the premises, with tables, chairs, linens, staging, and dance floor availability. Staging an event in this style of facility is considerably easier as it readily supplies power and water but also offers protection against the weather elements. Therefore, if the budget is limited, you are best advised to choose an on-site venue rather than an off-site.

Typical on-site venues include

Three-, four-, and five-star hotels	Reception halls
City convention centers	Theater rooms
University function centers	Designer stores
Art galleries	Restaurants
Historic homes or mansions	Concert halls
Sports clubs	Casinos
Museums	Private residences
Libraries	Dance clubs

Once you have selected an on-site venue for your event, make the following assessments of the site as part of your planning process:

1. *Measurements*

   Record the venue in length, width, and depth as well as the ceiling height. The points to be considered are (a) the number of guests, (b) the table setup, (c) the position of the stage or stages, (d) the dance floor (single or twin), (e) the number of food stations, (f) the number of bar stations, and (g) the side service tables used by the waitstaff.

2. *Walls*

   Note the wall colors and surface finish. Is the finish painted, papered, timbered? Record the existing décor elements, for example mirrors, artwork, lamps, pillars, ornaments, or draping.

3. *Floors*

   Note and record the floor finish. Is it timber, mosaic, polished cement, or carpet? As for the carpet, it can be wonderful in color or bold beyond belief. Always hope for wonderful, as that makes it far easier to dress the room. If the floor carpet has a distinctive and bold print with strong colors, as is often seen in casino hotels, I recommend that you select a one-color scheme based on the color that is least dominant.

As an alternative, if a carpet just happens to have wonderful neutral tones of beige, gray, or cream, then the color world is your oyster. You can possibly now introduce a color of your choice for the décor.

4. *Ceiling*

Record the height, style, and finish of the ceiling. The style and finish can vary from very ornately decorated to panels of mirror, sections of timber, or artistically draped fabrics. If ceiling work is programmed into the décor dressing, be sure to check any hanging points that you are permitted to use.

5. *Doors*

Pay attention to the entrance doors to the ballroom or function center. Will there be ease of traffic flow for the guests? Check that the doors leading to the back-of-house and the kitchens and the adjoining hallways are clear of unused décor, props, and empty road cases. Arrange to have such items removed before the event. At all costs, do not leave the walkways cluttered, as excess road cases or empty boxes can be disruptive to the flow of the evening.

6. *Fire Exits*

Recognize that fire exits must be clear of any type of decoration, staging, or technical equipment. The hotel security officer or engineer will be checking to make sure that all exits meet the requirements for the venue. Most important, the exit signs must be clearly visible.

7. *Service Elevators*

Inspect the back-of-house with the venue operator, who will explain the layout and point out any restrictions. Measure the hallways, service elevators, and elevator ceiling height. This information is essential for the loading in of equipment, such as staging rostrums, decorative props, and the many road cases required by the technical contractors. The venue operator will recommend the best service elevators for your team to use.

8. *Loading Docks*

Coordinate and maintain control of the scheduling for the arrival of contractors' trucks at the loading docks for the unloading and reloading of equipment and props. You do not want all the contractors to arrive at the same time. Good timing of this aspect can be a real money saver for you, especially if you are aware of the busiest service times. Poor planning can mean that the unloading and reloading can take twice as long, which adds extra labor hours. This is a cost you do not need and can avoid.

9. *Breakout Rooms*

Inspect the additional rooms required for the event. Specific areas are usually needed for administration, entertainers, bands, and your own team of contractors. Special breakout rooms will be necessary for clothing changes, band breaks, and crew meals. Again, communicate your requirements to the venue operator and inform him or her of the number of people you will need to care for and accommodate. Choose the crew menu, ideally a buffet. Entertainers and crew will eat at different times depending on the schedule, and buffet-style dining allows the crew to obtain meals, take the food to tables, and eat while on break. The crew will always appreciate continuous access to coffee or icy-cold soft drinks. Don't forget to provide freestanding mirrors and clothing hangers, which are necessities for the entertainers and their wardrobe.

10. *Preparation Workspace*

If the floral designers are working on location, a workspace area should be designated for them if the budget permits. Ideally the florists are best placed away from the technical and staging teams. You might ask why. Quite frankly, most florists are usually messy, regardless of having a well-organized area with tables, buckets of water, and well-placed waste bins. Additionally, the perishable goods required for an event need care, conditioning, and organizing, which take space.

Before the floral designers start work, cover the venue flooring by laying down plastic drop sheets to protect the floor from water spills and flower waste.

It goes without saying that the technical team and staging specialist will set up their own work areas within the designated space of the selected ballroom.

11. *Facilities for Guests with Disabilities*

Inspect all access points, such as entrances, exits, ramps, steps, and elevators, which may be required by those with a disability. Most venues today do have these accommodations in place, but be aware of their availability for use.

12. *Back of the Venue*

First, meet with security personnel in regard to the external use of the premises. The venue operator will introduce you and then you can inspect the back access areas that will be available to you when you are on the job. Advise security about your crew's arrival and departure times and obtain their approval. Respect any restrictions in this external area of the venue.

13. *Parking*

Inquire about the parking available to your crew, including all contractors, before and during the event. Usually only two or three spaces can be reserved, but each venue has different rules. If you are allocated a specific time for parking your car by the venue operator, you will often need to follow up with the necessary paperwork for the security division. This step ensures that all vehicles are booked through the security system.

In the events industry, doing the paperwork to confirm any arrangement made verbally is a must. Should any dispute arise, the paperwork confirms the terms agreed to.

14. *Risk Management Adviser*

I highly recommend hiring a risk management consultant to help minimize the risk to people or property. This step is intended to act as a safeguard in all areas. You may immediately think, "Well, I can't afford this adviser." But can you afford not to have this coverage? Rest assured, most clients will appreciate your suggestion to hire this expert at their expense, and they are surprisingly affordable.

15. *Technical and Staging*

Once the client approves the venue you selected, it will be necessary to meet at the venue at an arranged time with all the chosen contractors, no matter the size of the event. Be prepared for this meeting. It is vital that you share the creative vision and the business objective of the event with these contractors. The technical adviser, staging specialist, and other hired supply companies in particular must sight the venue itself and also inspect the interior, back-of-house, and exterior of the facility.

16. *Crew Meals*

Advise the venue operator or caterer prior to the event of any requests you may have regarding crew meals, whether it be for five, fifty, or more. (For on-site events, it is the hotel or restaurant that tends to provide crew meals and this cost will be approved by the client and carried onto the company invoice.)

For off-site events, you can ask the caterer to provide the crew meals at a cost and again this will be approved by the client and carried onto the company invoice. I have always been conscious of team care regarding good-quality food, ever-flowing but nonalcoholic beverages, continuous hot coffee, and breaks. Believe me, all these are truly appreciated.

17. *Venue Contract*

It is important that every line of the contract you sign with the venue operator be read and reread to avoid mistakes or misunderstanding in any area. Pass this information on to the client, pointing out clauses pertaining to progressive payments, restrictions, and limitations. In the case of the mega-event with the mega-budget, have your attorney review the document before you sign off on it. Read the small print; it is painful but necessary.

18. *Emergency Contacts*

With any job, be sure you have easy access to a range of contact phone numbers: for the police, the fire department, an ambulance in case a guest has a medical emergency, and a car service, as well as the cellular phone numbers for all contractors working on the job.

19. *Waste Bins*

If you are expecting excessive trash waste at the end of an event, prebook commercial waste bins and arrange for them to be positioned in the loading dock area of the venue. The waste will be controlled, and this method could possibly save you money on the cleaning of the ballroom or function center. The venue will usually do the cleaning after the event, but it is unacceptable to leave masses of rubbish lying about. You need to leave the on-site venue in a reasonable state for cleaners; if this is ignored, the venue will charge to have the cleaning done. For off-site events, it is the planner that hires cleaners for the post-event cleanup.

Your Event Team

Those who have attended my presentations at The Special Event conferences in the United States have heard me promote the "partner with a professional" approach to large event management. The technical adviser, staging consultant, catering director, floral decorator, set designer, and entertainment agent must be treated as part of your team. When we talk about working as a team, the emphasis is on *we*, not *me*. This approach ensures that everyone is working together toward a successful outcome. The experienced leader will share his or her vision, continually inform the team about any changes, and communicate clear and precise instructions to the entire team working on the event.

On-Site Venue: A Checklist

The following template will help you gather all the necessary information regarding the on-site event venue.

Venue Contact Information

Company name:

Address:

Contact:

Position: Cell phone:

Main office phone:

Fax: E-mail:

Main Room

Name:

Measurements: Length: Width:

Ceiling height:

Highest point: Lowest point:

Features:

Number of guests for a seated occasion with dance floor:

Number of guests for an occasion without dance floor:

Entrances

Number of entrances into the main room:

Bars for pre-drinks area required (yes/no):

Cloakroom facility:

Piano availability:

Stairs, steps, or ramps required:

Technical

Audiovisual availability: _____

Power availability: _____

Air-conditioning availability: _____

Cool room availability: _____

Speaker equipment: _____

Staging

Stage availability: _____

Steps, ramps, or platforms availability: _____

Dance floor: _____ Size: _____

Cost involved: _____

Equipment that needs to be rented: _____

_____

Tables

Number of rounds: _____ Size: _____

Number of rectangles: _____ Size: _____

Number of squares: _____ Size: _____

Persons per table: _____

Chairs

Number of chairs available: _____

Number of decorative chairs to rent: _____ Number of chairs to be covered: _____

Linen color: _____ Numbers: _____

Kitchens

Position: _____

Is a secondary kitchen required? _____

Breakout Rooms

Number required: _____

Same floor as the main room: _____

Located on level: _____

Green room for celebrity guests: _____

Back-of-House Information

Service elevator measurements: _____

Service elevator access times: _____

Service elevator restricted times: _____

Contract Review

Contract reviewed? _____

Checked the cancellation and restriction clauses? _____

Client saw the contract? _____

Parking

Guests parking: _____ Charges: _____

Staff parking: _____ Charges: _____

Security passes: _____

Restrictions

_____

Load-In / Load-Out

Load-out point of contact: _____ Cell phone: _____

Special instructions: _____

Travel time required to get to the venue: _____

Contractors' access time for load-in: _____

Contractors' access time for load-out: _____

Off-Site Venues

Off-site venues are more unconventional facilities, often outdoors and usually without any fittings or equipment whatsoever, and events at such venues require far more organizing by the planner.

Securing legal permits is first and foremost on the to-do list, and once the event is approved to proceed, the event planner can concentrate on booking the appropriate contractors and required equipment.

With an on-site booking, the client must be prepared to lay out more money simply because of the additional equipment setup required, the freight cost of carrying equipment to the location, and the labor involved on location. Another point to consider is that the planner may have difficulty gaining access to the site during the time leading up to the event, and therefore additional days may be required to complete the job. As a result, additional rental time for the facility would be required.

So why would clients ever choose an off-site location? More affluent clients may simply have their hearts set on a wedding on a picturesque beach in the Caribbean or a spectacular company celebration in an airplane hangar (see the case study on page 150). If the clients have their hearts set on an off-site location, they will need to be aware of and understand the logistics of an off-site event as well as the extra expense that it carries.

If you and the client do decide to go off-site for the event booking, be aware that there is generally a 35 percent overall increase in costs compared with a similar-size event in an on-site venue. The reasons for this are that with off-site venues, it becomes necessary to bring in all equipment to the chosen location, such as entire kitchens, tableware, floor and floor coverings, tables, chairs, linens, dressing rooms, mobile toilet facilities, and so on. A stage, if required, must be freighted to the site and then constructed on location.

Marquees, tents, and hoeckers may also be needed. These are defined as follows:

1. *Marquee* is a British or Australian term for a structure that can be used for a small- or medium-sized event. The sides and ceiling of the marquee are usually in white or alternatively can be clear.

2. *Tent* is an American term, and these structures are often very elaborate. A tent may have windows, glass walls, and multiple levels and is often referred to as a structure.

3. The word *hoecker* is a brand name for a tent, but event planners often use this term when 2,000 to 4,000 guests need to be housed.

Examples of off-site venues include

Beaches	Public parks
Horse racing facilities	Sporting arenas
Public and private gardens	Amusement parks
Rooftop facilities	Zoos
University or college grounds	University gardens
Harbor islands	Airport terminals or hangars
Museum grounds or gardens	Tents in unique locations

Once you have chosen an off-site venue, make the following considerations part of your event planning process:

1. *Location and Access*

   Note the entrance and exit roads that lead into your off-site location and check that three- or four-ton trucks have access to roadways. Check also that parking is available for the unloading and reloading of products and equipment.

2. *Tent or Open Air*

   Depending on the size of the tent or other temporary roofing structure you will be using, it is wise to allow enough days for the actual setup (check with your contractor on how much time he or she will need). Any days required beyond the event day must receive the client's approval, as additional facility rental costs will be incurred.

3. *Kitchen and Catering*

   Depending on the number of guests and the size of the off-site venue, one, two, or three kitchens will be required to serve the guests—liaise with the caterer to determine the number. The caterer should provide a list of necessary equipment.

4. *Air-Conditioning and Heating*

   The need for air-conditioning and heating depends on the time of year the event takes place and on the weather forecast for that day. Introduce the air-conditioning component if guests will be more comfortable and if the budget allows.

5. *Pathway Requirements*

Pathways require path lighting to prevent accidents. They also must be clearly lit for the comfort and convenience of the guests and team members. Furthermore, in wet weather, nonskid rubber mats may be required to prevent accidents.

6. *Disability Requirements*

To avoid any mishap for guests who have a disability, ramps must be included for wheelchair access.

7. *Security*

Think of the security officers as part of your team because they are essential crew members. Communicate your requirements very clearly and they will oversee the safety of all concerned. Provide them with industrial flashlights in case of emergency during events held in the evening.

8. *Weather Forecast*

It is always advisable to stay up-to-date in regard to the unexpected downpour, for which a contingency plan of walkers with umbrellas must be in place. The location will determine whether the event can potentially move from an outdoor site with a tent to an undercover venue. For example, if an event is held on a beach, the contingency plan might involve a nearby pavilion or restaurant. However, if an event is planned in a vineyard, an indoor venue may not be an option. The distance that an outdoor event would need to be moved to reach an undercover location may be the biggest hurdle to overcome when creating a weather contingency plan.

9. *Permits and Licenses*

Local community council approval for off-site events is essential, especially if alcohol will be served. Keep the approved documents in your briefcase to carry with you on location. If required, you will have to produce them on the job.

10. *Emergency Contacts*

With any job, be sure you have easy access to a range of contact phone numbers: for the police, the fire department, the ambulance in case a guest has a medical emergency, and a car service, as well as the cellular phone numbers for all contractors working on the job.

11. *Mobile Toilets/Porta-Potties*

Positioning the mobile toilets in the appropriate space is essential, particularly given that they are usually an unsightly commodity. If the budget allows, book staff to service this area throughout the duration of the event. It is then kept clean and hygienic and supplied with fresh toiletries. Consider whether you require a subfloor beneath the restrooms to compensate for unlevel ground.

12. *Fencing*

Does the event require fencing? If long runs of fencing are needed, you will need to review the type of material your contractor is considering—steel, wood, or plastic—and the required height of the fencing. High fencing is sometimes required on off-site locations, especially to keep a private function separate from public spaces.

13. *Power Information*

Involve the technical adviser from the beginning of the planning process. While you may be aware of the requirements, his or her expertise regarding the additional equipment and use of the power supply for the kitchens and entertainers is of primary importance for off-site events.

14. *Waste*

When the event is off-site, commercial waste bins must be booked. A specific time must be given to outside contractors for both the delivery and removal of the bins post-event. This is an added cost to be included in the summary budget of the proposal.

15. *The Contract*

Have the client review the contract and preferably sign off on it. This way, a certain amount of responsibility will be lifted from you. Make sure to point out to the client the restrictions, the limitations, and the clause relating to cancellation. Make the client aware of penalties pertaining to a cancellation of the event.

16. *Restrictions*

Any restrictions are usually listed by the venue operator in the contract but are often missed by event managers due to the amount of fine print. Read the contract carefully to be conscious of any point pertaining to restrictions, but importantly look closely at the cancellation clause that relates to the time and refund of monies in the event of an unexpected cancellation.

The Sequence of Off-Site Venue Setup

1. The steel skeleton or frame is erected.

2. The tent's exterior skins of walls and ceiling are erected.

3. The air-conditioning units are positioned.

4. The floors are completed and covered.

5. The technical ceiling truss is positioned for light and sound.

6. The staging or platforms are built and positioned.

7. The room is now ready for tables, chairs, side service tables, and bars.

The pre-event meeting with contractors will determine the specific time for each contractor to load in and begin setup. You can see from the sequence of actions why the floral designers are best positioned in a separate work area to avoid interruption of the flow of work.

Off-Site Venue: A Checklist

The template below will help you collect all the necessary information regarding an off-site event venue.

Venue Contact Information

Contact name:

Position:

Office phone: Cell phone:

Venue Details

Address:

Tent or other facility:

Measurements:

Length: Width: Height:

Features to note:

Guest numbers for seated dinner with dance floor:

Guest numbers for dinner without dance floor:

Coatroom

To be constructed:

Allocated position:

Tables: Hanging racks: Tickets:

Pre-Drinks Area

Allocated position:

Equipment required:

Signage: Placement:

Fresh plant rental, if required:

Other:

Technical Equipment

Light and sound: _____

Power availability and requirements: _____

Air-conditioning availability and requirements: _____

Heating availability and requirements: _____

Speaker equipment and rostrum: _____

Permits and license required: _____

Emergency handheld fire hydrants: _____

Outside and pathway lighting: _____

Staging Requirements

Stage positioning and requirements: _____

Steps, ramps, platforms, speaker podiums: _____

Dance floor measurement: _____

Other staging equipment requirements: _____

Kitchen Requirements

Installation and position of kitchen(s): _____

_____

Kitchen equipment: _____

_____

_____

Beverage Bars

Number: _____

Position: _____

Entertainment Requirments

Piano, stool, music stands, and band chairs: _____

Mirrors, hanging racks, and coat hangers: _____

Dressing room installation: _____

Position: _____

Tables

Availability of tables and chairs: _____

    Number: _____ Positions: _____

Flower arrangements: _____

    Number: _____ Style: _____

Tablecloths and chair covers: _____

    Number: _____ Style: _____

Professional Greeters

Number required: _____

Badges, uniforms, flashlights: _____

Security

Number required: _____

Security passes: _____

Parking

Guests parking _____

    Position: _____ Number: _____

Staff parking _____

    Position: _____ Number: _____

Load-In and Load-Out

Contact: _____

Position: _____

Number: _____

Time arranged: _____

Crew passes: _____

Portable Toilet Facility

Number: _____ Position: _____

Attendants: _____ Toiletries: _____

Restrictions and Cancellations

Contract scrutiny: _____

Floor Plan Variation for Venues

So much can be learned from studying and viewing CAD (computer-aided design) plans of floor layouts that have been created to show precisely what goes where in the room, such as the position of the stage, tables, and chairs. Such layouts show whether there is enough space for guests' comfort and adequate room between tables and chairs for the waitstaff to service the tables.

If you have done a lot of jobs in a ballroom of a particular hotel, you may feel as though you know it back to front and would rather forgo creating a CAD plan for your next event. But remember that every event is different, even if it is by the smallest element. So, a new job means a new CAD plan.

Your venue operator or catering director will have a CAD drawing done for you on request, once he or she receives confirmation of the event. The event producer, who acts on your behalf, can also take responsibility for this element. A final version should be presented for client approval. Copies are then forwarded to the contractors hired for the job.

Not all event planners chose to work using CAD plans. Some may settle for a hand drawing. Whichever way you choose to go, the client must get a visual representation to understand the intended seating arrangement of the guests.

Creating a library of such drawings for your reference offers a great advantage to you as the planner for a couple of reasons. First, you will be able to show some CAD drawings of past work to clients. They can then offer their opinion of the layouts, which will give you an idea of their likes and dislikes. Second, you can revise previously created floor plans and reuse them, which will save time in redesigning.

The following pages show a collection of CAD plan drawings for various venues in Australia and the United States, which have been generously provided by industry professionals. Feel free to add these plans to your new CAD plan library.

When you view a venue for the first time, you often immediately ask yourself, "What can I do that would be different?" I hope that these models will inspire you creatively and aid you in creating something original and fresh.

I have included a few examples that show how you can redesign the same space for different events—see plans 1, 2, and 3. Each of these events took place in the Grand Ballroom at the Four Seasons Hotel in Sydney.

1. Grand Ballroom, Four Seasons Hotel, Sydney.
   Courtesy of George Merkouris, catering sales manager.

In this beautiful ballroom for 300 guests, a two-tier elevation of platforms with guest tables is employed. The higher level is approximately two feet above the floor, and the lower level is one foot above the floor. Guest tables are placed on both levels and also on the floor level. This design solution provides a cabinet style of seating and is ideal when the entertainment component is extensive because it makes for easy and uninterrupted viewing of the stage by all the guests.

The event planner must consider that steps, as well as securely positioned handrails, will be necessary for guest and waitstaff movement between the three levels.

In addition, aside from the center stage, extra staging units are positioned around the room at two levels. Such extra stages are only used when the budget allows and additional impact is required.

This setup effectively brings a cabaret feel to the event and adds interest.

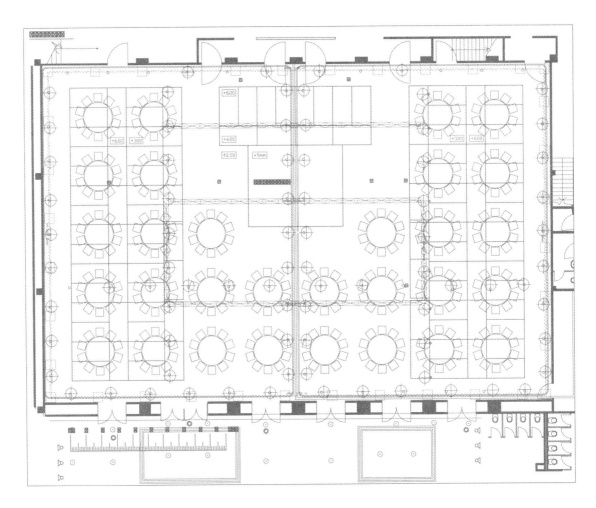

2. Grand Ballroom, Four Seasons Hotel, Sydney.

Courtesy of George Merkouris, catering sales manager.

This variation of table layout caters to approximately 300, with the tables arranged in cabinet style. Note that the tables are only three-quarters set to allow the guests clear sight lines to the central cross-shaped runway during a glamorous fashion parade and dinner.

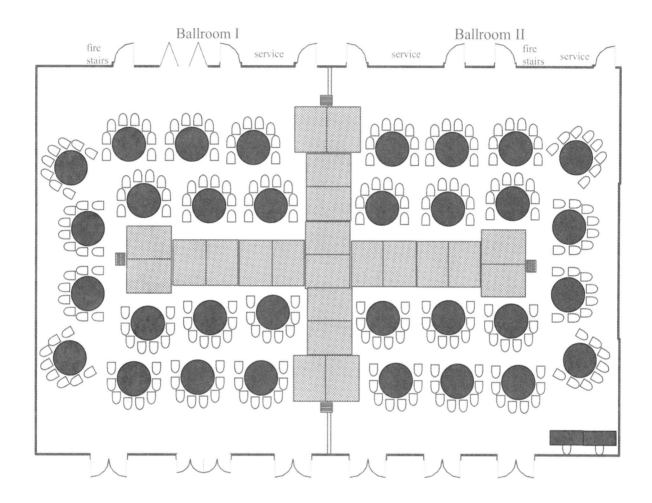

3. Ballroom, Four Seasons Hotel, Sydney.

Courtesy of George Merkouris, catering sales manager.

This is an interesting seating arrangement for an automobile launch over lunch or dinner. This ballroom can normally seat up to 400 guests, but for this occasion, four cars were driven in and seating was only needed for 152 people.

A twelve-foot floral tabletop could be placed centrally, at the cross of the tables. Miniature posies could be added, running down the center of the table approximately eight feet apart.

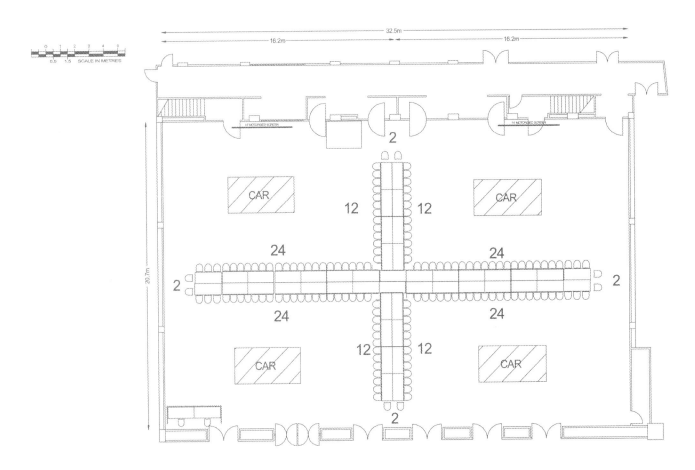

4. Westin Sydney Ballroom, Sydney.

Courtesy of Wayne Elstub of VenueCAD Pty. Ltd.

This ballroom happens to be long and narrow, and the chosen floor setup effectively works with this venue shape. The most interesting aspect of this layout is the introduction of the twin dance floors. Guests are close to the dance floors, allowing them to be fully involved in the evening's activities.

If only one dance floor is utilized and it is positioned to one side, or one end, some guests are seated well toward the back of the room and this is unavoidable with this setting. Alternatively, if a single dance floor is positioned centrally, it tends to split the guests into two groups. With this style of floor plan, there is little interaction among the guests until the dancing begins.

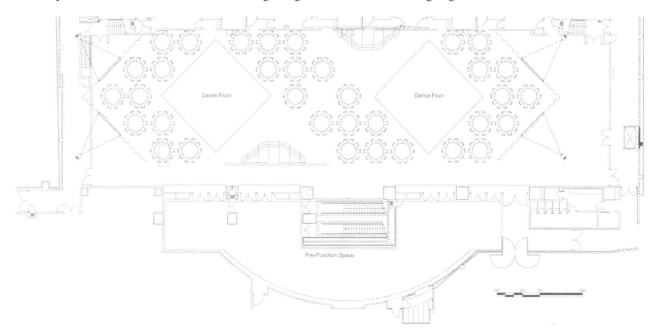

5. Sydney University lawn, Sydney.

Courtesy of Wayne Elstub of VenueCAD Pty. Ltd.

In this floor plan, the runway and water display are positioned centrally, so that all guests have the opportunity to see the models walk on the runway. The guests' tables vary, from the standard six-foot round to square and rectangular ones. This specific variation of table shapes was used to accommodate the number of guests attending this formal dinner.

Note the arrangement of the catering area. The chosen positioning gave easy access for the waitstaff providing the food and beverage service. The green room was for the models and the MC. As situated, they were able to move directly to the stage and runway. The third side room catered to the needs of the music band and crew. As space was a little restricted in this venue, the client decided to omit a dance floor from the evening. There was, however, a small designated dance area instead.

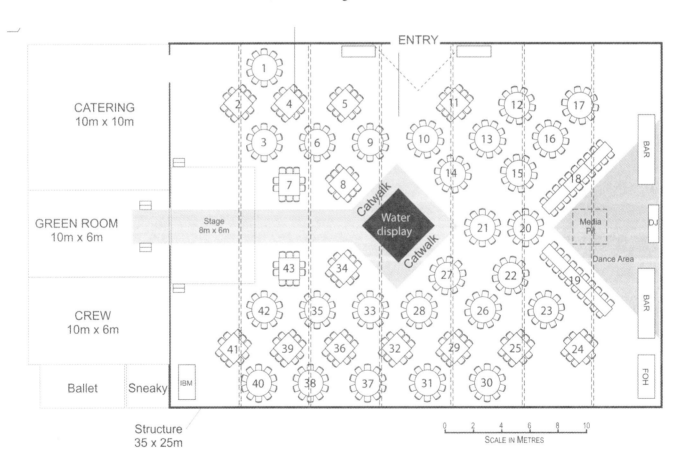

6. The Dome Royal Agricultural Showground, Sydney.

A Malouf event.

The Dome at the Sydney Showground is an interesting circular venue that seats up to 4,000 guests. The two biggest challenges during the illustrated event were, first, creating a floor layout to seat only 1,300 guests in this large space, and second, the fact that there was only one kitchen to service the guests. After many hours of discussion with the producer, technical adviser, and staging specialist, we decided to bring a four-tiered stage into the room. Black velvet draping was hung behind the stage, which effectively reduced the size of the floor space.

At the other end of the room, there is a line on the floor plan indicating a second black velvet drape (labeled "20M screen") that created a false wall, also intended to reduce the floor space. This solution allowed for a second kitchen to be set up. A tunnel entrance was created through which guests could walk directly into the room. The tables were arranged in rows and styled into blocks with six-foot-wide aisles between the blocks. This allowed ease of movement for not only the guests but also the waitstaff serving food and beverages. The dance floor was constructed in the shape of a diamond. One corner of the diamond pointed to the stage, which allowed the tables to surround the dance floor.

This event, which was titled "Gallactium," won an award at The Special Event conference in 2002 for the best event with a budget over $500,000.

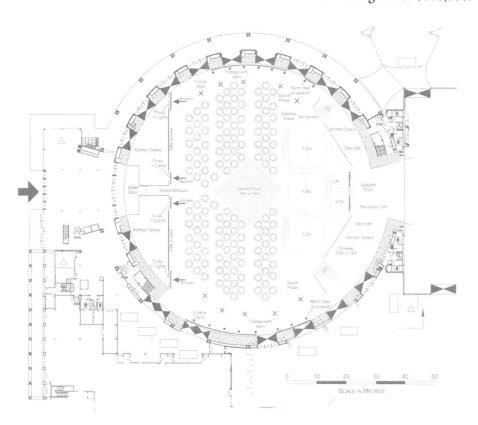

7. Sydney Showground / Sydney Olympic Park.

Courtesy of Andrew Roberts.

This floor plan shows an adaptation of the previous venue, which usually seats 4,000 guests, for an event of 1,750 people. As mentioned before, the problem in such instances is excess space. In order to overcome this hurdle, part of the main room was closed off into a pre-drinks area, where guests could enjoy cocktails and appetizers.

The walkways among table blocks were wider than usual, due to the large venue space, allowing for an efficient flow of a large number of people. Bars were placed strategically at the sides of the room to cater to a large number of beverage orders.

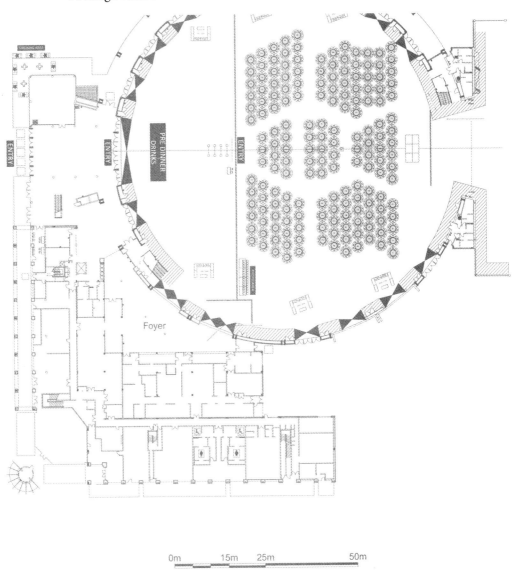

0m   15m   25m   50m

8. Hall 4, Sydney Convention and Exhibition Centre.
   Courtesy of Paul Davison and Sydney Convention and
   Exhibition Centre, Darling Harbour, Sydney.

The estimated seating capacity for this venue is 2,000 guests. Due to the vastness of the space, it is ideal for large corporate events and concerts. Note the placement and width of the walkways for waitstaff to use when serving food and beverages. The walkways are clearly defined on this CAD drawing, which is essential when you map out layouts for very large events and you view floor plans of considerable-size venues. The principle here: if it looks tight on paper, the movement will be restricted for waitstaff and guests throughout the duration of the event.

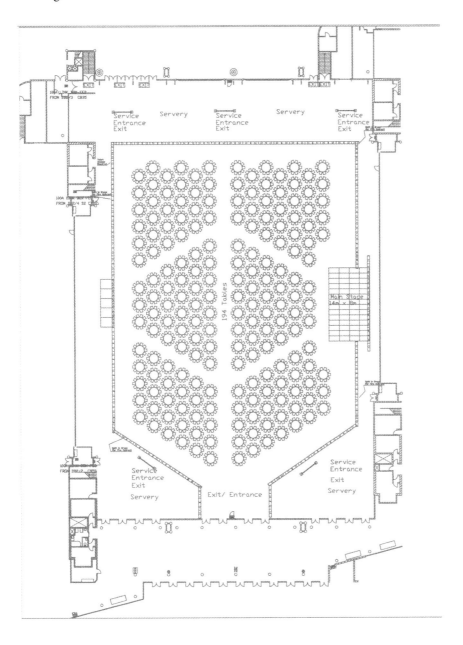

9. Sydney Convention and Exhibition Centre,
   Darling Harbour, Sydney.

A Malouf event. Courtesy of Paul Davison.

This floor plan was used for a Malouf company Christmas party. This venue usually seats up to 1,500 people, but here approximately 600 guests attended. Notice the four runways leading directly to the dance floor. This setup allowed the site performers and dancers to create impact as they each entered the room to perform their acts.

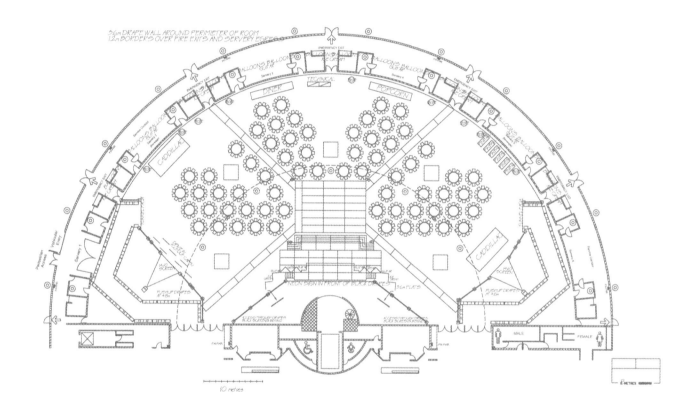

10. Treasure Island, San Francisco, California.

Courtesy of Andrea Michaels, Extraordinary Events, Sherman Oaks, California.

Andrea worked on this spectacular event for 11,000 guests in collaboration with Tom Bercu Presents. It was a hospitality event for the client George P. Johnson Company/VM Ware during a software conference.

The design and production teams were asked to apply their talents at "event visualization" and create a realistic experience of the streets of San Francisco in a building that hadn't been maintained for more than 10 years. They re-created seven of the city's popular neighborhoods, such as Chinatown and Haight-Ashbury, while at the same time also producing a block party carnival with a live concert featuring Smash Mouth for a mostly male crowd. There was something for everyone, and it all screamed "San Francisco." The numbers on this job speak volumes: 132,000 square feet of space to fill; more than 9 tons of food; 22,000 bottles of beer; 888 bottles of wine; 9,000 man hours to bring the event to life; 108,000 watts of light; a stage anchored with 32,000 pounds of cement; 10 generators; 4 water tanks; 9 restroom trailers; 52,000 square feet of custom draping; 172 renderings; and 1,200 crew members on-site.

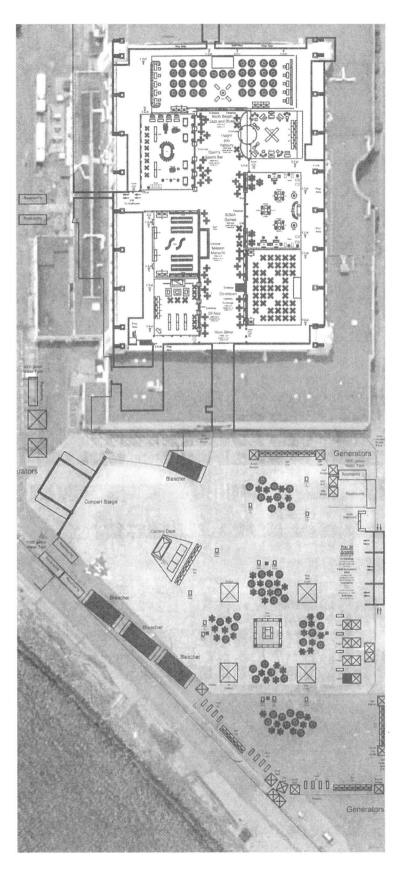

11. Private mansion, Malibu, California.

Courtesy of Andrea Michaels, Extraordinary Events, Sherman Oaks, California.

This event for 140 guests was a product launch for the client BMW International during the LA Auto Show. The client requested a hospitality event for "the ultimate driving machine" in a location described as "find us a place that looks like a BMW." The challenge for Extraordinary Events was to find a location that best represented the brand and then create a "totally BMW" evening.

The event planner located a private and very contemporary estate high atop the hills of Malibu and then created a menu and design that said "power and performance fit the bill."

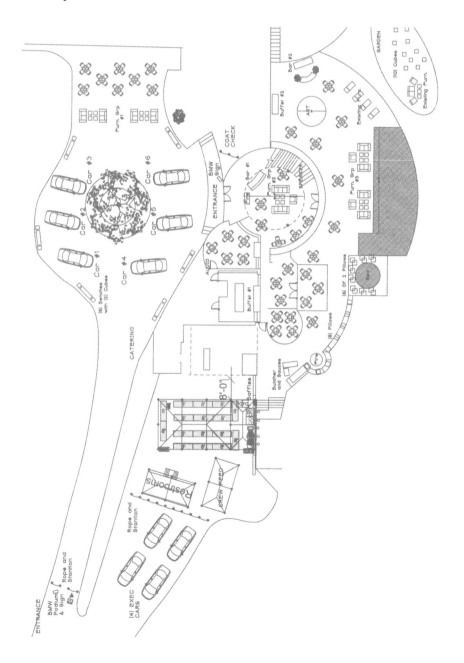

12. Long Beach Convention Center, Long Beach, California.
Courtesy of Andrea Michaels, Extraordinary Events, Sherman Oaks, California.

Every two years, American Honda Motor Co. holds an NH Circle World Convention. Each event is held in a different country and hosted by a different Honda division. The year Extraordinary Events was in charge of organizing the two-night global conference for 800 guests, the functions focused both on Honda's North America division as the host and Honda as a global family.

With such an international crowd, the event planner used the international languages of décor, entertainment, and food to convey Honda's message. This included a giant globe structure of the custom conference logo, living vignettes as buffet centerpieces, graphic globes, and custom Rubik's Cubes. Entertainment played a crucial role on both evenings and included mariachis, a Celtic dance troupe, the Three Waiters, the First AME Church Choir, a custom laser show, and the Zippers, to name only a few. All entertainment was carefully scheduled between dinner courses and executive speeches.

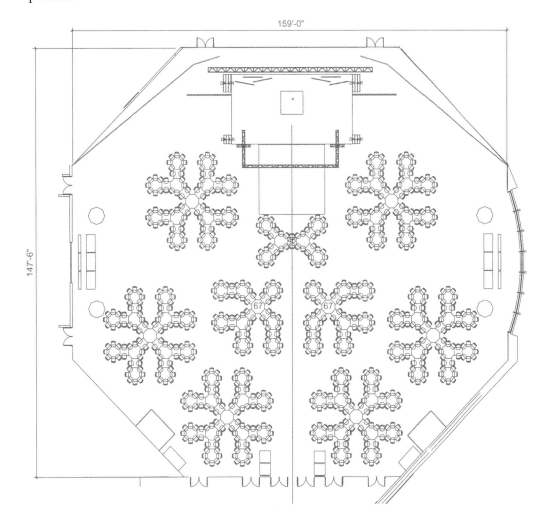

13. Hordern Pavilion, Sydney.

Courtesy of Greg Pullen and Play Bill Venues, Moore Park, Sydney.

Design of floor plan by Meri Took of Staging Rentals.

The Hordern Pavilion (www.playbillvenues.com) offers adaptability due to the squareness of the floor space. For this gala evening, a fully covered tunnel was built inside using truss and black velvet draping. Such tunnels are passageways created to add a wow factor at events. The tunnel was approximately 100 feet long and broken into five compartments. Each compartment offered a different experience appealing to one of the five senses: sight, smell, touch, taste, and sound.

The pre-function area was set up with bars and lounges opening up to the main dining area. Here, there was a central revolving stage and tables set up in three layers.

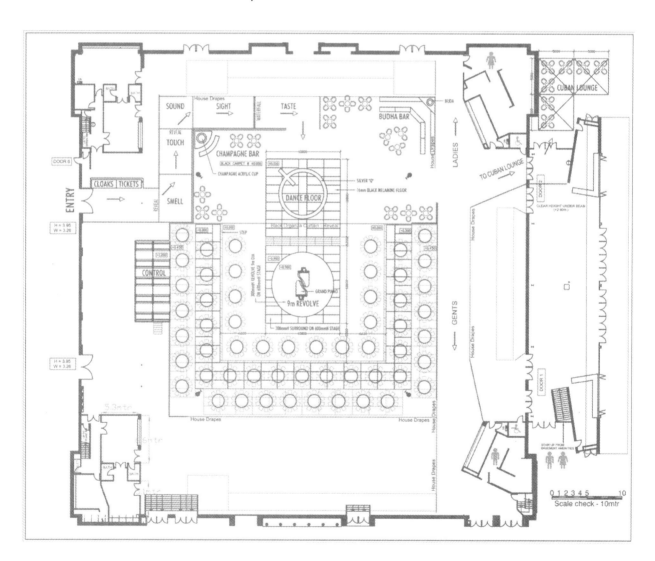

14. La Nouvelle Orleans Ballroom,
    Ernest N. Morial Convention Center, New Orleans, Louisiana.
    Courtesy of Kellie Mathas and The Special Event 2010 conference.

This inventive floor plan was created for a gala evening for The Special Event organization in New Orleans in January 2010. The table setup included a combination of wide rectangular and round tables and stylish 18-inch chairs. On walking into the main room, guests encountered a soft mist generated by a fog machine that beautified the lighting and made the room appear to be in a haze.

On one end, there was a lounge area where people had the opportunity to meet and network, while on the opposite end a dance floor, DJ, and a live music band were set up.

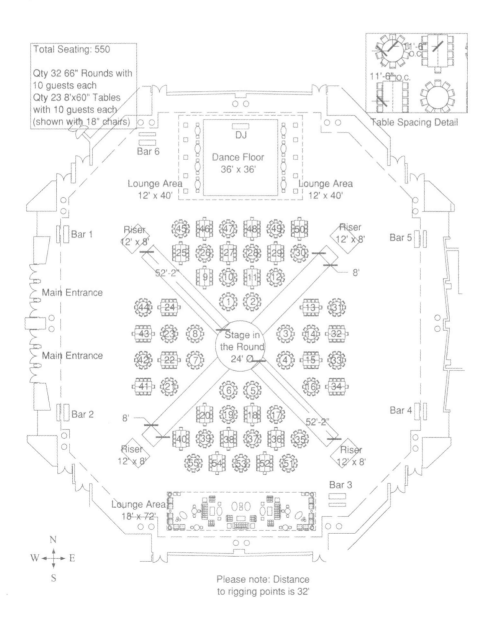

In the center, there was a 24-foot-high stage with four runways leading to it from the corners of the room, with a riser at the end of each runway. This gave prominence to the many entertainers performing at this event, from aerial artists and feature singers to New Orleans drummers and New Orleans dance groups.

One interesting feature of the décor was women suspended from the chandeliers. They dropped suddenly, as if out of space, hovered slightly above the heads of guests, and poured champagne. For photos of this event, see color plates, Figures 1–3.

When you are selecting a venue for your event, first look at the assets of the room under consideration and evaluate the ease of access to the building. Knowing these intricacies will help you select the best venue option and will save you time and money in the long run.

Manage the Money

ONCE YOU HAVE A CLEARLY DEFINED STRATEGY THAT WILL enable you to increase your client base, focus on managing the money.

Budgeting

Working within a budget is a winning formula if you wish to make money. It will ensure that your business remains viable in the long term.

For some events business owners, projected and actual budgets are a mystery. It does not have to be that way. We do not need to be highly sophisticated financially, but we must know enough to be able to manage our money. To increase your knowledge, you need to ask yourself certain basic questions to get basic information. You need to ask yourself the following four questions:

What can I spend?

Where is the real profit on this job?

What are my labor costs?

What stock can I purchase right now?

And once you have the answers to those questions, ask yourself:

Where can I make cuts without sacrificing the quality of the event?

When answering these questions, the word *honest* comes to mind. We can all hope that we will suddenly land 15 major projects, but the cold, hard truth is that we

What Does a Budget Do?

- Helps you plan for the future

- Allows you to make predictions about your business

- Shows you what incoming revenue to expect

- Exposes expenses that must be covered

- Shows the expected profit or loss on each job

- Produces targets for your business to aim for

---

probably won't; therefore, our working budgets should err on the side of caution. If those coveted contracts fall into our laps, we are in for a nice bonus.

Six months is generally the favored budget period, but a quarterly assessment is even better for an events business.

Fixed and Variable Business Costs

The following is a list of typical categories of fixed and variable costs for event planning businesses. Use this list to create spreadsheets that will help you generate your quarterly and annual budgets and spreadsheets for monitoring your actual business costs.

Fixed expenses are ones you must pay at regular intervals and are best described as recurring, such as property rent, equipment leases, and insurance. These are usually paid on a weekly, monthly, or quarterly basis. Once you decide to contract one of these costs, you undertake a long-term obligation to pay these bills.

Variable expenses, such as freight and office supplies, are more irregular, and the amounts and frequency of recurrence vary. They pertain to expenditures that are more flexible and offer the principal an opportunity to save with careful planning and ongoing monitoring. Variable expenses are costs of doing business that are separate from costs assigned to the everyday running of the business.

Fixed Expenses

Rent

Bank charges

Office cleaning

Insurance

Interest on loans

Depreciation on vehicles, equipment, and machinery

Industry memberships dues

Utility bills, such as electricity, water, gas, heating, and air-conditioning

Employee salaries and wages

Communications, such as telephone, fax, and Internet service

Office equipment rental

Business taxes

Waste disposal

Motor vehicle (registration, gas, and maintenance)

Variable Costs

Transport

Temporary employees

Travel

Accountancy and financial services

Advertising

Conferences and conventions

Consultants

Couriers

Contractors' commissions

Magazine subscriptions

Employee bonuses and rewards

Employee gifts

Freight and cartage

Fines

Gifts for clients

Office supplies

Mailing

Office repairs and maintenance

Staff amenities

Legal costs

Promotional materials, such as company stationery and Web site design and maintenance

Making money for the business is very much like personal savings. You see something you love, and you have to make the decision about whether it is a necessity for the business or an unneeded extravagance. The key is to think before you twitter the dollars away. Consider adopting a wise principle and personally approve all purchases for the business and sign your own checks.

We must look back into our operation periodically and review every single cost related to the business. The advantage of doing this is that if there can be a small saving on every variable cost, there will be a considerable amount of money saved at the end of the year. For the small business that may have annual revenue of a quarter to a half million dollars, a savings of $200 a week on the variables will result in a $10,000 gain at the end of the financial year. We must look for areas where we can save and search for improvement in the way we operate and the way we manage the finances.

The best leaders realize that the need for improvement is continuous. They have a sheer determination to make financial progress. They must set their sights higher and higher. Standards and systems can be fixed in this game, but with budgets we must be willing to work within that framework and make each accepted job profitable.

Financial Adviser: A Necessity, Not a Luxury

Larger companies can often afford the assistance of a full-time financial adviser. Smaller businesses cannot afford this luxury, but even then, a financial adviser must be involved on a part-time or freelance basis. When choosing a financial adviser, consider working with someone who has an understanding of the events industry and, particularly, a working knowledge of the financial aspects of the business. The advice you expect from this specialist should be focused wholly on the bottom line.

This professional may oversee incoming revenue and outgoing expenses and guide the business with an eye on growth. This guidance gives you clarity on your financial standing and hence allows you to position yourself to maintain your existing clients and simultaneously take on new accounts.

A good financial adviser will help you manage your finances beyond just making sure there are sufficient funds to pay the current bills; he or she will offer suggestions for creative allocation of funds. He or she may offer procedural solutions to improve your cash flow, so funds become freed up to organize a marketing campaign or purchase new office equipment. Other ways of allocating financial resources could be setting some aside as reserves and investing for future times of need.

You will also be advised to look closely at your operation and look for potential problem spots. There are companies that tend to carry too much stock, for example. Some people like to stockpile so they're not caught short. Overstocking your studio is very expensive because it lowers your cash flow—your money is trapped in the stock that is sitting and waiting to be needed. And low cash reserves can cripple your business.

A business adviser will also make it clear to you that it is pointless to spend time and effort winning an event contract, delivering a spectacular show, and sending out invoices if you then fail to collect the amounts due. The adviser will remind you that you are in business to make money.

With the guidance of this professional you will be able to take your business to a new level.

Spotlight Aspects of Your Enterprise for Review

If you're not sure why you aren't making as much money as you should be, go back to your projected budget and check it against reality—the actual revenues and expenses. Another way to perform a financial analysis is to focus on the different aspects of the business one at a time, to ensure you are actually turning over the expected profit in each area.

Most businesses find that with every passing year their overhead tends to rise more rapidly than the volume of sales. Because business owners find it difficult and time-consuming to apply a continual study of all factors of overheads, I advise you to apply the "spotlight" method to one aspect of your business a month to assess whether this area is profiting you or merely contributing to loss.

The following list shows a few specific areas of business to review for changes that may prove to be money savers.

> *Conferences.* Review the list of conferences you normally attend for the betterment of the business and your professional growth. If expense cuts need to be made, limit your and your staff's attendance to the conferences that are going to bring some financial return.

> *Organizations.* Only remain in organizations that benefit your company in a tangible way.

> *Couriers.* Courier services are expensive and it is best to have a policy to avoid this expense unless absolutely necessary. Even if you avoid routinely using these services, you may find yourself resorting to calling a courier; this may happen when you are on a job and suddenly find that due to a packing error necessary goods are missing, or when returns were not made on time and late fees threaten. A way to avoid courier costs is to plan well. When

preparing for a job, have a packing list of all necessary items or equipment. This list can then be passed on to the packers for reference. Remember to check and double-check.

Communications. Bundle your communications package and negotiate for landline, cellular phone, fax, and Internet services. Doing this will result in considerable savings for the business.

Contractors. The costs of outside contractors can get high if you fail to keep control of their hours of work, excluding breaks and lunch hours. It is advisable to have contractors sign on when they start the job, and sign off when their work hours are complete. I have mentioned before the advantages of taking an assistant or administrator onto the job with you; this person will be responsible for recording staff times and correctly checking their working hours. I seriously recommend planning the contractors' work hours ahead of time, during contract negotiations, so that there are no surprises when they send in their invoices for payment.

Money can also be saved on contractors if you stagger their hours of work by making sure you only bring them in when they are needed. This avoids having them waiting around for others to finish before they can commence their work. This particularly applies to set designers and florists.

Design Materials. You can always save money when a prototype of the décor prop or floral design is done for the client's approval. This strategy helps avoid excessive spending on a range of decorative materials or fresh flowers that would be wasted if the client did not approve a design.

Fines. Encourage your drivers to park correctly and observe speed limits regardless of the location. Parking tickets of $200 to $300 each are an expense your business doesn't need. Be sure to communicate your wish to the drivers in regards to fines and speeding; if you clarify that incorrect parking or speeding fines are their financial responsibility, rest assured, the drivers will observe the rules.

Office Supplies. Buying office equipment and stationery in bulk is one idea for savings. It is also wise to do a price comparison when you buy in bulk. Avoid last-minute purchases, as they add up to a substantial figure at the end of the year.

Salaries. Adopt the Trump philosophy of "hire slow, fire fast." This means giving new employee candidates a careful review before committing to a long-term contract. Employ them on a trial basis or for one to three months, with a review for full-time employment after that time.

One way of arranging to absorb an increased overhead without reducing profits or increasing sales prices is to plan an increase in the volume of sales as discussed in Point 4, "Build the Business" (page 21).

As a business owner, you must be business conscious. It is necessary for all members of your team to play their part in keeping profits up and the waste of financial resources down. A business that keeps asking itself questions and takes the necessary actions to improve and profit is well on its way to becoming a commercial force in the industry.

Pinpoint Profitability of Each Event

It can pay off considerably for you to learn to calculate the expected profit of each job and become aware of hidden costs that could eat into the programmed profit.

I conducted a workshop with 60 participants recently, and I asked them if they knew the profit of each job before they went into it. Shock and horror: only 20 percent put their hands up! I always remain surprised at just how many event principals commit to jobs without knowing the actual profit. Take the time to work out the profit of the job before a loss of profit occurs.

Budgeting for an Event

A template is a must when you start working on the budget for each event. I use the template on pages 80–84 even on smaller jobs to avoid missing an item when charging the client.

Proposal

Under the costing template, the management fees can be the main fee for the organization of the event.

Many event planners ask me whether they can charge for the time-consuming preparation of the proposal itself and/or the creative concept. My response is usually no. If a client calls you into his or her office to give you an event brief with the intention of giving you work and your response is, "Thank you, but I will have to charge you for the proposal and concept," within seconds you will be shown the door.

On the other hand, let's say the same client calls you to brief you on a particularly big event. You realize that this proposal in presentation form will run from $500 to $5,000 and it is not certain you will get the job. In such situations, I advise that you request from $500 to $1,000 for the detailed proposal and budget, but make it clear that this amount will be refunded if the client wishes to proceed. If clients like and trust you due to the past work you have done for them, they will likely be agreeable to this request. Bear in mind that a proposal for a mega event will far exceed $1,000.

CONCEPTUAL ART

Some events require artistic impressions of the proposed concept to illustrate the idea or look, and for such artwork it is legitimate to charge from $500 to $3,000 and even more in some cases, so inform the client of this fee. But you may decide to absorb the cost of this artwork, especially if you feel it adds to the value of the presentation and will assist you in winning the job. As a point of interest, if you review the mega event that Andrea Michaels organized on page 65 you will find that 172 drawings were required. Another example of conceptual art can be seen in the 1920s stage illustration on page 182.

Administration

Most of the entries in this section cover communication costs of each individual job, whether it is staged in a ballroom, tent, or field. These are "on-location costs." The general practice is to charge 1 to 2 percent of the total cost of the event to cover these expenses; for example, if the event total is $100,000, you can assume that basic administrative costs of your office alone are $2,000.

LEGAL COSTS

Some events require legal documents prepared or require attorney's advice, and these fees need to be considered in the budgeting stage and shown to the client for approval.

COURIER AND TAXI

If a client makes a specific request that requires courier, limousine, or taxi service during production or on the day of the event, such as picking up a forgotten guest, you can charge the client for fulfilling these tasks.

Entertainment

If you feel that a rehearsal of the entertainment is necessary to achieve maximum client satisfaction, then costs of rehearsal space are incurred. Also, the musicians and entertainers need to be booked to come in a few hours prior to the event, and this means an additional expense. This extra cost must be incurred with the approval of the client only, but if you point out the advantage of the rehearsal, the client usually approves.

Remember that not all venues have pianos or music bandstands, so sometimes you will need to rent these and charge the client for the rentals.

Catering

It is a usual practice to include crew meals and refreshments as a cost billed to the client. Crew meals are usually not the same meal that is served to the guests, but a wholesome two-course staff meal will suffice.

Décor

This section of costs covers all venue decorations, including decorative props, floral designs, fresh plants, fairy lights, or anything pertaining to the dressing of the event. Remember to include decorations for all areas: the main room, pre-function or drinks area, stages, entrances, gates, and/or similar positions of the venue.

Waste

When the job requires a massive amount of décor or flowers, or when the number of guests is high, there is going to be a massive amount of waste. The commercial waste bins will need to be ordered with the approval of the venue and positioned in the allocated back area of the venue with the approval of the venue operator. On the other hand, the venue may let you use its waste units.

Printing/Promo

This section covers any printing that you may need to do on behalf of the client, from invitations and menus to place cards and promotional materials.

Labor

In this section, you want to include the costs of labor for your staff plus the hours contracted to the casuals employed for the job. Taking the time to calculate the hours for each team member is a necessity as it will give you the accumulated hours for the labor component. Then multiply these accumulated hours by the wage team members are paid per hour. This will help you arrive at a profit, not a loss, on a job.

Costing Template for an Event

Item	Budget	Actual	Contractor Cost
PROPOSAL			
Creative concept			
Conceptual art			
MANAGEMENT			
Event planner's fee			
Producer's fee			
Stage manager's fee			
Consultancy fees, if any			
ADMINISTRATION			
Phone			
E-mail and fax			
Staff travel			
Staff amenities			
Insurance for event			
Legal costs, if required			
Courier and taxi			
Dry cleaning			
ENTERTAINMENT			
Rehearsal space			
Piano and other equipment rental, if required			
Feature artists' fees			
Bands' fees			

Item	Budget	Actual	Contractor Cost
Speakers' fees			
Additional artist			
Costume re'			
Transfe'			
Sp'			
Adu.			
Food			
Beverages			
Waitstaff and bar staff			
Storage supply area			
Dinnerware			
Glassware			
Silverware and utensils			
Refreshments for crew			
Crew meals			
Uniforms			
Equipment rentals			

Item	Budget	Actual	Contractor Cost
TECHNICAL			
Technical adviser			
Lighting equipment			
Lighting operator			
Audio equipment			
Rigging equipment			
Video and special effects equipment			
Projection system			
Camera and operator			
Special effects			
Stanchion and ropes			
Spotlights and platforms			
Microphone			
STAGING			
Main stage			
Side stages			
Stage skirting			
Stage steps			
Dance floor			
Podium			
Scissor lifts			
Ladders and trolleys			
Room blackout			
Ceiling truss			

Item	Budget	Actual	Contractor Cost
DÉCOR			
Décor on stage			
Décor for ceiling			
Décor for pre-function/ reception area			
Décor for full or part of the room			
Lighting rentals			
Sets of flowers			
Floral urns			
Floral tabletops			
Floral accessories			
Table linens (including chair covers and napkins)			
Table gifts or party favors			
Balloon artistry			
Other special décor effects			
WASTE			
Trash systems, if required			
Transfer of waste			
VENUE			
Venue rental if on-site			
Rental fee for off-site			
License and permits			
Cancellation costs, if any			

Item	Budget	Actual	Contractor Cost
Parking costs			
Storage costs			
Breakout rooms rental			
PRINTING/PROMO			
Invitations			
Place cards / hold-the-date cards, if required			
Menus			
Flyers and posters			
Programs			
Signage and banners			
Directional signs			
Badges and ribbons			
LABOR			
Staff wages			
Contractors' wages			
Cleaning staff			
Other labor costs			

Setting Your Fees and Invoicing

In regards to setting your event management fee, a general practice is to charge 15 to 25 percent of the total event budget.

There are two methods used in the industry for invoicing the client.

1. The client receives an invoice with only one charge listed on it. This number covers the event planner's fee, the costs of all the products that were necessary to purchase or rent, and the costs of all the services the planner subcontracted, such as the artist's, technical contractor's, or the floral designer's fees. The event planner takes care to include an additional fee of 10 to 15 percent of the subcontractors' charges for serving as the broker.

2. The event planner charges a fee for organizing and managing the event and invoices the client just for this fee. The planner selects the contactors, from floral designer and caterer to technical and staging help, and they each invoice the client for their products and services. The client pays each contractor directly. All the invoices from the contractors are addressed to the client; however, they are first reviewed and approved by the event planner and only then forwarded to the client for payment. When using this method, planners need to impose a greater management fee because the client is utilizing the best of their knowledge and their recommended contractors. This method is known as "open invoicing" and is requested quite frequently.

Whichever invoicing method you choose, or the client prefers, be upfront with your client in regard to the payment process.

Present the Proposal

THE PROPOSAL IS THE DOCUMENT THAT YOU PREPARE IN writing and present to the client, often accompanied by visual aids, in response to his or her request for a proposal (RFP). This document outlines how you would go about staging the client's event, and it reflects your organized approach to event planning, your expertise, and your standing within the industry as a professional.

Maximize Your Chances of Winning the Job

Proposals that fail are usually not persuasive in conveying the visual aspects of the event, or they fail to demonstrate the event planner's flexibility and capability to meet the client's budget. A well-prepared, well-worded proposal shows a process that is systematically programmed to take the job beyond expectations for the client. When the client receives your written proposal, make sure it represents your best effort.

Combining the proposal with skilful face-to-face presentations can increase your business. Meeting clients in person will increase your chance of the clients getting to know you, and if they like you, they will buy from you. This is what is called "relationship selling" and, of course, remember that this first impression of dress, manner, and behavior reflects your professional image.

Such a meeting also provides an opportunity to present visual aids that refer to the job, such as the floor plans that will be crucial to the flow of the evening and the color scheme of the proposed decorations.

But there are times when a face-to-face presentation is not an option. The client is then left to select the event planner from written submissions. Therefore, you either fall behind in the way you have written the document and hence fail to get the job, or you stand out entirely due to the finished proposal and win the job. Lack of face-to-face interaction leaves you vulnerable to the possibility that the client will misunderstand your ideas or not realize that you have the flexibility to adapt to his or her needs. It doesn't leave space for the client to get a sense of your personality and work style. In a face-to-face presentation, you can monitor the client's body language and dispel doubts immediately, before they take root in the client's mind.

You can standardize the following components of your proposals:

1. List the services you provide.

2. Insert the financial formula detailing the form of payment, that is,
   (a) 50 percent paid upon confirmation in writing, with a further 25 percent paid two weeks out from the job and the balance paid on completion;
   or (b) an alternate progressive payment plan that is negotiated with the client.

3. Define the cancellation clause of the venue.

4. Include a confidentiality clause.

5. Provide your company portfolio and contact details.

Word the document so that it reads like a discussion. Use the heading "discussion proposal" because then the client will understand that the document is not "set in cement." Present the entire document in a consistent layout style, using headings and subheadings.

What cannot be standardized are the creative elements of any event. These will change from one project to the next, as you may need to write up a proposal for a corporate breakfast with a budget of $2,000, a corporate luncheon for $20,000, or a gala event for $200,000.

When you write a proposal, you write for the decision maker. He or she could then sign off on it simply because he or she has an amicable relationship with the event planner. Alternatively, a decision maker who is highly analytical will immediately look at the costs. To him or her, in this case, the creative elements then become a secondary consideration. However, try to recognize the personality of your client when communicating (see pages 213–221, which define behavioral personalities).

How to Create a Proposal: Step-by-Step

1. ***Do your homework.*** Before creating a proposal for a company you have not worked with before, and especially before meeting with a new client face-to-face to discuss the project, research the client company to become familiar with its history. The informative Web site www.Hoovers.com, for example, is a good starting point for company information.

2. ***Establish the client's objective.*** You must observe exactly what the client wants to achieve from this event. Listen carefully to the client to clarify the appropriate brief as he or she discusses and informs you of his or her wants and needs. Try not to interrupt the person speaking, as it will be disruptive to his or her line of thought. Ask questions after the speaker has finished.

   The following list gives a few examples of corporate objectives for special events.

   (a) It can be intended to expand the client's database.

   (b) It can be an incentive program to motivate the company's sales staff.

   (c) It can be a part of the marketing business plan for the company.

   Get answers to the following key questions:

   Why is it being held?

   What is the client objective?

   When will it be held?

   Where will it be held?

   Who will be attending?

   How will it be budgeted?

3. ***Define the creative plan.*** Research the concept specifically requested by the company and come up with your creative concept.

   (a) The style of the event

   (b) Décor and color scheme

   (c) Technical specifications for light, sound, visions, and special effects

(d) Entertainment components, including photographs and bios of the feature artists and bands that you are proposing

(e) Catering, including a profile of the caterer with a suggested menu

4. *Walk the client though the story.*

(a) Let the written word express the visualization of the event.

(b) Make the visual aids (conceptual art, drawings, and photos) support the concept.

(c) Include a table layout on a floor plan.

(d) Present the first draft of the event's schedule. To some planners, it may seem early to be discussing such a schedule, but this will truly give the client an idea of how the evening is going to flow.

5. *Stipulate the specifics.*

(a) The financial formula payment

(b) The cancellation clause

(c) The confidentiality clause

(d) Agreement and confirmation

A Proposal Sample

I have always found that it is far easier to formulate a proposal plan by viewing a sample document, so you may care to compare the following template to your existing proposals. Let it serve as a guideline and modify it to suit your style.

Discussion Proposal for the Star Company

Date: _____

Name: _____

Address: _____

Contact: _____

Telephone: _____

E-mail: _____

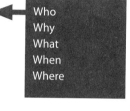

On your letterhead, add full client contact details.

Attn: Mr. Star, CEO

Star Company

Who
Why
What
When
Where

- A company 50th anniversary celebration

- An appreciation gala dinner

- January 2013

- Museum auditorium

The Event Overview

This gala dinner will reflect the formality befitting the celebration of the 50th anniversary of the Star Company for 500 VIP invited guests.

Describe the event in one or two paragraphs (approximately 150 words) so the client can imagine and visualize the evening.

This special evening will be sophisticated in format, visually stunning, and stylishly staged. This beautifully dressed venue, in black and silver, will provide a dramatic effect, both emotionally and physically.

This grand celebration evening offers a series of special events, wonderful entertainment, and surprises that will delight your guests.

1. Arrival

Refer to photographs, pictures, or pen drawings to illustrate the proposed decoration for this area.

- Lighting effects enhance the exterior of the building with the Star Company logo moving forward and back across its face.

- A series of 10-foot-high fresh cypress trees create an impressive entrance.

- The concierge assists guests as they arrive and directs them onto the black carpet runway under a stylish black and silver striped awning, preceding the entrance doors.

- Guests enter the interior for coatroom access and use.

- The Star concierges assist guests into the entrance. Guests will then be directed to the tunnel to experience five senses: smell, sound, sight, touch, and taste, which leads to the pre-function space where champagne cocktails are served.

The Detailed Creative Plan

The Floor Plan

Present a floor plan, preferably in size A3 laminated copies, and explain the flow of the evening in detail. Be brief and precise.

The Event's Schedule, First Draft for Discussion

2. The Five-Senses Tunnel

- Guests enter a unique 80-foot tunnel, constructed within the auditorium. The walls and ceiling of the tunnel are covered with black velvet. The tunnel is broken into five segments that are approximately 15 feet square and 9 feet high. Each segment represents a different sense: smell, touch, sound, sight, and taste. As guests walk through the tunnel and into each compartment, they have the opportunity to experience it sensually.

- Guests pass through in groups of 20 and concierges stand by to assist with the flow of guest movement.

(a) Segment 1: The Sense of Smell

- Beautiful florals are traditionally arranged and heavily perfumed with essential oils. Silk fabrics spill from the back of the urns, providing a lavish floor look.
- Soft specialty lights on the floor and ceiling enhance the look of the floral décor.
- After approximately 90 seconds, the black velvet curtains dividing the segments are automatically opened and the group moves into Segment 2: The Sense of Touch.

(b) Segment 2: The Sense of Touch

- A special effect is featured on the floor and walls. With the touch of a hand, visuals emerge from an otherwise blank canvas. This is an out-of-the-ordinary effect, fully expressing the sense of touch.
- After approximately 90 seconds, the black velvet curtains dividing the segments are automatically opened and the group moves into Segment 3: The Sense of Sound.

(c) Segment 3: The Sense of Sound

- This area is completely blacked out as the sense of sound comes into play through very clever sound effects. Arrow lighting on the floor acts as the directional sign to lead the guests into Segment 4: The Sense of Sight.

(d) Segment 4: The Sense of Sight

- In this segment, there is a special effect of water flowing on a wall.
- The technical use of lighting brings to light a distinctive look for this sense.
- After approximately 90 seconds, the black velvet curtains dividing the segments are automatically opened and the group moves into Segment 5: The Sense of Taste.

(e) Segment 5: The Sense of Taste

- Segment 5: The Sense of Taste opens to the pre-function area where guests mingle.
- As guests experience the fifth sense, the waitstaff is on standby to serve the guests cocktails and appetizers. The floor plan shows the specifics of this room layout from its conversational velvet lounges to the specialty champagne bar, the daiquiri ice bar, and the starlight bar.

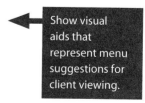
Show visual aids that represent menu suggestions for client viewing.

- The pre-function area is completely carpeted in black.

- A feature of this area is the viewing of the full room through a ceiling-to-floor black organza curtain that will be lifted when guests are to be seated. This is also clearly illustrated on the floor plan.

- The magic of the evening begins with aerial artists dancing in space. The aerial tissues and swings fall above the heads of guests; the artists dance in the air while guests enjoy cocktails and canapés. The soft sounds of the 16-piece orchestra are heard and at the appropriate time guests are ushered to their tables to be seated.

3. It Is Time to Dine

Points 1–8 in this proposal write-up include a lot of details, so that every aspect of the event is covered. I consider the numbering of each element essential, as it will aid you in creating and adjusting the event budget as it changes through the planning process.

- At the scheduled time, the black organza curtain lifts to the ceiling to expose the dining area. Guests are ushered and directed to their tables by waitstaff.

- The stage is a feature and is central in the room. It is 4 feet high in elevation so that it can be seen by all guests. The stage will also revolve on call. A shiny black melamine dance floor is positioned in front of the stage as shown on the CAD plan.

- Black velvet skirting surrounds the stage apron, while the steps to the platform are mirrored and lit.

- Tables of 10 are set on different levels, creating a cabaret-style design.

- Two grand pianos are displayed (one black, one white) as part of the orchestra.

4. The Event's Design Elements

(a) Tablecloths and Chair Covers

Take photographs of the tablecloths or samples of the fabric to show the client.

- There are 50 tables of 10, allowing for 500 guests.

- The BBJ linens are floor-length imported black and silver brocade tablecloths with black velvet chair covers and ties. The black brocade napkins are dressed with black and silver trim.

- The floral chandeliers are suspended from a ceiling truss and measure 4 feet in diameter.

(b) Tabletops

- The canopy of flowers is designed to stand 5 to 6 feet high. It is also designed to form a canopy over the heads of the guests. The flowers are lilies, roses, and orchids, with a variety of choice foliage.

Show samples of the flowers you propose to use, as well as photographs of your suggested tabletops.

5. Staging

The stage for this event is a feature of the room, built in its center and elevated 4 feet high so that guests can view the entertainment comfortably. The stage is black. Two pianos are placed centrally.

Consult with your staging specialist and describe what your staging will look like.

6. Technical Brief

As the guests walk into the main dining area, intelligent lighting creates a soft wall wash that complements the overall color palette of the décor. As a feature, every tabletop is pinpointed with light to enhance the centerpieces. Decorative units around the room and on the stage are specifically lit with floor lighting.

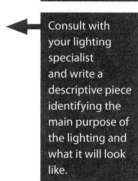

Consult with your lighting specialist and write a descriptive piece identifying the main purpose of the lighting and what it will look like.

7. Entertainment

Two professional piano players from the Sydney Recital Group serenade guests throughout the evening. They play a mixture of classical music and jazz, providing both relaxing and upbeat music.

Show promotional materials from proposed entertainers.

8. Catering

Menu

Appetizers

Peking duck crepes with spring onions and hoisin sauce

Roulade of smoked salmon with lemon crème fraîche and dill

Zucchini and red pepper frittata with sun-dried tomato pesto

Seafood tartlet with prawn, rocket, and cashew sauce

Chicken satay skewers with peanut dipping sauce

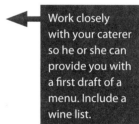

Work closely with your caterer so he or she can provide you with a first draft of a menu. Include a wine list.

First Course

A choice of:

Steamed mussels in a spicy broth

Lamb and rocket salad with black olive dressing

Grilled haloumi cheese served with Italian bread and fresh garden salad

Main Course

A choice of:

Marinated leg of lamb with spicy char-grilled vegetables and garlic-yogurt sauce

Ricotta and spinach gnocchi with brown butter

Crispy-skin salmon with braised chickpeas and herbed yogurt

Dessert

Mango and passion fruit trifle served with vanilla bean ice cream

Carrot and almond cake served with freshly whipped cream

This first draft of the evening schedule is presented to the client to provide a general overview of the evening. Once this is approved in concept by the client, a very detailed minute by minute schedule will be finalized.

9. The Event Schedule

Time	Activity
7:00 p.m.	Guests arrive and are guided to the coatroom by the concierge. Groups of 20 enter Segment 1, and the process continues until all guests enter the pre-function area.
7:40 p.m.	Guests enjoy cocktails and appetizers. A ceiling-to-floor black organza curtain partially conceals the total look.
8:00 p.m.	The black organza lifts up to the ceiling as a surprising revealing. Two pianists at grand pianos are seen and heard. Aerial tissues and swings fall from the ceiling. Aerial artists perform for 5 to 6 minutes.
8:10 p.m.	The celebrity MC asks guests to be seated.
8:25 p.m.	The first course is served.
8:50 p.m.	The first course is cleared.
8:55 p.m.	The feature artist performs for 20 minutes.
9:15 p.m.	The main course is served. The two pianos resume through dinner, playing softly to allow conversation at the tables.

9:50 p.m.	The main course is cleared.
9:55 p.m.	The MC thanks artists and introduces the main performer.
	The 10 performers emerge from different areas and elevations of the room, entering at different times. They perform for 25 minutes.
10:25 p.m.	The MC invites guests to mix and mingle.
	Guests serve themselves from the buffet table or movable trolleys of desserts and coffee tables set in conversational areas.
	The big band takes the stage and dancing commences.
10:45 p.m.	Segments 1, 2, 3, 4, and 5 open on the side of the room, allowing guests to wander back into the pods to further indulge the senses.
12:00 a.m.	A spectacular special effect in the form of a glitter drop indicates the end of the evening.

The Event Plan Components

10. The Summary of Event Costs

Event Personnel

Executive producer consultancy/management fee	$
Producer	$
Creative event stylist	$
Stage manager (3 days)	$

Technical Components

Staging	$
Technical adviser and lighting	$
Audio and sound operator	$

A summary of estimated costs is also a necessary component of a proposal, and quite often the client company will go to this page before considering the creatives.

The event planner or management fee is generally 15 to 20 percent of the budget. This cost is included here under "Executive producer consultancy/ management fee."

Technical Components (continued)

Vision	$
Communications headsets, etc.	$
Risk management consultant	$

Venue Rental

Rental fee (4 days)	$

Food and Beverages

Catering (including food and beverages, waitstaff, bartenders, kitchens, dinnerware, equipment)	$
Crew meals	$

Entertainment

Pianos	$
Other equipment rentals	$
Entertainer special requests	$
Entertainment director	$
Entertainment quote	$
Décor, sets, and florals	$
Cloths/covers/napkins	$
Conceptual art (optional)	$
Load-in/load-out	$

Furniture and Bar Rentals

Bars	$
Lounges in conversational nooks	$
Provisional Budget	**$**

Presenting the expected costs in a table format gives you a handy and visually friendly reference in meetings and allows you to easily enter budget adjustments.

Financial Clause

The required amount is to be paid in three installments so arrangements can be made for the pre-event aspects; 25 percent is to be paid on acceptance, 50 percent is to be paid two months out from the event, and the final 25 percent is to be paid on completion.

Cancellation Clause

If cancellation occurs, the following charges will be imposed for services and work undertaken to date:

Days Prior to Event	Percentage of Budget Billed for Cancellation
Up to 120	10
Less than 90	20
Less than 60	60
Less than 30	90

The specific terms of the cancellation clause presented here are a general guideline.

Confidentiality Clause

The documents accompanying this communication may contain information that is legally privileged. The information is intended only for the use of the intended recipient named within. If you are not the intended recipient, you are hereby notified that any disclosure, copying, distribution, or taking of action in reliance on the contents of this copied information, except its direct delivery to the intended, is strictly prohibited. If you have received this correspondence, fax, or e-mail in error, please notify us by telephone to arrange the return of the original documents.

All props, linens, and tablecloths remain the property of our company. In the event of theft or damage, a wholesale cost will be invoiced to the client.

Important Points to Remember
When Preparing Your Proposal

- I repeat, use the heading "Discussion Proposal" for any written proposal. It shows flexibility and adaptability because it implies you will make appropriate changes to fit the client's business objective and budget.

- Number each component of the event to assist you with the final write-up to be signed off on.

- Number every page in the lower right-hand corner, making reference easier when the proposal is under discussion with the client.

- Prepare copies for each person expected to be sitting in on the meeting. Do not arrive with just one copy.

Written Confirmation

Any event can only be confirmed when the client has paid the requested deposit and signed off on the proposal. If one or both of these fail to happen, you are best advised to consider the job a nonevent. To start any job based only on verbal confirmation can be a costly mistake and one you do not need to experience. If you have seen my presentation at The Special Event conference, you have heard me say, "If you don't want the paperwork, don't do the party."

The Event Cabinet

ERFORMERS ARE ONLY AS GOOD AS THEIR LAST CONCERT, authors are only as good as their last book, and event planners are only as good as their last event. And your last event is only as good as your team. This is an industry that can't be handled solo. Due to the sheer amount of work required to create a spectacular event, you need people with you every step of the way. These people—whether you hire them as full-time or part-time employees or whether they are your freelance contractors—are your team cabinet; they're the core of your business.

Now, if you are an event planner who has just ventured into business ownership, I am of the opinion that there is no alternative but to hire professionals on a contract basis at first. You will be able to afford experts who are more seasoned, since you will be hiring them for specific projects and paying them per project or per hour. These experienced professionals bring in a level of expertise to the project at hand, assisting you in achieving maximum client satisfaction, and you can learn from them as well.

Every member of your team will be an individual, with specific talents and a specific role to play. Together, this group of salespeople will move as one like a well-oiled machine. Yes, I said salespeople. Because your team members sell your business every day—be it by the way they answer the telephone, the attention they pay to details of design, or the attitude they show toward clients. And this is what you should aim for: a well-oiled machine should sell you and your business.

Unfortunately that ideal is not always easy. Sometimes it can take one disruptive team member to destroy the emotional well-being of all other members and create disharmony. As the team leader, you have to weigh that member's contribution and then deal with that person accordingly.

Perhaps all it will take is for you to voice your displeasure and request a change in attitude. At other times, more drastic measures will be required. Be prepared to do whatever it takes. Yes, it is hard to let a very talented artist go, but a person who refuses to work as a team player will only cause you heartache and perhaps loss of work. Be prepared to cut your losses if necessary.

Someone on your team is someone on your side. Your team members are beside you fighting for the same cause, working toward the same goal. They're prepared to go the whole mile for you and with you. If you have employees who are motivated by threats and domineering direction, they are simply a group of individuals who are working for you because they have to be; their jobs are a means to an end. Such employees do not have the ability to share in the spirit of the team.

Creating great teams takes strong leadership—teams don't just magically bond. They are guided from the top.

Your Responsibilities as a Team Leader

Your team members will take their cues from you, the leader, so the messages you impart must reflect how you want them to treat you and their fellow team members. Lead as you would want them to follow.

The key word here is *respect*. *"Worthy of respect"* heads the list of the necessary traits of a team leader. And it is a two-way street: when we give it, we usually get it back.

Leaders have a responsibility to walk the talk and lead by example—this is essential. Leaders know the importance of being levelheaded during an event crisis. They are acutely aware that crises are overcome by quiet strength and guidance. They also recognize the importance of enthusiasm for the project at hand, as this trait is contagious.

Being a Leader: An Action Plan

1. *Instill Accountability*

   I have always believed that if you want the best from someone, you must expect it. Expecting the best from someone is a huge compliment, as long as the employee is able to handle any pressure that this may create. (If not, perhaps he or she is better suited to a different part of your organization.) As a general rule, people try to live up to expectations. We want to be thought well of: we want our colleagues to know we're reliable, and we want our boss to know we're up to the job. Remember: if you set your expectations of employees too low, that's what you'll get.

2. *Reveal the Plan*

   Your team members aren't mind readers. In order to perform a job well, they first have to know what that job is. They need to know what they are personally responsible for and to what extent. They need to take full ownership of that position and those responsibilities. But first you need to ensure they fully understand what it is that's expected of them.

Communicate your firm's ideals and repeat them often. Each member of your team must be able to recite your firm's mantra. Each one must live and breathe the morals and ethics of your firm. They need to uphold your standards and be as horrified as you at being asked to deliver anything less.

3. *Know Your Employees*

You, as the leader, must be aware of your team members' strong and weak sides. Then recognize and utilize the strengths and dismiss the weaknesses. It is just common sense to position people where they are going to shine. For example, an analytical team member is best assigned to detailing the administration and organization of the event, while creative set dressers are best allowed to focus on hanging fabric, arranging florals, or decorating a ballroom interior.

4. *Measure the Results*

Team members need to know that they're getting it right, which is why we have a performance appraisal system built into our office culture. Those of us who are diligent and honest welcome a review, particularly in the post-mortem of each produced event. What could we have handled better? What did we learn?

Time is critical, so you may choose instead to build in a quarterly review with each team member. Whatever the frequency you settle on, I recommend employee performance reviews as one way of staying on top of problems or shortfalls. It is also a way of encouraging your team members to learn how to "think around corners." Thinking around corners is a term I use in the endeavor to avoid mishaps and mistakes. For example, if I am on a job and decide to make a change to a décor unit or the placement of a flower design, I immediately think about whether this change would affect the lighting placements or perhaps interfere with guests' view of the stage. The change can be implemented if it won't potentially cause problems. Experience in this industry pays dividends when the leader and the employees develop an ability to avoid mishaps and mistakes by thinking ahead in this way.

Clients will be happiest if their expectations are exceeded, but in order to achieve this standard level, the methods of operation within your company must be reviewed regularly—otherwise standards have a tendency to drop.

It is important to speak in honest terms with your team, but make it clear that performance feedback is not meant to bring the reviewed person or group down through criticism. This is simply a means of encouragement

Post-Event Review Survey: A Template

The following survey, which can be anonymous if you like, can help you evaluate the teamwork on a particular project. It is intended to improve performance and eliminate mistakes in the future.

What aspects of this event did you like the most? _____

_____

What aspects of this event did you like the least? _____

_____

Who was the most helpful and cooperative person on the job? _____

_____

What issues on the job concern you most? _____

_____

What two things caused you to waste time on the job? _____

_____

What are your ideas for improving the next event? _____

_____

Were the instructions you received clear and precise? _____

_____

Could you have received clearer instructions? _____

_____

What changes would you like to see for more effective performance? _____

_____

Do you feel the crew care on the job was adequate? _____

_____

to lead to a higher performance level as a team. Through learning and self development we grow.

Employees must be encouraged to speak frankly, and they should feel their comments are making a valuable contribution to the team. Adopting this attitude during review sessions can negate any tension and make the meetings more profitable in terms of knowledge and insights learned.

You will find that post-event review meetings that encourage an open discussion are advantageous. To continually strive for excellence, a desire must be present to improve our performance with every event that we take on. Consider the template on page 104 as a feedback tool for these occasions.

5. *Diffuse the Dramatics*

True leadership doesn't start and end with meetings. Nor does it appear only when it has an outside audience or when there's a job to be done. True leaders carry their leadership attitudes into every aspect of their professional lives.

Your team members need to be able to observe you at any time and see consistent, fair, and rational behavior. If you want them to respect your clients, show them that you give respect. Don't complain about the clients, and always maintain a professional stance.

To go further, avoid any trace of backbiting, sarcasm, and pettiness toward your team members, as such attitudes drain the team of energy.

From my experience, there is the occasional time when the full-time staff designer feels threatened if freelance floral designers or set dressers are booked to work on an event of considerable size. The full-time employees might, due to their insecurities, show undesirable traits of negativity, such as sulky behavior or unhappy or unpleasant demeanor. If you foresee a similar problem, plan for its elimination early. In the case just described, advise all full-time staff members that their positions in the company are not in jeopardy and that freelancers are employed to assist with the current project. Stress the importance of all team members working as one.

6. *Listen, Be Flexible, and Adapt*

The "my way or the highway" approach in the leader is a surefire killer of team spirit. You employ people for their individuality and flair, so listen to their ideas. If an employee's idea has merit, acknowledge it and decide if it is an appropriate action for the circumstances at hand. If the idea doesn't have legs for this occasion, point out why and then still thank the employee for his or her input. You want your team members to feel confident that there will come a day when one of those ideas will be adopted and solve a major problem, and you'll be thanking your lucky stars that you have assembled and nurtured such a talented and creative team!

7. *Offer Internal or External Training*

Continue to train your people and develop their skills while on the job, but know their strengths and talents so you don't push them in a direction that will undermine their confidence.

Train your team members on specific event projects, but plan it well and in advance to ensure the success of both the training and the event. Communicate clearly the tasks you assign to each team member and advise them on the process you have planned. Map out the event journey in a series of small steps. All team members must clearly know their position, their role, and the tasks they need to execute. When team members try on new roles or responsibilities, careful oversight and feedback afterwards are also important elements. Supervise the event progressively to make sure all team members are completing their tasks to the best of their abilities.

You might ask at this point, "Is there any cost attached to this in-house training program?" The answer is yes, because any meetings in regard to this type of training are best done outside normal business hours. So show your team members you care and order in food and beverages for their enjoyment.

External training happens when team members participate in outside training programs pertaining to sales, management, or design. When suggesting external workshops to your employees or approving their suggestions, keep in mind that allowing them to experience other aspects of the business than the ones that are part of their current position encourages them to expand their skills. Research professional development courses and make an allowance in your budget for your team to attend.

Is there a guideline as to the cost of external training for an event company? It is relative to the gross turnover. For example, if your business is bringing in half a million dollars in revenue, you may consider budgeting 7 to 9 percent for all external training, including industry publications and conferences, provided the business brings in profits. However, it's best to seek specific input from your financial adviser.

Sculpting Your Team

A high-quality team member is one who is reliable, takes pride in his or her work, and aims at being the best in the chosen field of expertise. Learn to spot talent, and if you have a team member who is outstanding in a specific area, be sure that you continually utilize and stretch that creative talent. This is where your guiding skills come into play.

A great leader has to be something of a psychologist and be able to recognize talents that team members don't realize they possess. To be able to do that, the leader has to remain very observant. To test a theory, you could hand over a small part of a bigger job in an area you think this person could excel in and watch how he or she handles the task. This strategy will help you find the best people in your organization for particular jobs and tasks, and it will also make the employees more fulfilled and hence more satisfied with working for you.

Motivation and Rewards

How do we reward a job well done? There are times when your staff members have met their targets, won accounts, completed proposals, or even exceeded expectations, and you wish to reward them.

There is a balance to be perfected here. Everyone loves rewards, but if they are given too freely, they may not have the desired effect of motivating employees, making them feel appreciated, and giving them a feeling of satisfaction with their working environment. Excessive rewarding can be taken for granted at times and result in a net zero benefit for you, the principal. Then, on the other hand, if we give rewards too infrequently, employees can feel undervalued, unappreciated, and disgruntled toward management. You want neither of these extremes.

The primary factor that motivates any team member is knowing that he or she contributes to the overall success of the company. Be sure to tell your employees regularly of their value to you. It makes people feel good and builds a greater sense of commitment.

In terms of individual rewards, first, work out what you consider to be a reward that is fair and that will be appreciated by the given employee. For example, if the employee's salary is above average, more dollars in the pay packet may not be appreciated as much as a gesture would be. In this case, dinner for two at an exclusive restaurant may be an appealing option. A weekend at a resort is always a favorite; alternatively, one or two days off with full pay usually works very well. A store gift card is also always well received. These are just some ideas for rewarding employees; you will need to determine what rewards are appropriate and affordable for your firm.

Another reward alternative is the system that encompasses the biannual or annual bonus. This is usually set with the salary package. Some companies find that bonuses are a tool that helps motivate employees to work at their maximum level all year long.

There is yet another way of rewarding your employees, and it is actually a favorite of mine. Send your key personnel to an industry conference in another city, or better still, overseas. This reward will be seen as a real bonus, as most people love to travel; furthermore, they will have the opportunity to network with people in the same industry. Apart from the reward factor, this is also a training program that will allow employees to develop new skills. Money spent in this way will come back to you in their working roles.

Apart from individual rewards, host a company dinner. This type of occasion brings your people together. It allows them to bond on a more personal level, which makes for a happy working environment. The way your staff members feel about their work and your company is carried through directly to the client, and the clients want to work with people who enjoy servicing them. If your employees feel important and cherished, it will show in all sorts of positive ways for your company. And that is a huge bonus for you! It's sort of like rewarding in reverse.

The most important goal for you as the principal is to convey that your people are all important. Often, in our own minds we are putting our people first; we know they're important. But just as often, we don't let them in on the secret. Yes, always put your people first, but let them know it, too.

Expanding Your Knowledge Base

There is always so much to learn, and as event planners we should continually develop our skills and lift our competency level. Build on your knowledge through regular exchanges with peers and mentors in the events business.

I highly recommend that you participate in trade shows or attend conferences that are held on an annual basis. See page 224 for industry associations; their Web sites are a good starting point to learn about training programs, special event conferences, seminars, and workshops. These special educational gatherings and events are where you will find the mentors you can observe and perhaps meet in person.

Aside from networking with peers and learning from mentors, don't overlook the importance of expanding the product knowledge related to the events business at large. You might have entered the industry with a business degree or as a floral designer, but you are now in a position of hiring stage designers, lighting specialists, and caterers; you rent table linens and work with graphic designers and printers on invitations and menus. Learn more about these adjacent disciplines that you aren't formally trained in. Find out what's hot in these fields.

One way to do that is through gaining accreditation in the industry. You don't need to become an expert in each discipline, but it is a big advantage to have a general knowledge of each aspect of the business.

We all have buddies in this small world of event planning; often these are people we have hired in the past or people we have heard about and may hire in the future.

If you need to know what's happening in catering, floral design, or the special effects field, call your buddy who specializes in this field and make an appointment to view his or her stock and equipment and spend time talking to that person. Such specialists should include light, sound, and vision companies; catering establishments; and floral studios. And don't overlook staging and various supply rental companies.

People at these companies want to meet with you because they want to make a name for themselves as well. They want to get more business and sell you their services. They want to use the latest and greatest—and they want you to know about it so you can sell their concepts to the client.

The lighting person, for example, may show you everything he or she has on hand, from the simple par can floor light to the intelligent lighting systems of today. View the many colored gels so you get a feel for the enhancement that they provide for décor units. Also get some advice on the best ones to use.

Such research and peer involvement help you build a broader knowledge base in subjects that are outside your main area of expertise, which gives you more tools when coming up with your creative concepts and makes you more knowledgeable when talking to the client.

Clients can relax when they realize you have a solid working knowledge of these fields and are easily able to put the pieces of their event puzzle together. That's what they want—an assurance that they are in good and capable hands.

Role and Responsibility Checklists for Team Members

The following checklists are intended to present the role and responsibilities of each team member involved in a special event in an at-a-glance format. These checklists apply to events of almost any size, regardless of budget.

The Ideal Team

To put the ideal team in place, you must first know where your own strengths lie or, more important, what your weaknesses are. If your strength or expertise is creative planning and designing, then the first full-time or part-time team member for you to add to your event cabinet must surely be the person with organizational talent. Alternatively, a principal with administrative knowledge may find it a major benefit to employ a creative director or designer at the onset to combine talents.

1. Administrative Assistant

Perform administrative tasks during the event ☐

Handle accounting pertaining to the event ☐

Handle insurance for the event ☐

Know the emergency numbers of police, ambulance, ☐
and fire department

Have a list of the contractors' cellular phone numbers ☐

Be familiar with the event timeline and schedules ☐

Gather post-event reviews ☐

Request deposits and implement final invoicing ☐

An administrative assistant is usually a full-time employee, but occasionally a part-time staffer or a contractor; it depends on the size of the event company. The newcomer to the business is best advised to at least contract this function, even if for only four hours a week. Don't think that you cannot afford this expense; in my opinion, you cannot afford not having the assistance of this professional.

Every team and company needs a person who has administrative talents and who can sequence the order of the work. This person's strength is organization. This is also the person who can handle all the paperwork, including the final drafts of the proposal. He or she puts together the proposal document based on the agreed plan. Then, he or she will follow up with the client to arrange for the agreed upon money deposit—and here is where frequently the newcomer to the business will make a mistake. In the excitement of winning the job, he or she will proceed without attending to the formality of the financial arrangement, and this will surely lead to loss of money. You should never proceed to working on the job until the deposit is received.

I find it essential to have an administrative assistant on location the day of the event if it is an event for 250 guests or more. The assistant's job is keeping the incoming paperwork under control, recording staff time sheets, handling incoming and outgoing deliveries, and dealing with minor issues that may occur with the venue or with contractors. He or she can also organize the food and beverages for the crew.

2. Producer

Perform site inspection and manage site ☐

Communicate with venue operator ☐

Style and manage the stage ☐

Know the venue logistics and coordination ☐

Prepare a brief for all contractors ☐

Oversee interior room setup ☐

Oversee tent setup if off-site, including exterior walkway lighting ☐

Check on insurance for contractors ☐

Prepare a floor plan with table layout ☐

Arrange for table and guest seating signage ☐

Oversee hiring of technical specialists (light, sound, and vision) ☐

Review artists' special requests and contracts ☐

Communicate with MC and speakers ☐

Manage load-in and load-out schedules ☐

Follow weather forecasts regarding a contingency plan ☐

The producer of the event is the person responsible for overseeing the total concept. For new event planners or firms that are still small, the principal usually performs the function of producer if production is his or her area of expertise; alternatively, a producer can be partnered with or hired on a freelance basis.

It is important to know your own position in the company. Is your strength in the production side of the event or does your strength lie in the creative role? There are cases where the business principal is the owner and is aware of what is required but not specifically skilled or accredited in either stream. Such a principal relies on employees who bring the appropriate skills to the table. What is important here is that you must recognize exactly what and who is needed to meet the client's expectations.

As the company grows, and there are many accounts to handle, a producer on staff is usually assigned to oversee each particular project.

The producer's role carries quite a responsibility, from assisting and advising on the site, to communicating with the venue operator, mapping out the floor plans, working with the technical rental and other companies, communicating with the catering director or entertainment agent, and drawing up the event-related schedules.

The producer usually chooses his or her stage manager, and this specialist becomes invaluable to the principal of the business.

3. *Venue Operator*

Advise on food and beverage packages ☐

Advise on use of interior and exterior of venue ☐

Advise on kitchen(s) and their access ☐

Provide floor plans and room layout on request ☐

Advise on available power supply ☐

Advise on rigging requests ☐

Advise on availability of tables, chairs, and dance floor ☐

Prepare contract for client ☐

Provide details on cost limitations and restrictions ☐

Provide crew meals ☐

Advise on air-conditioning or heating components ☐

Advise on the use of elevators and exits ☐

Advise on coatroom and additional rooms ☐

A venue operator is the contact at the venue. Once the venue is booked and confirmed, the producer must keep the venue operator in the loop regarding the event. For this professional to perform well, he or she must be given all the necessary information regarding the event. Make this specialist feel like he or she is part of your team. The venue operator understands that a truly successful event will lead to more bookings with his or her venue in the future.

The venue operator will make sure that the details of the event are confirmed in writing. He or she advises the producer on what the venue can or cannot supply and will work together with the producer on a series of necessary tasks, from mapping the floor plans with tables and staging choices to pinpointing the best times that contractors should be given access for the load-in and load-out of equipment. The venue

Where to Find Contractors for Your Events

All kinds of freelance help can be found by searching the Web these days, but I highly recommend that you source event specialists through the International Special Events Society (ISES) based in Chicago (see www.ises.com and click on the "Find a Member" tab).

operator will also provide information concerning limitations, restrictions, and power availability and use. The producer depends on the efficiency and thoroughness of the venue operator and vice versa—the venue operator must also work within the framework provided by the producer.

4. Creative Director

Communicate with show director and scriptwriters	☐
Liaise with artists regarding wardrobe	☐
Oversee production of invitations and promotional materials	☐
Oversee any promotional gifts or programs	☐
Oversee memorabilia displays or guest mementos	☐
Oversee banner and poster placement	☐
Oversee tent (marquee) dressing if off-site location	☐
Oversee stage design and any VIP areas	☐
Oversee dressing of the pre-drinks area	☐
Oversee design and sets continuity of room and tables	☐
Oversee dressing of auction displays and registration tables	☐
Oversee the look and finish of room and other areas	☐

Depending on the size of the event, a creative director may be contracted to join the event team for a specific project. His or her responsibility is to art direct the floral designers and set dressers as to the overall decorative look at the venue. The creative director may be requested to interpret the concept brief received from the client and translate that brief into an executable creative vision. This professional is informed of the event's budget and it is his or her responsibility to stay within the confines of the budget. Other responsibilities could include oversight of the design and printing of any printed matter, such as invitations, menus, and promotional materials.

The creative director is also responsible for conceptual art or drawings that may be required. He or she submits these items to the producer along with cost projections. This professional may also be called upon to write scripts for either guest speakers or the MC.

If banners, signage, vintage cars, or auction tables are called for, this person's role is advising on the choices and overseeing placement. As the décor comes together, the creative director checks the look of all components, such as the tables, the stage, any decorative and associated props, and the overall room design. He or she makes sure everything looks harmonious and has the intended visual impact.

5. Technical Director

Present technical drawings ☐

Prepare briefs for light and sound ☐

Prepare brief for vision, special effects, or lasers ☐

Supervise load-in and load-out for crews ☐

Coordinate technical schedules ☐

Supervise technical rehearsal ☐

Implement stage designs for lighting ☐

Check speaker equipment for main room setup ☐

Oversee radio communications ☐

Ensure correct power usage ☐

Liaise with venue engineer or electrician ☐

Seek quotations from subcontractors ☐

Oversee special effects, video, and vision ☐

The role of the technical director is of vital importance because events depend heavily on the knowledge, skill, and technical expertise of this person. A contractor is usually hired to cover this area, and it is either a company or an individual specializing in light, sound, and vision. The size of the event determines how many technical people are required for the job. Small events (up to 150 guests) may only require one to two technical operators, while much bigger jobs (up to 1,000 guests) will require up to four or five such operators.

Staying Cool and Organized on the Day of the Event

The day of the event is a culmination of weeks, or months, of preparatory work, and while there is a lot of excitement and anticipation of how well all this planning will turn out, there can also be moments of stress, panic, or crisis for the event planner and his or her team.

There could be the temptation, especially for the less experienced event coordinator, to pull staff members from their regular jobs to help out elsewhere. But I believe in letting experts do their jobs, and I have specific people for each job. This strategy results in an organized progression of work no matter how big the event—and not in a chaotic approach. The exception occurs when there is a full-blown crisis. Then it goes without saying that it's all hands on deck until the job is back on track and the crisis has been averted.

The technical director is also responsible for the technical drawings, the power supply at the venue, and the rigging of the technical equipment; he or she makes sure that all required speakers, other technical equipment, and special effects are included. The list of necessary items and equipment compiled by the technical director is forwarded to the producer for approval in regard to the budget.

The technical director attends meetings organized by the producer, and he or she communicates with the producer and stage manager on a regular basis prior to and during the event. This person will need to have access to documentation and drawings to aid in the technical setup. Then this specialist or an entire crew will orchestrate the technical setup according to a schedule received from the producer. The installation team will usually stay on-site during the event to operate the technical equipment.

6. Catering Director

Advise of menu choices and packages	☐
Respond to specific briefs	☐
Provide a food and beverage plan for staff	☐
Inspect site if off-site location	☐
Provide dinnerware, glassware, cutlery	☐
Provide uniforms	☐
View service areas	☐
Provide trolleys and kitchen equipment	☐
Provide tables, chairs, and linens	☐
Ensure appropriate refrigeration and electrical requirements	☐
Check power	☐
Handle waste disposal	☐
Book breakout and additional rooms if required	☐
Provide catering schedule	☐
Take responsibility for load-in and load-out access	☐

Catering plays an important role in the success of any event. The quality, presentation, and serving of food can make or break an event. It is a difficult and sensitive discipline. The product is fresh, the product is delicate, and it must be served to please, whether it is chilled to perfection or served deliciously hot.

A catering director is the head of catering and the contact person who liaises with the event producer. This person is often employed by the venue, especially if it is a hotel or a reception hall. In such cases, the in-house catering team is ready to work with you.

However, for most off-site and certain on-site venues (see pages 38 and 46 for definitions of off-site and on-site venues), it will be the event planner who hires a catering company. Independent catering companies each have a crew of employees: chefs, prep cooks, assistant kitchen hands, dishwashers, and waitstaff.

Independent caterers must be able to visit the site to determine their needs. They must be informed of the expected number of guests as well.

One of the catering director's responsibilities is to estimate the waiter to guest ratio, which will be determined by the budget. With small budgets, the ratio is 1 waiter per 20 guests, while with more generous budgets, it could be 1 waiter per 15 guests. What is highly desirable if the budget permits is the ratio of 1 to 1½ waiters per 10 guests.

For off-site events, the caterer will be in charge of installing and positioning the kitchens. The catering director will work with the event producer to factor in all the necessary costs and to figure out the logistics of the workflow.

7. Head Floral Designer

Know the number of floral designers required	☐
Review the producer's schedule and work to it	☐
Review the proposed designs for tabletops and rooms	☐
Know how may designs can be produced per hour	☐
Plan the work area within the venue	☐
Check the equipment required: floor covering, tables, buckets, bins	☐
Know the unit cost of each tabletop and other floral décor pieces	☐
Supervise the floral crew and assistants	☐
Prepare the fresh flower arrangements and other floral decorations required	☐
Oversee the quality control of the floral work	☐

The head floral designer is in charge of all the florists working on the job. The floral design team is responsible for arranging the flowers for the event, from, for example, large urns of flowers at the entranceway to all the centerpieces for the guests' tables, plus any additional floral work that may be required.

Hiring junior floral assistants is an advantage and a real cost saver. I recommend that juniors be hired to help not only the head designer but also the supporting floral designers. They can fetch, cart, carry, and prepare flowers and foliage so this material is ready for the seniors to work with.

They can also act as a "runner" to place the centerpieces or tabletops on the guests' tables when completed. You want to avoid wasting the time of the head floral designer with simple tasks like these. Imagine an event for which 200 centerpieces must be placed on the guests' tables, and estimate the approximate time that would take. You can see the advantage of delegating this task to junior-level people.

The head floral designer must ensure that the production schedule provided by the producer is strictly adhered to. It is imperative that the schedule be followed to the letter; delays could affect other teams, which could lead to a disaster.

The head floral designer is also responsible for the overall quality of the designs. Even if a large number of floral pieces are required, piece number 200 must look as crisp and clean as piece number 1.

8. Set Dressers

Adhere to event schedule received from producer	☐
Review the proposed set designs	☐
Check the event units that are being used for decoration	☐
Check that the fabrics are pressed and free of creases	☐
Perform assigned set decorating tasks	☐

There is no time to deal with display divas on-site on the day of the event, so choose your set dressers carefully. Select set dressers who will blend in and harmonize with other staff and whose record shows an ability to get the job done with the least fuss.

The work of set dressers can range from decorating the ceiling with fabric, mirror balls, or large lanterns to decorating the stage with event props, such as columns, pillars, or other decorative units that tie in with the design concept.

It is usual practice for the set dressers to work directly under the creative director and/or the producer of the event.

9. Staging Specialist

Observe the pre-working schedule of the producer	☐
Liaise with the technical team and producer	☐
Liaise with security of venue	☐
Book scissor lifts and other equipment rentals if required	☐
Oversee activity in back-of-house to avoid a clash of times	☐
Program the appropriate staging, catwalk, seamless flats, theatrical drapes, platforms, handrails, risers, bollards, lecterns, bars, dance floor, and other staging equipment required	☐

A staging specialist is an independent contractor who specializes in equipment pertaining to staging. The event planner hires this contractor on a freelance basis.

This contractor works in the background, designing, testing, and building the staging for the desired thematic concept. Staging specialists possess unique construction capabilities and are able to offer a whole range of stage design options, including painted MDF, Perspex tables, stage flooring, carpeted platforms, panels with digital print or custom finish, and more. They can hang interior wall draperies, using fabrics such as stunning satins, silks, sheers, or velvets.

Again, it is the producer who liaises with this contractor and coordinates the load-in and load-out schedules.

For an example of an interesting staging concept and its execution by Staging Rentals in Sydney, see color plates, Figure 26. Contact information for the company can be found on page 226.

10. Stage Manager

Assist the producer with any request	☐
Coordinate production of printed matter if requested (invitations, menus, programs, posters, etc.)	☐
Oversee promotional activities and contractors	☐
Oversee the communications of radio, microphones, etc., if requested	☐
Oversee the program according to schedule for the contractors	☐
Liaise with security staff	☐

A stage manager serves as a right hand to the producer. There is constant communication between the producer and the stage manager; in fact, they must work as one. The responsibilities of this specialist can vary considerably, depending on the needs at a particular event and the preferences of the producer as to which tasks he or she would like to delegate to the stage manager. A stage manager is usually a freelancer, and this person tends to be hired for events of some size. He or she can assist with communication with the venue operator and catering director, preparation of floor plans, promotions, and more.

Newcomers to the business handling smaller events will not necessarily need a stage manager as long as the producer can handle the workload.

11 Entertainment Director

Source and book feature artists and atmospheric performers	☐
Source and book music bands and atmospheric performers	☐

Prepare artists' contracts ☐

Handle artists' special requests ☐

Adhere to the producer's event schedule ☐

Adhere to any rehearsal requests ☐

Book the piano, music stands, mirrors, and racks if required ☐

Inspect the venue and know the stage size ☐

Check back-of-house for access ☐

Coordinate production requirements for artists ☐

Discuss the style to present the artists' repertoire if requested ☐

Source and book the choreographer if required ☐

Confirm all the above in writing ☐

Make any travel and accommodation arrangements for artists ☐

Request dressing room space ☐

Request times for sound checks for speakers or artists ☐

Be present at the event if possible ☐

An entertainment director is a contractor who is hired to book all artists, entertainers, music bands, and feature performers for the event. He or she works closely with the producer. The entertainment director provides the producer with price quotations, artists' special requests, and contracts for approval. He or she oversees the artists' involvement throughout production, especially their adherence to the schedules.

The producer communicates schedules with this specialist, as well as all the necessary details regarding the event concept and documentation such as the floor plan and stage dimensions, so that everyone is on the same page.

12. Security Staff

Liaise with producer ☐

Liaise with stage manager ☐

Meet with event planner ☐

Understand the style of the evening and number of guests ☐

Adhere to special requests ☐

Procure a copy of pre-working schedule of contractors for parking ☐

Know the fire codes and the emergency numbers of police, ☐
    ambulance, fire departments, and car service

Today many venues have their own security staff in place for both on-site and off-site locations (see pages 38 and 46 for definitions of on-site and off-site venues), but even if security staff is not attached to the venue, most event planners today hire security staff on a contract basis, especially if the guest list is celebrity or VIP driven. Examples of events that require security staff would be gala fundraisers with international speakers attending, official government gatherings, rock concerts, and movie premieres.

The number of officers required for an event is decided at the discretion of the client or organizers and is usually determined based on the status and number of guests.

The primary responsibility of the security staff is to observe the crowds and ensure the orderly conduct of everyone present.

It is important that the head of security receive the event schedule so that he or she will know what is planned from the start to the end of the event.

13. *Truckie*

Review the size of the load to be carried to the venue ☐

Book trucks or vans required for the job ☐

Present the budget cost of truck to the principal for approval ☐

Check the driver's licenses and insurances of all drivers ☐

Sight the venue and meet the security personnel ☐

Review the main room access ☐

Check back of house access ☐

Check the ceiling height of elevators if bringing in tall decorative units ☐

Estimate best time for load-in of stock and props ☐

I categorize the truckie as the hero of the show. This is the person who is responsible for bringing in all the equipment, stock, and décor items to the venue and actually unloading it all, and then removing it all at the end of the event.

The truckie is the first point of contact with the venue operator and venue security, and much depends on his or her efficiency. This person will also act as your representative, so it is crucial that he or she have a pleasant manner and be able to communicate clearly with the venue personnel.

The truckie is the jack-of-all-trades. If you get a good one, never let him go, as the song goes.

I have worked with one such load in and load out coordinator, Ian Murphy of Sydney, for many years. He knows every part of the event as well as I do. Not only can he orchestrate loading a truck so that the stock fits together like a glove, but he creates goodwill with venue staff due to his pleasing manner. He always makes himself known to the staff prior to the event day, and he anticipates potential holdups or problems with getting the stock unloaded and carried into the venue. All this is communicated to his team of assistants, so they can plan their job. Then, on the day of the event, once everything has been loaded in, Ian sticks around to wear his jack-of-all-trades cap, ready for whoever may need him.

PART TWO

All About
DESIGN

Turning a beautiful bunch of roses into an artistic display or transforming a ballroom or tent into an environment with a fantasy atmosphere does not happen by chance. It happens when the artist, whether a floral designer or set designer, has studied the principles of design, and has combined them with artistic talent, creativity, and practical experience.

I hope that the following pages will help you advance your design know-how and that you will find here an inspiration for your creativity. No matter how much experience one has in the industry, we can all do better; we can all improve our level of competence and skill.

Tabletops and Other Décor Props

THIS CHAPTER LOOKS AT THE FOCAL POINT OF A BEAUTI-fully decorated venue where the guests are attending a sit-down function. The place they spend most of their time dining and socializing is, of course, the table. The elements surrounding the table and placed on it must work in harmony to create a pleasing, fitting, and memorable effect.

When decisions are to be made, a discussion is to be instigated, or a celebration is to be had, we head for the table. For any formal or informal gathering, the table is part of the picture, as it is a meeting place, a neutral territory that encourages communication.

Dining at a special occasion will carry with it many expectations, from the physical (the actual eating and excitement of being served and experiencing something different) to the emotional (the need for company, or to be seen) to the psychological (enhanced self-esteem). If one or more of these expectations are not met, a dissatisfied customer is born.

How can the event producer be responsible for meeting all these expectations? His or her expertise will ensure not only that every aspect of the event, from décor to food to entertainment, is the best, but that all the components blend to create a magical ambience that envelops the attendee.

Tables, tablecloths, and seat covers have changed dramatically over the years, from that white linen three-quarter-length cloth with the posy of roses to a stunning table dressed with a glamorous tablecloth and matching napkins and chair covers (see color plates, Figures 4–14).

Main Considerations for Seating Layout and Table Décor

Before you decide to jump in and decorate a table and its surroundings, there are many points to consider.

1. *The Reason for the Event*

    It is essential to know the reason that the event is taking place—whether it is a fundraiser ball or a bar/bat mitzvah—so that tables can be dressed to suit.

2. *The Overall Color Scheme*

    Considering the overall color scheme agreed upon for the event is essential, as a harmonious color combination must be carried through to the smallest detail of the napkin tie or its trim. Attending to such minute details gives a distinctive quality to the look of the complete table setting.

3. *Available Table Sizes and Table Layout Options*

    Naturally, the size of the table determines how many guests can sit at that table and the size of the tablecloth needed.

    Generally tables are uniform in size, which makes the procurement of the covers not too difficult. Always ensure you have the right-size tablecloth for the right table; nothing looks tackier than cloth that barely covers the table, or an overly large cloth dangling onto the floor.

    The first and probably the most fundamental decision regards the type of table that is to be decorated and embellished. Tables come in a variety of shapes, including rectangular, round, and square. Square tables can be achieved by placing two rectangular tables together.

Rectangular Tables

Standard Rectangular Table Measurements

4 ft. × 24 in.	121 cm × 60 cm	seats 2 classroom-style
4 ft. × 30 in.	121 cm × 76 cm	seats 4
4 ft. × 40 in.	121 cm × 101 cm	seats 4 to 6
5 ft. × 30 in.	152 cm × 76 cm	seats 4 to 6
6 ft. × 18 in.	182 cm × 45 cm	seats 3 classroom-style
6 ft. × 24 in.	182 cm × 60 cm	seats 3 classroom-style
6 ft. × 30 in.	182 cm × 76 cm	seats 6 to 8
6 ft. × 40 in.	182 cm × 101 cm	seats 6 to 8
8 ft. × 24 in.	243 cm × 60 cm	seats 4 classroom-style

8 ft. × 30 in.	243 cm × 76 cm	seats 8 to 10
8 ft. × 40 in.	243 cm × 101 cm	seats 8 to 10
8 ft. × 48 in.	243 cm × 121 cm	seats 8 to 10

The information in the table above has been kindly contributed by Kool Party Rentals in Phoenix.

Rectangular tables can be configured in various ways, depending on the desired effect. A setting in the shape of a cross can be created, as can a hollow square, a square U shape, or a square (which lately has been extremely popular for sit-down dinners).

Beginning with the simple shape of a rectangle and extending your creativity to see how far it can stretch is a perfect example of thoroughly investigating every single option or element to see it through to its absolute creative limit. What follows are some options for table layout using the rectangular table as a unit.

- The cross is used where an open style is desired, particularly in formal situations; it has recently increased in popularity and is now used for informal lunches and dinners as well.

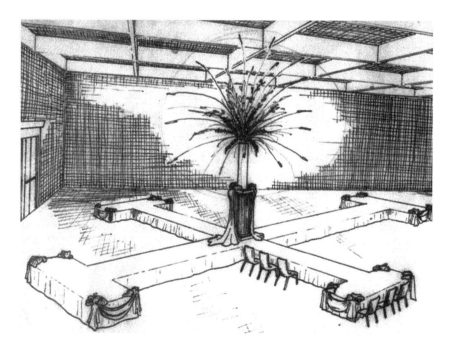

- The hollow square is a versatile style and is often used for conference sessions, with all guests or delegates facing toward the center.

- The square U shape is a popular choice for conference-style events or lunches with a keynote speaker.

See also pages 56–59 for illustrations and examples of practical applications of various table layouts.

Round Tables

Standard Round Table Measurements

48 in. diameter	130 cm	seats 2
54 in. diameter	137 cm	seats 6 to 8
60 in. diameter	152 cm	seats 6 to 8
66 in. diameter	167 cm	seats 8 to 10
72 in. diameter	183 cm	seats 10 to 12

The popular round table is often used for events at which guests are seated for breakfast, lunch, or dinner. The shape of the table, whether you decide to go for round or square, is mostly up to the choice of the client, although space can also be a factor in determining the table shape.

Square Tables

A square shape is achieved by placing two 6-foot trestles side by side. It provides seating for 10 guests. This shape is an alternative to a round table and is sometimes chosen for design reasons.

What could be such reasons? One consideration is the shape of the venue. Another is whether symmetry is part of the desired effect (symmetry has long been considered more pleasing to the eye). Square and round tables both allow for a tabletop centerpiece to be placed in the center of the table to make the table look pleasing from all angles. Square and rectangular tables can also be used in combination with round ones to achieve a unique look (see CAD plan, page 60).

A Creative Layout: Two Rounds and One Rectangle

This is an interesting table layout with a rectangular table centered and two round tables on each of its short ends. This style setup allows for 16 to 20 people to be seated at one "table."

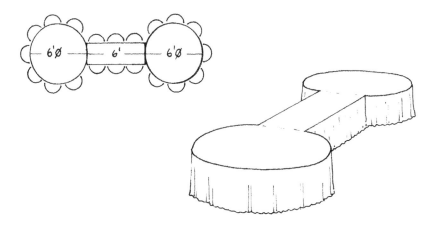

4. *Table Linens*

The next element to be tackled is the dressing of the table (and chairs). Linens come in a multitude of fabrics and in different colors, patterns, thicknesses, and textures. Unless made to order, seat cloth sizes are reasonably standard.

There are many qualities of linen available for either rental or purchase and the choice, which ranges from Irish linen, cotton, damask, sheer, satin and brocades to synthetics, such as polyester and viscose, would be selected to tie in with the type of event you have planned.

A Few Expert Words on Table Linens

The following information regarding tablecloths, chair covers, and napkins is included courtesy of Bill Pry, the vice president of BBJ Linen, which has showrooms throughout the United States.

Color Comes First

Color plays an important role in the event planning industry, and table linen companies strive to offer every season a palette of colors that matches every mood, with linens running the gamut of color and hue options, from bold and energetic to calm and relaxing.

Reds and Pinks—What's hotter or sweeter than red or pink? How about red and pink combined for a lively, bright, and lovely night? Vibrant and feminine all at once, reds and pinks are the bold choice for a remarkable evening. They are available in a spectrum of shades, patterns, and fabrics, but proceed with caution, because these colors ignite.

Purples and Blues—Regal and sophisticated, purple and blue fabrics set the tone for elegance and classic style. Serious yet glamorous, inks and violets command attention and cloak the evening in a cool, polished glow that manages to wow and welcome at the same time.

Teals and Greens—Drawing inspiration from nature, teals and greens are modern and inviting. These colors can be bright and playful or refreshing and light, and can help create moods from sassy to subtle.

Oranges and Yellows—Nothing says modern, warm, and bold like oranges and yellows. Brighten up an evening event or saturate a daytime one. Either way, these statement colors provide a stunning backdrop. Ethnic, sunny, pleasant, and strong, oranges and yellows fill a space with life.

Neutrals and Browns—Deep and shimmery or traditional and subdued, neutrals and browns provide a stable, timeless, yet dramatic look consistently. Every event can benefit from the warmth and elegance they provide. From stripes to dots to florals, the possibilities are infinite.

(continued)

Blacks and Grays—Chic, urban, and so easy to work with, blacks and grays form the basis of many unforgettable looks; they are the go-to staple. Whether for a night of sophistication or a simply elegant afternoon event, there are myriad applications, patterns, and styles.

Whites and Ivories—White and ivory fabrics tend to steal the show. In classic damask or more modern patterns, these colors provide a wide spectrum to work with. Make it shine or give the room a soft glow; everything looks clean and fresh in this color palette.

Fabric Galore

The linen fabrics available on the market today include lamour, bishon, lamé, bengaline, sheer, sparkle sheer, chiffon, metallic shag, damask, plaid, denim, shantung, and velvet. Pattern options include plaid, classic checks, spots, stripes, and more.

The Importance of Napkins

On the well-dressed table, the focus is the napkin. It serves not only a practical purpose, but also when folded stylishly and dressed with bows, beads, or flowers, it enhances the setting with style. The perfect napkin setting completes the table.

---

5. *Invitation, Place Card, and Menu Design*

The design of the invitation to the event offers a creative opportunity, and the same design can be carried through on place cards. The invitation is the first glimpse the attendee has of the upcoming event, the first inkling as to what sort of event it will be. Therefore, the invitations are a very important aspect of the event. Remember, the emphasis is on *creative.*

Printed menus also follow the event's creative concept in pattern, color, and style, discreetly displaying the company logo if it is a corporate event. They can be designed as an individual distinctive gift souvenir for guests or, alternatively, one may be placed between two people. Menus are considered part of the décor. They can be designed creatively to enhance the table setting; however, they must never detract from the table's otherwise pristine setting or make it look messy.

6. *Dinnerware*

On-site venues, such as restaurants and hotels, will provide their own dinnerware to be used during an event. However, for off-site venues, such as tent or garden settings, caterers often supply the dinnerware, using either their own supplies or those rented on demand. The event planner must confer with the caterer as to the style, design, and color. Orange napkins and trim won't go with puce pink dinnerware, no matter how hard you try to dress them up to match.

Still, the event producer should be familiar with dinnerware sizes and uses.

Plate Sizes

Item	Diameter	Item	Diameter
Side plate	7 in. (18 cm)	Starter/dessert plate	7 in. (18 cm)
Pasta plate	11 in. (28 cm)	Soup plate	9 in. (23 cm)
Dinner plate	10 in. (25 cm)		

Breakfastware Sizes

Item	Fluid Measure
Breakfast plate	n/a
Cereal bowl	8 fl. oz. (23 cl)
Tea cup with saucer	8 fl. oz. (23 cl)
Coffee cup with saucer (demitasse)	3 fl. oz. (8 cl)
Coffee pot	Varies
Teapot	0.5 pt. (28.4 cl)

You should also be familiar with the following miscellaneous items, as they are needed on some occasions:

- Oval serving platters
- Bread and butter plates
- Dip bowls
- Soup cups
- Consommé bowls
- Salad bowls
- Espresso cups and saucers
- Creamers
- Milk jugs
- Mugs
- Sugar bowls
- Butter dishes
- Water pitchers
- Gravy boats

7. *Glassware*

In terms of glasses, a good wineglass should be clear, allowing the color and vivacity of the wine to sparkle through. The stems should be sturdy enough not to snap at the merest touch, but also not cumbersome. The right glass will ensure that the wine is shown to its best advantage. Take care to use the appropriate glasses for red, white, and rosé wines (for the latter, wineglasses with a slightly shorter stem and a "curled" lip are customarily used—the so-called Riedel glasses, named after their designer).

The preference today is for champagne to be served in tulip glasses or champagne flutes rather than martini-type glasses, as the narrow shape helps retain the sparkle and effervescence.

Glassware Sizes

Glass	Size
Standard red wine glass	14 fl. oz. (41 cl)
Standard white wine glass	12 fl. oz. (34 cl)
Standard rosé glass	12 fl. oz. (34 cl)
Champagne flute	6 fl. oz. (18 cl)
Martini	10 fl. oz. (30 cl)
Old-fashioned glass	6 fl. oz. (18 cl)
Shot glass	1.5 fl. oz. (4 cl)
Sherry or port	6 fl. oz. (18 cl)
Highball	8 fl. oz. (23 cl)
Lager glass	12 fl. oz. (34 cl)
Brandy snifter	9 fl. oz. (26 cl)
Liqueur	2.5 fl. oz. (7 cl)
Tumbler	12 fl. oz. (34 cl)
Collins glass	12 fl. oz. (34 cl)
Beer	12.5 fl. oz. (36 cl)
Hurricane glass	23 fl. oz. (68 cl)
Coupe (or champagne saucer)	8 fl. oz. (23 cl)

8. *The Menu*

It is usually preferable to have the professional caterer create the menu for the event. Have the caterer build up three or four course selections and present them to the client for choice and approval. Often the client will mix and match to suit personal tastes, but it is wise to recommend and organize a tasting for your client, preferably with the venue operator or coordinator.

However, while you'll allow the other experts to do their job, never forget your reputation is always on the line when you are the ultimate producer. Become familiar with the most popular gourmet offerings and if something is suggested that you feel will not work given the number of people or the food service area, then you must speak up. Check that the client is happy with the final choice and confident that the caterer can handle the job at hand.

The room can be dressed or decorated beyond belief, but if the food does not meet expectations, the client's company objective has not been met. Every area requires energy and expertise. Nothing can be taken for granted.

9. *Kitchen to Table Access*

For events where the kitchen is on the premises, when you inspect the venue site, pay particular attention to the location of the kitchen in relation to the service that needs to be provided to guests, whether it be table or buffet-style service. Does the kitchen's location work well? How will it affect your floor layout as far as ease and speed of service?

10. *The Waitstaff Ratio*

For a seated table of 10, a formal occasion may require one to two waiters per table if the budget is generous. If a budget is restricted, you may only be able to afford one waiter for every 20 guests.

11. *The Weather Forecast*

For an outdoor event, have a contingency plan. If the predinner drinks and hors d'oeuvres are to be served by bar staff and waiters in beautiful grounds or a garden, have a fallback plan in case of bad weather. If the main plan is to have tables for a sit-down dinner set up in a garden, source an alternative dining area as a precaution. All clients imagine that on their day the weather will be perfect, but unfortunately, not every day of the year is.

Terrific Tabletops

When it comes to the absolute talking point of a function's table—the centerpiece is usally the focal point—the sky is the limit when it comes to the creative license and options. However, the budget can restrict the creativity here. A clever event planner will understand the client's financial limits and will adapt the props or décor accordingly.

A delightful centerpiece can be achieved with the intelligent use of inexpensive elements and a minimal use of fresh flowers. These artistic creations often end up even more appealing than ones made with lots of fresh flowers and triple the money invested in them. It is all about creativity, illusion, harmony, balance, and visual impact.

See color plates, Figure 18, for an example of one tabletop design that requires only a small budget. A colorful paper shopping bag is filled with foam to hold various decorative units inserted from the top. Candy-colored paper whistles are arranged as the top placement with clusters of mini feathers, circles, and a butterfly. Light balls from Fortune Products are placed at random for effect.

With a theme party, you can draw from the obvious elements known to typify that theme; for example, art deco of the 1930s is synonymous with white ostrich feathers, pearls, and green ruffled ferns. In contrast the 1920s is synonymous with red carnations, red roses, and the glitz of the silver sequin. To achieve height, introduce the use of Perspex rods, wooden dowels, or cardboard tubes.

This is clearly illustrated in the ideas that follow, which can be used when creating tabletops of distinction. Construction advice has also been included so you are aware of the necessary materials when creating your own pieces. Following these directions will ensure that your decoration is stable and will not topple over halfway through the event.

Tower Tabletops

A tower tabletop exceeds the standard height of 12 to 18 inches and is specifically styled to rise above the heads of guests, but without obstructing their view across the table. It creates a strong impact.

A simple construction made of a wooden base and a postal tube has untold uses for events. The diagram below shows an 18-inch square base made from 1-inch-thick plywood. The base has a central hole drilled allowing for the postal tube to be inserted and hot-glued in place. The 6-inch wooden square at the top has an empty tin can nailed in place (the can is not visible in the diagram, as it is slid into the top of the postal tube). Inserting the tin can into the top of the tube prevents movement of any kind and increases the stability of the structure. Paint the base, tube, and top a color of your choice or cover them with fabric. This basic structure can be decorated with embellishments of your choice—fabrics, florals, and props.

To get an idea of how this construction can be dressed for a stunning effect that

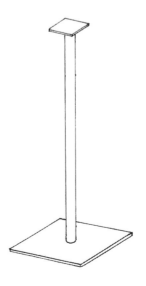

will wow your guests, see color plates, Figure 17. A "disco design" tabletop is shown, with lime green and hot pink circles, and with the base covered with matching fabric.

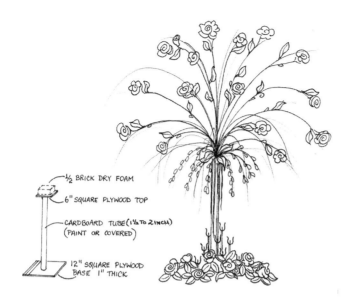

The design above will tower over the heads of guests. The construction is similar in design to that of the preceding centerpiece. The base is a 12-inch square cut from 1-inch-thick plywood and, as in the preceding design, a hole is drilled centrally to hold a 1½- to 2-inch-diameter Plexiglas or postal tube (purchased at the post office or hardware store) in place. The 6-inch square timber top holds a bowl and a wet Oasis foam brick, into which a selection of flowers and foliage are arranged.

The diagram below shows a variation of the preceding style using different materials: rope, twine, and vine are used to decorate the base, and tortured willow explodes from the foam brick at the top. A cross, made from a dowel and wound with vine, is attached to the top, and miniature Chinese lanterns are dangled from the ends.

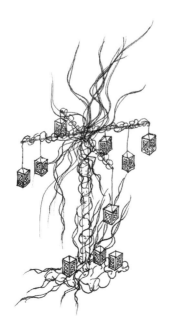

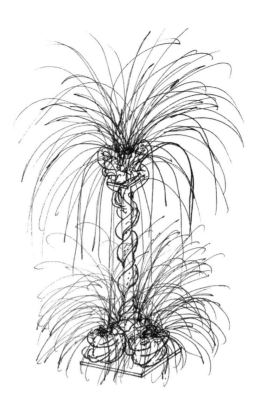

The diagram above has the same construction style as in the preceding examples, but it is dressed to be appropriate for a safari, jungle, or similar theme. For a safari theme, you can use leopard-print fabric and savanna grasses (grasses can be sourced from a floral shop), and for a jungle theme, you can employ real leaves, ferns, and foliage.

Remember: the bases for the tall, pillar tabletops can always be recycled for use at more than one event. If you take care when constructing the bases, and they are adequately secure, you can dress and redress them as many times as you like.

Glass Accents

Glasses and vases are an appealing accessory when it comes to the centerpiece. They offer a range of options simply because they can be filled with fresh fruit, rose petals, seashells, sand, or tinted water. They can be designed to tie in with the overall color scheme and theme of the event.

Vases of this nature can only be used with fine-stemmed blooms and must be light in weight because otherwise they tend to topple. Review the color plates, Figures 19, 20, and 21, for examples of glass-accented centerpieces.

- Figure 19 features a glass and apple spray that takes very little effort to create and is a budget-conscious choice. Such a tabletop would be appropriate for a fall-themed event.

- Figure 20 uses a lace glass vase placed among five martini glasses, all of which are lit up at the base (the LED-light base was sourced from

Just Before the Guests Arrive: A Checklist

Before the arrival of the first guests, it is imperative that you take the time to review the following list to prevent any embarrassing moments and ensure that your event has a slick and professional look and feel.

- ☐ Make sure all tables are positioned so that all guests face the stage.
- ☐ Check that no chairs have been removed at rehearsal time.
- ☐ Make sure all table linens are even, with seams going in one direction.
- ☐ Check that every guest has a napkin.
- ☐ Check that no pieces of foliage are trailing over flames or guest plates.
- ☐ Make sure there are no wilted flowers.
- ☐ Make sure that all foliage is clean, crisp, and glossed.
- ☐ Have the candles lit 15 to 30 minutes prior to the guests' entrance.
- ☐ Place menus, place cards, and cutlery in line with each guest's seating.

Fortune Products; see page 225 for company contact information). The martini glasses are filled with pink pebbles, creating a soft pink glow. The light shining all the way up the stem of the lace vase creates a unique sparkling effect.

- Figure 21 features a glass duo. Two clear vases are filled with green foam cubes and wire collars created at the tops of the vases. Fresh roses and scattered rose petals provide a color contrast and bring in an element of freshness, delicacy, and lightness. This centerpiece is not expensive to make (the foam cubes and wire collars can be sourced from Smithers-Oasis; see page 226 for company contact information).

Pillars and Pedestals for Your Venue

Pillars and pedestals are items that can be used to decorate rooms that have large areas of empty space. These items are much larger than the tabletops and are designed to stand on the floor rather than the tables. Pillars and pedestals are made in the same way, the difference being that pedestals are shorter than pillars and will always hold something on the top, such as an urn of flowers. Both are good to consider, especially when faced with a venue that has a number of unsightly walls, nooks, and crannies. In addition, pillars and pedestals can allow you to further extend and accentuate your theme. As you browse through the following ideas, remember that many of the decorative ideas for pillars can be used for pedestals and vice versa.

Pillars

Pillars are essentially used as a focal design feature and are tall enough to tower above the heads of guests. They can be used individually or be placed around the room or in a row, joined together with fabric.

To create pillar backbones, you will need industrial tubes made of durable cardboard, as well as plywood, wire, and duct tape. Industrial tubes in different diameters and sizes can be purchased from building and construction suppliers.

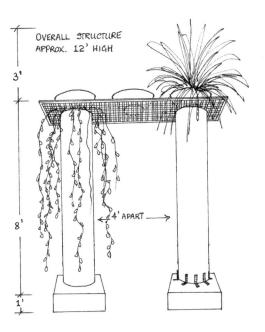

Above is an example of a versatile unit consisting of two pillars. The external faces of the tubes can be repainted or recovered as needed for different events. For safety reasons, it is essential to ensure that the tubes are inserted deep inside the base timber or plywood boxes, and that they are attached to the boxes securely and firmly. With this strong support, other units can be placed on top of the pillars as decoration, whether they are bowls with flowers or mirror balls.

The two industrial cardboard tubes used here measure 9 feet in height and 18 inches in diameter. The cardboard is ¾ inch thick. The timber boxes measure 24 square inches and are made of 1-inch-thick plywood. This thickness is necessary to add weight at the base, giving the unit stability. "L" brackets screwed into the columns and secured to each box hold the pillars in place.

The next step is to place a piece of garden trestle or a piece of plywood across the tubes. This trestle should measure 6 to 7 feet in length by 3 feet in width . Large terra-cotta bowls can be placed on top and filled with a variety of foliage and flowers.

Ivy, ferns and trailing vines can also be arranged around the edges of the terra-cotta bowls. Let this first layer of foliage surround the base of the bowls and cascade to the floor. To make this arrangement, you need to be on a ladder, with an assistant handing you the materials.

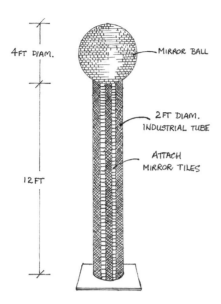

The pillar in the diagram above was painted with a white undercoat and allowed to dry, and then two coats of black paint were used for a good finish. When the painted tube was completely dry, broken pieces of mirror were glued to it at random, making it an ideal event prop for a party with an outer space or disco theme. Alternatively, you could paint or spray the pillars silver or gold and then glue on the mirror pieces. Such a pillar could be used to dazzle any viewer at a gala event.

Using several pillars (or pedestals) decorated in the same way makes a statement for staged, wall, or entrance walkways, as shown below.

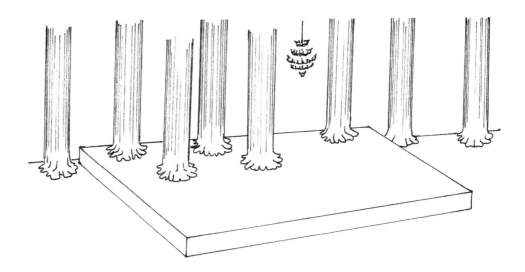

For the repeating vertical look shown above, eight units of 10-foot-high staging truss can be draped with velvet: an inexpensive but effective solution. The backbone is created from a steel vertical truss and a hula hoop, which holds the curtain drop over the vertical truss. The hula hoop is cut open and threaded through the top of the curtain. The curtain is then hemmed to the hula hoop. The hula hoop with the attached curtain is subsequently balanced on top of the truss and wired on where the two sides of the curtain meet and where the cut to the hula hoop was made.

This prop is visually dramatic, especially when used in units of two, four, six, or eight. The best fabrics for this design are velvet, colorful cotton, satin, or sheers. This diagram shows a layout variation in which some of the eight columns are placed forward and some back to create a dimensional effect.

The drawing below shows a setup of two vertical units connected at the top with a horizontally placed beam. The entire construction is made of the aluminum truss or

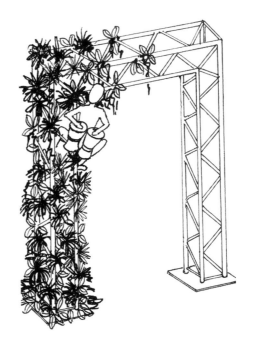

steel frames typically used by stage designers. A unit of this shape is often overlooked as a viable prop. A series of such units could be used to create a tunnel or walkway at venue entrances. Alternatively, a single unit can be used as a stage feature, or several units could be placed along the walls. The diagram shows yet another decorating idea: the skeleton is decorated with flowers and an African drummer prop is attached high up—suitable for a safari-themed party. It is necessary to work with a staging specialist when implementing this design, as he or she will ensure that appropriate security measures are taken when erecting the steel construction and later decorating it (scaffolding may need to be used to reach the upper truss).

Pedestals

Pedestals are ideally used as an individual event prop for corners and entrances; however, they can also be used as a design element scattered around the room, which can sometimes help tie a theme together.

A basic pedestal (below, left) can be constructed in the same manner as the pillar described previously or rented from a staging or special event rental company. (One advantage of subscribing to *Special Events Magazine* is that it will provide you with resources for any type or style of product that you might need to rent or buy.) This type of 8-foot-tall, 18-inch-square pedestal can be painted or covered with fabric or vinyl sheeting.

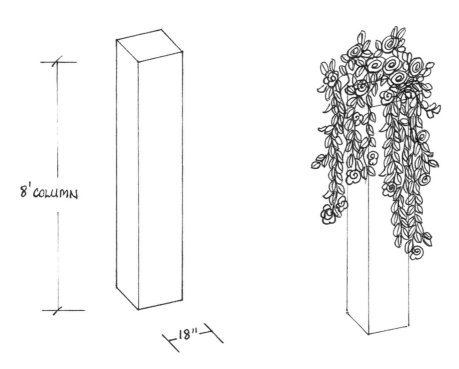

The basic pedestal shown in this diagram can be finished with a large flower arrangement placed on top as shown above at right. If using fresh flowers, place them inside a bowl, vase, or another waterproof vessel.

The design below at left uses a trio of pedestals varying in height and dimensions. This look is ideal for a room corner or an entrance.

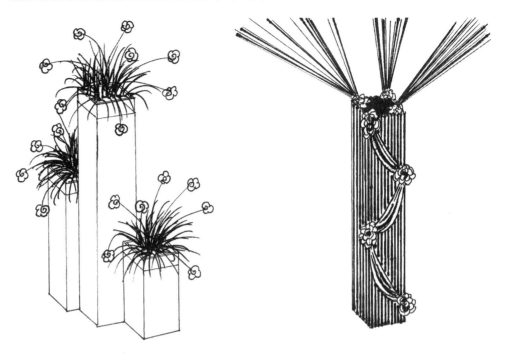

The same basic pedestal is shown above at right decorated for an absolutely dramatic effect. It is painted white and 2-inch-wide black ribbon is stapled on in vertical strips. Then silk flowers and strips of fabric are attached to the pedestal, and thin strips of black-and-white fabric are extended to the ceiling and attached.

Below is an example of a pedestal made of a stage truss and dressed with bunches of flowers and foliage. The idea is to hang the bouquets at three different levels for a

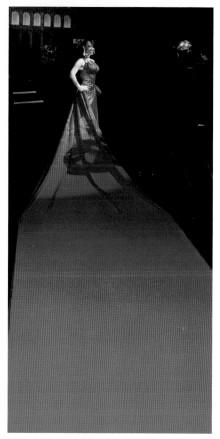

FIGURE 1 (*above*). This beautifully styled room was designed by Kellie Mathas for The Special Event conference's gala award evening in New Orleans in 2010. The beautifully set tables create a high-impact look at the entrance of the ballroom.

FIGURE 2 (*far left*). The chandeliers come to life for an added "wow" factor: A beautifully dressed model suspended in space from the chandelier gracefully filled the champagne glasses of the guests at each table.

FIGURE 3 (*left*). The Lady in Red made the red carpet a stunning entrance piece for the awards presentation. The train extended for yards and yards, but when the model walked away, the Velcro™ attachment released so the fabric simply fell to the floor. All photos on this page provided by USA Hosts.

FIGURE 4 (*top*). The undercloth of yellow lamour in this table setting provides a dynamic lining to the floor-length white-lace tablecloth. Photo by Artist Group Photographers, provided by Premier Bride.

FIGURE 5 (*left*). A blue-and-dusty pink motif gives a look of sophistication. Photo by Scott Patrick Photography.

FIGURE 6 (*above*). The crisp, fresh style of this luncheon setting on the beach is the perfect complement to a beach wedding. Photo by Audrey Snow Photography. All photos this page: Linens by BBJ Linen.

FIGURE 7 (*left*). This "amber twist" tablecloth dresses up a high-style cocktail table. The table linen is gathered along the table stem and trimmed there with a fabric rose. Photo by Art Engel, provided by The Flower Firm, Signature Room. FIGURE 8 (*bottom*). The richness of chocolate linen against crisp white napkins makes a statement at any formal occasion. Photo by Art Engel, provided by Party People. All photos this page: Linens by BBJ Linen.

FIGURE 9 (*above*). Lush and intense: the color combination of apple green and cerise sets a strong mood for the evening. Plexiglas chairs are a perfect complement. Photo by Amber Strickler, Zasey Photography, provided by iCatching Events. FIGURE 10 (*right*). A series of dressed cocktail tables add glamour to a cocktail party in a construction setting. Photo by Armosa Studios, provided by *Alabama Weddings* magazine. FIGURE 11 (*below*). The style of setting shown here, with the napkin and place setting positioned on the dinnerware, brings beauty to any table. Photo by Jai Gerard Photography. All photos this page: Linens by BBJ Linen.

FIGURE 12 (*above*). The look here is fashion and passion combined, resulting in the most elegant of settings. Photo by Boutique Photographers, provided by Janice Rosenthal of Party Productions.

FIGURE 13 (*left*). This stunning outdoor table setting is a delightful look for a corporate lunch or Sunday brunch. Photo by Mark Silverstein Photography.

FIGURE 14 (*below*). Achieve ultimate style even with an informal table setting by choosing a tablecloth fabric with a sophisticated feel in a brilliant hue. Photo by Frank Carnaggio Photography, provided by *Alabama Weddings* magazine. All photos this page: Linens by BBJ Linen.

FIGURE 15 (*right*). The matching components of this traditional-style table, from the cloth, napkins, and chair covers to the florals and handcrafted place card, are a specialty of designer Tim Lundy of Atlanta. Photo by Karen Gordon of Karenscapes Photography.

FIGURE 16 (*below*). Beautiful branches with blossoms, maple leaves, and orange roses create a stately look for any table setting. Photo by Craig Ferré.

FIGURE 17 (*above, left*). This versatile tabletop in lime green and hot pink is made of affordable components: a plywood base, a cardboard tube, dry foam, fabric, and colored plastic disks.

FIGURE 18 (*above, middle*). This colorful paper shopping bag is filled with foam to hold decorative units. Paper whistles are arranged as the top placement and are surrounded by clusters of mini feathers, with light balls at the base.

FIGURE 19 (*above, right*). The geometric glass vase is dressed with two artificial red-lacquered apple sprays twisted around the vase for an artistic effect.

FIGURE 20 (*below, right*). A beautiful lace vase holds a single rose and is surrounded by martini glasses filled with pink pebbles.

FIGURE 21 (*below, left*). A pair of glass vases are filled with lime green foam cubes. At the necks of the vases, soft collars made of wire (a Smithers-Oasis product) are arranged. The fresh roses and rose petals complete the look.

FIGURE 22 (*left*). Newspaper is artistically used as a background panel to a huge lamé bow. Newspaper is inexpensive to use in décor, and it can easily be pasted onto foam core.

FIGURE 23 (*above*). The lime green and purple panelling creates a backdrop for an island of decoration. Such panels can be used when an accent is required to the side of a stage or in a ballroom corner.

FIGURE 24 (*right*). Nine-inch-wide ribbons decorate a royal blue background. Lion Ribbon has a beautiful range of choices.

FIGURE 25 (*far right*). A pink flamingo stands in a stately manner against nine-feet-tall branches with blossoms. Exotic flowers complete the look.

FIGURE 26 (*above*). This stage and background were constructed using AllySTAGE, with aluminum and Plexiglas, resulting in a very modern look. Lighting enhanced the aluminum and Plexiglas, making the stage a standout feature of the room. Photography by Peter Flowers/Regina King. Designed by Peter Jones of Melbourne, the stage was constructed by Staging Rentals in Sydney.

FIGURE 27 (*above, left*). This steel stand is covered with foliage. The flame bowls, available from Fortune Products, create an illusion of real fire, safely.

FIGURE 28 (*above, right*). This high-style centerpiece uses a variety of foliage, ferns, and leaves affixed to a moss-like base. The frogs suspended in swings are a fun addition.

FIGURE 29 (*right*). Black baby's breath is designed into the top tier of this tabletop. The baby's breath is dried and everlasting but creates a soft and dramatic look. Teardrop pearls are attached to a fishing line and dropped into space. Cyclamen orchids are scattered through the composition.

FIGURE 30 (*left*). Short-stemmed white roses and clusters of white net provide interest and texture, while beaded drops and sprigs of foliage fall in a cascading effect. Elegant wide, white ribbon is used to cover the cardboard tube.

FIGURE 31 (*below*). This massive arrangement was created for the International Catholic Youth Congress 2009 mass held in Sydney. Six floral units are joined together by lengths of silk to give the illusion of one decorative backdrop. The fabric is secured at the back of the arrangements and extends to the floor. These designs stood 16 feet in height and covered 16 feet in width, making an impressive statement.

FIGURE 32. In this Italian setting, the tables are covered with a silk tablecloth with white-and-red check. Wrought iron chairs suit the look. The floral arrangement placed on the floor against the inside wall of the tent measures 10 feet high by 6 feet wide and features cascading lengths of foliage with roses.

FIGURE 33 (*above*). In this blue and green room setting, the tables are dressed with white lilies, purple liatruis, cyclamen orchids, moss, ferns, shells, and gilded pods.

FIGURE 34 (*left*). Pieces of dried seaweed painted blue are the key feature of this glamorous tabletop. The base is a plastic tray with Plexiglas rods of varying lengths. Ferns, moss, and cyclamen orchids finish the look for an underwater-themed party.

FIGURE 35 (*top, left*). The main, 15-inch mirror ball in this arrangement (available from Fortune Products) is positioned on a round, moss-covered oasis frame. A round piece of dry foam is hot glued at the top, allowing the ribbons, smaller mirror balls, and berry strands to cascade down.

FIGURE 36 (*top, right*). This stunning ceiling décor was designed to suspend over the heads of guests (see pages 198–199). Artificial roses cover a 48-inch-diameter foam wreath base. Fresh asparagus fern was added as it can hold without watering for up to 48 hours.

FIGURE 37 (*left*). This fun party tabletop is created using strands of optical fiber from Fortune Products. The tray is filled with pink glass pebbles and rose petals.

FIGURE 38 (*left*). For these unique centerpieces, hundreds of white dendrobium orchids were attached to the branches of white manzanita trees. Accents included candles, orchids, and crystals. Photo by Abby Ross Photography.

FIGURE 39 (*below*). A surprise after-party was revealed when the drapes in this dinner room parted dramatically. The focus of the design was a zebra-print dance floor and crystal chandeliers. Photo by Abby Ross Photography. Designs this page: Designs by Sean.

FIGURE 40 (*above*). This tent was positioned in the forecourt of the Sydney Opera House, a stunning off-site venue location. Photo provided by Stephen Thatcher of Pages Event Hire.

FIGURE 41 (*right*). These distinctive raw aluminum cast-iron finish urns and pedestals are beautiful and timeless for event décor. They can be lavishly dressed with an abundance of fresh flowers as a decorative event piece or used as a pair for a stage or ballroom entrance. Urns by Accent Décor, Inc., Montego Collection; photo provided by Accent Décor, Inc.

FIGURE 42 (*below*). A sensational look for a wedding, this eye catching tabletop features Halo glass vases filled with varying depths of water and floating candles. Blooms of pink roses and cyclamen orchids are lavishly arranged to cascade down the center of the table. Photo provided by Accent Décor, Inc.

tiered effect. It is achieved by using the so-called casket bat (which is an Oasis foam brick available from Smithers-Oasis; see page 226 for company contact information), encased in a plastic cage with a hanging device. This idea is particularly effective for weddings or galas, where flowers take on primary importance.

Decorating Ceilings

Ceiling work is always difficult for a number of reasons. First, the ceiling has a limited number of hanging points from which to display props or suspend fabrics. Second, the types of decorations that can be used are restricted because items need to be hung above the heads of guests. Finally, when dressing the ceiling, you need to be extremely specific with your timing, as the whole floor will need to be cleared of people before the hanging can take place. With this in mind, an invaluable tool to the event planner is a timber grid available in many nurseries (see the diagrams on page 144). It is a panel made of timber trellis that opens up to a 6 x 4 foot rectangle. This tool can be utilized in a variety of ways when decorating ceilings.

Here are some tips to keep in mind when decorating ceilings:

- Seek approval from the venue engineer or principal before proceeding with any décor intended for ceiling beautification.

- Consider the schedule leading up to the event when deciding on the timing of the ceiling dressing. Be prepared with the swags of fabric and other material or decorative units, but make sure the ceiling décor work does not hold up the staging or technical team in any way. Book the scissor lift for the projected time required for the ceiling decorating.

- Consult with a staging specialist in regard to your design, especially for safety reasons.

Examples of Ceiling Décor

Chinese lanterns are suspended from a timber grid. This is a great decorating idea for events that are themed; all you need to do is suspend the appropriate props in place of the Chinese lanterns. Think lightweight disco balls for a 1960s party or bats and ghouls for Halloween.

Below at left is a variation of the previous design with items hung on a timber grid, but here hanging baskets are filled with artificial flowers and decorated with flowers and ribbons. In ceiling design, artificial flowers are often used rather than fresh because they are lighter and do not require watering. If this idea is going to be implemented with a basket and fresh flowers, the ceiling grid itself must be stronger and the hanging chains thicker.

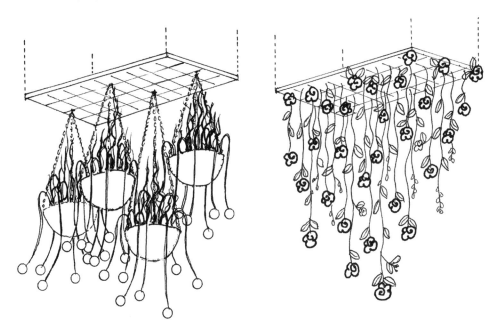

The design idea shown above at right uses the 6 x 4 foot expandable timber grid and silk or ribbon flowers dropping from it toward the floor. Using 12 to 20 such ceiling units over the dance floor would create a beautiful canopy effect, appropriate for a wedding.

Below is yet another take on a ceiling structure using the timber grid: 6-inch-wide strips of fabric are stapled to both of the short sides of the panel. The hanging ends of the fabric could be knotted or frayed.

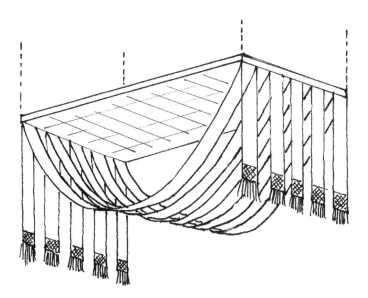

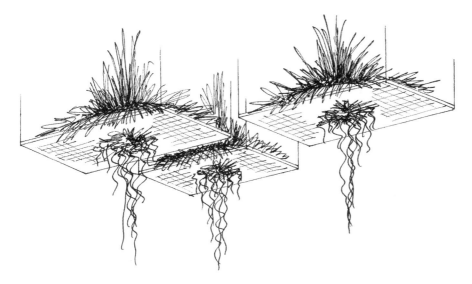

The set of ceiling units above uses the timber grid as the backbone of each unit. An abundance of grasses is arranged in Oasis foam bricks and suspended from the panels toward the floor.

Floor Panels

You will find that some venues have areas that are somewhat unattractive; for example, in an old warehouse, there may be pipes running out of a wall. Floor panels, which can be dressed with fabrics or flowers, are a perfect way of screening off such areas to make the room more aesthetically pleasing. They can also be used to condense space and give the room a more intimate atmosphere if you are working in a large venue but only have a small number of guests. You can also use a combination of ceiling panels and floor panels as shown below, or just floor panels, to create a decorative feature for your event. Some of these ideas are explored in greater detail in the following diagrams and directions.

Floor panels are constructed in the same way as ceiling grids, using a wooden trellis; however, the grids will be slightly larger, with standard dimensions of 8 x 4 feet.

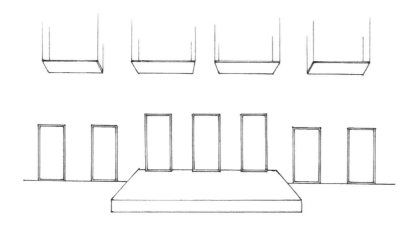

To make the frame freestanding, a timber bracket can be made from 2 x 1 foot timber batons that are secured by a hinge to the back of each panel.

Timber grids are easy to work with, are light and thus easy to erect, and, when decorated, create a dramatic effect.

The design above uses floor panels and ceiling structures decorated for a dramatic look for a stage or wall. The same floor panel and ceiling unit layout could also be decorated with ribbons and silk flowers for a different look.

Using the same layout idea shown in the preceding diagram, fabric can be intertwined among the ceiling panels as shown below, and also threaded creatively through the floor panels to make a strong statement in almost any setting.

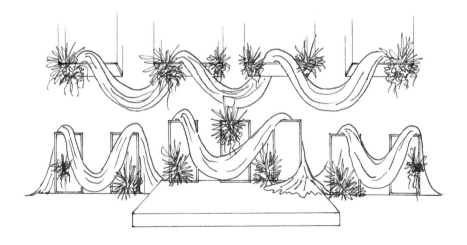

Figure 26, courtesy of Staging Rentals and Construction Services of Sydney, shows a white stage background lit up with contrasting colors. The stage, including a runway off to the side for feature artist James Morrison, is created using clear Perspex. The Perspex picks up the light shining on the white background, creating a stunning effect.

Islands of Décor

Dress up the odd spots in a room by creating islands of décor. Such islands also work well positioned in the pre-drinks area or the corners of the venue. See color plates, Figures 22–25, for examples of these islands of décor.

In Figure 22, newspaper is artistically used as a background panel with the addition of a huge lamé fabric bow, accented with bowls of flowers.

The lime green and purple paneling in Figure 23 creates a backdrop for this island of decoration, which features beautifully wrapped gift boxes and masses of colorful dried branches. Delphiniums, cyclamen orchids, and baby's breath add the finishing touch.

A ribbon story is featured in Figure 24. Here an extremely wide ribbon is used to decorate a royal-blue velvet backdrop, along with bows and a collection of fresh flowers.

Figure 25 shows a flamingo standing in a stately manner against 9-foot-tall branches with blossoms. Exotic blooms of anthuriums and aspidistra leaves add to the striking look.

Using Fabrics for Effect

Fabric can be used in myriad ways to decorate a venue: on the ceiling, walls, or floors, or even to accentuate props. Fabric allows the event planner to cover large areas, and, with some fabric choices, it can give a luxurious feeling to a room. When fabric is correctly lit, it can create an impressive feature for your event. Best of all, you can find fabrics to meet all your decorating needs, whether you are planning a themed beach luncheon, a sophisticated corporate dinner, or a lavish wedding reception.

Creative Event Concepts

T HE PURPOSE OF THIS CHAPTER IS TO PROVIDE YOU WITH examples of creative event concepts, or event themes that are workable, bankable, and appealing to clients. The event planner will tackle the choice of concept for an event for the first time at the proposal stage. On some occasions, the client will approach the planner with a theme idea ready or somewhat formed. For example, the client might say he or she wants a picnic, or might describe the desired affair with key words, such as upscale, sophisticated, fun, or fantasy. Whether the client offers early input on the topic or not, there will be a lot of room left for the planner to brainstorm the theme creatively and flesh it out into a full, definite, feasible idea. The planner will present the discussed ideas as part of his or her proposal.

The concept that eventually will be agreed upon between the planner and the client will be developed through further discussions, ensuring that the client's wants and needs are expanded to meet expectations. A budget can only be developed once a specific brief is created. The next step for the event planner will be to source the most suitable venue for the concept that the budget will allow.

The Purpose of Event Décor

Décor is, in effect, an artistic, visual interpretation of the creative concept for the event, of the story that is being told. Wrapping up the room with décor is an extension of window dressing and therefore a highly specialized art form. But, of course, the window is much longer, much wider, and certainly much higher. Décor may involve transforming a ballroom, tent or marquee, luxurious home, garden, or, heaven help us, an airport hangar.

Where to Go for Concept and Décor Ideas

I am often asked, "How do you keep coming up with fresh ideas?" The answer is, there is nothing new about the procedure for generating ideas. Keeping up with trends, being aware of changes in the industry, and constantly checking out new available products and samples enable me to deliver creative ideas for clients.

The important point here is, regardless of your years in the business or experience in the industry, view the world with an open mind because it is like a parachute: when it opens, it takes everything in and when it is closed, creativity is static.

That said, one way to get new ideas for creative concepts and the associated décor is by widening our horizons through travel, thus experiencing different cultures and exchanging conversations with people from other countries. Comparing different types of architecture and landscapes allows us to form a broader impression of life, and that enhances, inspires, and extends creativity.

Event Planning in an Airport Hangar: A Case Study

The following case study has been presented courtesy of Lehman & Associates of Sydney, the company that staged this event.

A well-known international airline requested to have their anniversary celebration staged within the Sydney International Airport hangar. The hangar was in its original state, with large beams and a workshop area; it was very authentic—which the guests loved, as this was a high-security area.

Guests were invited to the event with a pseudo–airline ticket, handed "passports" on arrival, and greeted by "check-in staff." The event organizers decided to divide the hangar with white sheer drapes to allow for a revealing effect during the event.

Guests were seated for a gourmet lunch and then came the showcase: the white chiffon drapes were pulled back and in came the actual first plane ever owned and used by the airline company, all engines blazing. The cross-check procedure was performed, the doors opened, and out walked the captain of the first flight for the company. He was accompanied by the first child to fly on the flight from Europe to Australia with this carrier, who was nine years old at the time. The sounds of "Fly Me to the Moon" in an up-tempo arrangement could be heard in the background. What an experience. What an event.

For years, I have made a point to collect sketches, drawings, books, magazines, posters, invitations, and even advertisements that I found inspiring and that could one day possibly kick-start an idea for an event or even lead to a complete concept.

It is always to your advantage to observe the phases of interior design in contemporary living. Learn to develop a third eye for creative inspiration, as so many things around us can act as a source for creative stimulus that will help you flesh out that theme you have been struggling with.

The study of Ikebana (the art of Japanese flower arrangement, Sogetsu School) made me very aware of nature's unending inspirations. This study taught me to question and as a result, I question almost everything. Constant questioning is the very trait that will give you the constructive, vital, and practical knowledge to make you the best you can be in the industry.

Whenever you see something appealing, photograph it or note it on paper and place it in your ideas file. I promise you, there will come a day when this comes into play. A visit to an art gallery or museum, an early morning walk in the park, a shopping trip around the city, a movie, or a theatrical performance can be the beginning of an inspirational concept.

The following example illustrates this point. When I was last in Chicago, a large department store displayed two mannequins dressed in designer jeans and accessories artistically in the window. Apart from the window floor, which was massed with soft brown autumn leaves, the only accent in that window included long drops of very thick rope knotted from top to bottom. These lengths of rope were stapled to the window ceiling and fell to the floor in a series of vertical lines. I photographed this window display and recorded it in my ideas file when I was back in my office in Sydney. Sure enough, a few months later, I used that idea for a "Pirates' Party."

Now, does an idea like this fit only one thematic concept? Not at all. Those long drops of knotted rope could serve as a decorative prop for a "Treasure Island," "Safari," or "Marooned" event.

I also draw on the publications related to the industry, such as the monthly educational magazine *Special Events,* a Penton Media publication (see www.specialevents .com to obtain a subscription). You only have to look at the outstanding event decoration in the beautiful books by Preston Bailey (see Select Resources, page 223) to feel new waves of inspiration. These are great volumes to have in your library.

Finally, never underestimate the input from a close associate in the industry. Gone are the days when you were unable to partner with a professional and pick the brain of a working pro. You will find that the event professional of today will be happy to share his or her experiences and expertise. Our industry has moved forward and grown in numbers, and the amazing delivery of events today is a testament to this. A conversation between two event planners is a key way for both parties to exchange information and build on the industry experience.

Inspiration Block

Every planner gets to the stage where he or she feels like all possible creative ideas have already been exploited. When this is the case, I advise that you create space for yourself, which provides a time for mental stimulus.

Utilize quiet time to research past trends and styles (see page 182 for information on past decades to get you started). Alternatively, meet with industry partners and colleagues to discuss ideas and seek creative assistance; a conversation with your peers could very well result in distinctive and original ideas.

The newcomer in the display world generally has problems generating ideas due to lack of experience. He or she may lack the ability to bring the decorative components

Tips for Avoiding Mental Blocks

1. Look back on what you have done in the past. Maybe the materials used can be substituted for units that give a smarter look.

2. You may only need to change the color, fabric, or board to create something new. Review past events to kick-start the imagination.

3. Isolate yourself completely and designate time to totally immerse yourself in the task at hand with absolutely no interruptions. Space and quietness are key when searching for something new.

4. Research is vital. Surround yourself with reference material, such as books on theater, classic movies, children's books, and *National Geographic* magazines to gather information on your theme. Jot down every possible idea you can think of initially. Build on the key features to support the concept.

5. Feature three key décor elements rather than display a series of mismatching elements that are scattered around the room.

6. Know your venue: its assets and its limitations. Study the site inspection chart carefully and appraise what can be done. Seek advice from other professionals to resolve any issues in your "too hard" basket.

7. Study the color wheel, as color sets the mood for the event. Discuss color with your lighting designer and creative director to achieve an atmospheric result. Lighting will enhance any scheme.

8. If designing is your strength, work it to the best of your ability. If another discipline is your primary strength, be smart enough to partner with a person with outstanding expertise in the creative aspect of your job.

9. When the budget is low, concentrate on decorating the stage and tables only. These specific areas in a venue will carry the look.

together to create a total and well-coordinated look. If you are a newcomer and employed within a special events company, I encourage you to seek advice from peers within the organization. Direct observation of creative and experienced set dressers at work can also be a valuable education.

Remember that you can obtain maximum results with just one smart idea. Mastery of the art of display does not happen overnight, but you can lift your level of competence if you put time into studying this creative field. You can learn from seeing other events, from viewing event décor done by others, and by attending special event workshops and event trade shows. You can also continue educating yourself through industry magazines and other publications.

Environment Dictates Décor

The environment of an art gallery will call for a completely different theme or concept than an airport hangar or empty warehouse. An art gallery already has an atmospheric environment; therefore, the décor will be minimal. On the other hand, an airport hangar or warehouse will typically require maximum décor; props will be needed to fill spaces in order to deliver the desired theme.

Budget plays a key role when determining the best décor and venue to execute the creatively planned concept. If you select the option of the art gallery, you already have a furnished venue with ambience and in some cases need a minimal décor budget. Alternatively, a tent in a unique location will usually require a large décor budget because of the bare space of the structure itself.

If the budget allows, it is ideal if the venue can be "blacked out" with either thematic painted canvases, sheer white fabric, or velvet drapes in the color of your choice hung from a truss around the four walls. The "blank canvas" starting point offers a wider scope for event décor.

With this scenario, any theme can be styled into the venue, from "Prison Break" or "An Evening in Space" to "The Glittering Gala" or "The Ice Heist." The "blank canvas" is the first choice for the event planner as room décor is not hampered in any way by venue embellishments, such as wall finish, specific paneling, drapes, mirrors, lamps, or ornaments.

If the budget is restricted, seldom does it allow for the "blank canvas" look due to the expense of hanging fabric from ceiling to floor. If you are organizing an elegant corporate affair that lends itself to a more formal setting and decoration is needed, source a beautiful ballroom, art gallery, or even a five-star restaurant. Then the feature of the décor can be beautiful table centerpieces massed with candles and fresh flowers.

Groundbreaking Party on Lot 165: A Case Study

The following case study has been provided courtesy of Cheryl Fish of Cheryl Fish and Associates, based in Las Vegas.

A groundbreaking party was planned for clients about to build their dream house on Lot 165. They had just approved the architectural plans for the home, so doing the party on the lot seemed the perfect choice.

The invitations were designed to replicate the blueprint of their new home, and the party details were noted on the professional blueprint rendering.

The 205 guests were scheduled to arrive at a country club, where they were met by "construction worker" waiters and subsequently transported to Lot 165 on large golf carts. Upon arrival, they were escorted to the "Cocktail Construction Site" where "Lounging on the Lot" took place.

Sounds from the famous "Rat Pack" filtered through the air, and the guests enjoyed taking photos with the strolling look-alikes. Later the photos were framed and prepared for the guests to take home as mementos. The lush lot featured groupings of chic outdoor lounge furniture. The tables were dressed with silk-screened runners and replicas of the invitation, complemented by clear paint cans filled with munchies. Food carts offered pretzels and popcorn. The chef cooked up appetizers that were served on personalized trays.

As the sun set, the guests were transported back to the country club for more surprises. A tent was set up there, bathed in primary paint colors that swirled throughout the night. Long tables, dressed in blueprint-design linen with white paper overlays, featured wheatgrass, garden florals, and construction-inspired centerpieces, such as enormous pencils, paint cans, yellow construction boots, rulers, caution tape, and rotating caution lights.

A hearty barbecue dinner was served on the terrace. For dessert, an array of decadent delights was served, including cupcakes featuring individual tools made of fondant: saws, hammers, and "under construction" signs.

As the guests were departing, they stopped to pick up their framed photo mementos. The "Night Construction Crew" was on hand to say good night and present each guest with a yellow LED flashlight with an attached card that read "Thanks for lighting up our night!"

"Build it, and they will come"—that is exactly what happened at the groundbreaking party on Lot 165.

Allow your décor selection to complement or suit the venue environment so that the space works for you and not against you.

Design Principles and Décor

There are art principles that have been set by master artists of times past, and these principles guide the artists of today, including event planners, in their work. The following discussion of balance, scale, and color can help you create original and successful event concepts.

Balance

Balance is the key to effective use of display materials. A sense of balance entails a great deal of visual accuracy and requires a certain sense of feel through sight. If any display is completely off balance, it will be seen or noticed through the eye immediately. The "less is more" technique can be applied when trying to achieve a balance of the individual units.

The inexperienced display person tends to use everything he or she can think of and scatters décor units around the room without a sense of purpose. This approach is madness, not method. It is just as important to know what to leave out as what to put in. A venue can be dressed so that it is either symmetrically or asymmetrically balanced.

With a symmetrically balanced display, what happens on one side of the room is mirrored on the other. In short, symmetrical balance is simply a reversed replica. In earlier days display professionals only had to style up half a window because the other half was just repeated.

Asymmetrical balance is best applied in a display when decorative units vary in style, color, and size. This type of balance is best suited for the cocktail evening where guests are moving and mingling as they network. This style is also utilized when the décor props vary in look but are similar in size, and the placement of those individual props is balanced by optical weight.

To position decorative units to bring either symmetrical or asymmetrical balance into play, you need to create various levels with the individual props. One prop, for example, can be attached to or suspended from a piece of truss. Another prop can be placed slightly lower, working the units from the height toward the floor. The eye will then naturally flow from prop to prop, from top to bottom, and therefore make the optical weight or stability easier to achieve. Balance merely directs the flow of the eye from one decorative point to another.

Scale and Size

The size of the props used to decorate a venue is important because such props provide impact in relation to the size of the space in which they are placed. For example, let's assume that room A has a ceiling height of 12 to 15 feet, as could be the case with a restaurant or banquet room that seats up to 100 guests. The tallest prop appropriate for such a room will be 8 to 10 feet in height. As another example, room B has a ceiling height of 20 to 40 feet; here, props can be 12 to 16 feet high. Venues that have very high ceilings—50 feet and higher—require much taller props. In such venues, decorative ceiling units are often introduced in addition to standing props, to help make the space come together. Work off the ceiling height as a starting point to decide the optimal scale and size of props for your venue.

Color

The color scheme you decide on can make or break the event; it can enhance or diminish the impact of all other décor elements. As a guideline, it is helpful to understand the power that each color represents within the decorated venue.

Red

- Red is considered a hot color with strong visual influence.

- Red is a color with impact.

- Red's heaviness can be lightened by introducing tones of the same color.

Orange

- Orange is a popular and harmonious shade when teamed with apricot, salmon, peach, and clay tones.

- Orange is dramatic when combined with red.

Yellow

- Yellow projects brilliance and brightness.

- Yellow can be used in conjunction with orange tones for a harmonious effect.

- Yellow can be used in conjunction with violet-purple to create contrast.

Green

- Green is a safe color and can be included with any other color.

- Green teams well with shades of teal, aqua, and purple.

Blue

- Blue expresses coolness, distance, and space.

- From the palest blue to the richest royal, blue creates a harmonious look.

Violet

- Violet, lilac, and mauve evoke tranquillity.

- Violet contrasts with and combines well with yellows.

Gray

- Gray can be used stunningly when combined with silver and black.

- Gray is a neutral tone that acts in harmony with other colors.

Brown

- Brown tones have a neutral influence and work with earthy themes.

- Brown can be highlighted with aqua or turquoise.

White

- White is an important color, whether used alone or as a pivotal neutral.

Black

- Black is considered a neutral; black can be used in contrast with any other color or be combined with any other color.

- Black can be a featured color with the addition of any strong color, such as hottest pink, silver chrome, or dazzling gold.

Color Schemes

Color schemes are a systematic color plan carried throughout the event, from table linens, florals, invitations, and the menu to event props. The following are examples of pleasing combinations.

The Direct Complementary Color Scheme
(any two colors directly opposite each other on the color wheel)

Yellow combined with violet

Blue combined with orange

Red combined with green

The Analogous Color Scheme
(any three adjacent colors on the color wheel, plus one primary color)

Red combined with red-orange, orange, and yellow-orange

Blue combined with blue-violet, violet-red, and purple

Yellow combined with yellow-green, blue-green, and emerald

The Monochromatic Color Scheme
(the principle of working from the lightest tone of one color through to the deepest shade of the same color)

Royal blue combined with basic blue into pale blue

Yellow combined with daffodil into cream

Burnt orange combined with orange into apricot

The Neutral Color with Primary Color Scheme

Black combined with the primary color red

Gray combined with the primary color yellow

White combined with the primary color blue

If you want your event to tell a story, the use of color can cleverly evoke a sense of vitality and excitement.

Color and Lighting Design

Fortunately, the lighting designer will specifically create the technical lighting program to fit or enhance your thematic concept, including your color scheme. Lighting can make or break the design.

Event Product Analysis

With any scheme you choose, after brainstorming your color scheme, décor, and entertainment, you should perform a product analysis for the project so that you can accurately assess your prop and equipment requirements for the event. This will also assist you with a budget check.

The following is an example of a working document for a "Jungle Jive" theme.

EQUIPMENT LIST FOR A "JUNGLE JIVE" EVENT

Decorative Props

5 canvas backdrops	50 black tires for ceiling	20 timber planks for elevations
30 flats with scenic art and braces	5 huts with straw roof	3 rolls of burlap
20 decorative jungle trees	10 bundles of tea tree branches	2 rolls of black ground cover
30 sandbags	10 timber boxes for elevations	20 bags of black floor color
40 camouflage nets	20 drums for elevations	6 bags of coconut fiber

Plywood Cutouts or Two- and Three-Dimensional Props

7 elephants	8 ostriches	20 small and medium monkeys
4 gorillas	10 zebras	8 snakes
3 leopards	3 panthers	12 wired animals for lights
10 giraffes	6 large monkeys	10 boulders
3 lions		

Plants

600 fresh palms and assorted varieties

20 ruffle ferns

Linens and Accessories

80 black floor-length cloths	800 napkins trimmed with
80 safari overlays	snake
800 black chair covers/sashes	400 hats

Tools and Other Equipment

2 scissor lifts to order	4 rolls of wire or twine
3 ladders	2 floral kits

Tabletop Requirements

80 premade tabletops, 1 per table	All foliage and fillers ordered	240 batteries
80 torches, 1 per table	160 coconut halves and candles, 2 per table	400 binoculars
480 toy snakes and spiders, 6 per table	240 small electrical lamps, 3 per table	

Lights

50 extension cords	3 rolls of black gaffer tape
20 double adapters	400 yards of flexi-lights

Uniforms and Miscellaneous

40 staff T-shirts	Soft drinks and mineral waters
Coffee urn, cups, napkins, teaspoons	First-aid kit
	Fire extinguisher

Why is such an equipment list necessary? For a few reasons:

1. It is a comprehensive product list required for the job, and stock and product cannot be missed.
2. The props required are specifically needed for the event, and the list allows the team member assigned to packing the truck to do so systematically.
3. You can use the list to establish which items will need to be unpacked first and hence their optimal arrangement in the truck. When the truck arrives at the venue, the large props and the ceiling décor, which were packed last, can come off first.
4. The list allows for double-checking against what is required.

Creative Concepts and Ideas to Inspire

Any theme you choose has been used before at one time or another, possibly even by another event decorator in another place. This should be of no concern to you because it is how we interpret the theme that matters. "The Cotton Club," for example, can be done three or four different ways, depending on who creates the story. If a given themed concept works, learn to modify it for future events because usually you will be entertaining different groups of guests and catering to different tastes.

The following pages introduce 15 conceptual schemes that may kick-start your imagination if you are searching for something new, different, and original. Stories such as these will assist you when you are researching concepts from a client's brief and writing up the proposal. Each theme can be used for a variety of events, such as the following:

- Corporate dinner
- Press conference
- Product launch
- Wedding
- Gala dinner
- Cocktail party
- Fundraising or charity event
- Incentive dinner or program
- Bar or bat mitzvah
- Birthday or anniversary celebration

15 Thematic Concepts to Kick-Start Your Creativity

1. Jungle Jive

2. The Housewives' Desperate Cocktail Party

3. An Invitation to a Bollywood Bash

4. Prison Break

5. Launching the Jewel

6. Rock Around the Clock—the Fifties

7. Chinatown Charade

8. Carnival, South American–Style

9. Step into the Outback

10. Art Deco Garden Party

11. Theatrical Experience

12. Wild Wild West

13. The Ice Heist Fundraiser

14. Oasis Sanctuary

15. Walk Like an Egyptian

Jungle Jive

Swing into the jungle, where the natives are friendly, the joint is rocking, and the vibe is hip, hippo! With this theme for all ages, the mood is tropical, the room is colorful and leafy, and the cast of characters runs from Tarzan to Jane to Dr. Livingstone.

From the pre-drinks area, African drummers in full dress lead guests into the venue and into the excitement of a fantasy evening. Drums pound and African rhythms vibrate through the pre-function area, where the electrifying hum of cicadas resonates. Stylish sets and décor transform the ballroom into a jungle. White fog and animal sounds add an air of mystery and magic, and waiters stand ready to serve cocktails and canapés as guests savor the experience.

Dressed in khaki shirts and shorts, waiters serve drinks as guests marvel at an array of assorted palms and tropical plants, interspersed with huge models and cutouts of African animals—giraffes, lions, and zebras—while model monkeys hang from ropes and vines suspended from netting covering the ceiling.

Theme colors are khaki and earthy tones. Napkins are tied with rope, and table coverings are khaki-colored floor-length cloths with sackcloth overlays. Centerpieces feature candles wrapped in twine, birds of paradise, and crumpled burlap fabric.

Color Palette

All earth tones of brown, beige, caramel, black, and burnt orange with masses of green fresh foliage.

Décor and Prop Design

Plywood cutouts of assorted safari animals

Painted scenic canvases for walls

Masses of vines and ropes

Camouflage netting made of burlap/hessian swags

Assorted trees and foliage plants

Tree trunks, logs, and branches

Safari hats, binoculars, and toy snakes and toy spiders for tables

Lanterns, lamps, and torches

Coconuts and fruits for tables

Jungle huts

Waterfall units—rented panels of painted birds and tropical flowers

Entertainment

Fire-eaters

Snake charmers

Witch doctors

Tribal dancers

Tarzan

The Housewives' Desperate Cocktail Party

The smash-hit TV show *Desperate Housewives* has become one of the most talked-about shows since *Sex and the City*. This is an ideal theme for any corporate Christmas party or an evening for the company staff.

As guests arrive, they are handed a choice of fluffy slippers, gardening gloves, or shower cap. Picture guests elegantly dressed in cocktail dresses and heels being served drinks and canapés by some waiters wearing smart black pants, shirts, and bow ties with skin-colored surgical gloves, and other waiters wearing black bathrobes. The waitresses wear knee-length satin dressing gowns and rollers in their hair. To complete the look, their footwear can range from stiletto heels to black sneakers to satin slip-ons.

The stage is adorned with a collection of household embellishments, including a clothesline strung from side to side from which hang sexy lingerie and black silk stockings. The ladies' apparel is strung high on the stage to avoid annoying the band. Colorful laundry baskets painted in black and silver are piled on the apron of the stage for effect.

Urns of black feather dusters or black ostrich feathers further glamorize this theme and add an impressive accent. Tabletops can include blackened branches with a range of kitchen utensils, kitchen sponges, steel wool pads, painted wooden spoons, and oven mitts in silver and gold with strings of diamanté. The possibilities are endless for this fun scheme. See color plates, Figure 29, for an example of décor appropriate for this event concept.

Color Palette

Black, silver, and hot pink

Décor and Prop Design

Brooms painted black and glittered

Blackened branches with diamanté drops attached

Cutouts of kitchen utensils

Swags of black or hot pink satin fabric

Fluffy slippers, hair rollers, bathrobes

Plastic laundry baskets piled with washing

Clotheslines strung overhead with clothes and sexy lingerie pegged to them

Colorful linen sheets for wall hangings

Black and hot pink feather dusters

Black silk stockings

Colorful dishcloths and kitchen utensils

Entertainment

Sexy gardeners

Male strippers

The "Hugh Hefner" Bunnies

An Invitation to a Bollywood Bash

Bollywood has arrived on the international entertainment scene, with vibrant colors, costumes, music, song, and dance. This Bollywood theme is derived from the Indian movie influences that we experience today, as well as India's exotic restaurants and interior décor, which features decorative lamps, basketware, and accessories made of brass and glass.

Guests enter an exotic-looking ballroom and hear the constant tinkling of bells evocative of Indian culture. This sound comes from the miniature brass bells that are attached to the aprons of the waitstaff, dressed for the occasion in saris and turbans.

Snake charmers, palm readers, contortionists, and belly dancers are featured throughout the evening as site performers. They delight guests as they move around, or, alternatively, these site performers can be featured as a main act.

Fresh palm fronds painted gold are arranged in tall black ceramic urns (24 single palm stems per urn are required). These urns are placed on 5-foot-high pedestals to provide a floral feature that exceeds 12 feet in height. This will make a stunning impression. Urns of this size can be featured on the stage, on the side of the stage, or in the corners of the ballroom to reflect the tropical Indian climate. Burnt orange silk is attached at the back of each urn and spills onto the floor in a pool effect, which adds a lavish look to these eye-catching designs.

This event provides the perfect showcase for the ballroom buffet, where the food is presented to support the theme, from pappadums and samosas to rich, fragrant curries, with an assortment of tropical fruits and Indian desserts.

Large cutouts of bejeweled elephants, peacocks, and snakes become part of the scenic sets, and the centerpieces feature feather, fake gems, and gold fabric, as well as strings of gold beads and chains.

Color Palette

Gold, burnt orange, chocolate brown, and splashes of turquoise

Décor and Prop Design

Painted canvas to hang from internal venue walls

Cutouts of bejeweled elephants, snakes, and peacocks

Colorful bowls of flowers and huge silk cushions

Colorful silk umbrellas or decorative cutouts

Gold silk swags for draping ceiling

Beaded curtains for ceiling suspension

Jewel boxes with beads and coins spilling out

Towering urns of gilded palms and peacock feathers

Fresh palm leaves or magnolia leaves painted gold

Baskets of tropical fruits and birds of paradise blooms

Collection of basketware and terra-cotta pottery

Entertainment

Palm readers

Snake charmers

Fortune-tellers

Group performing as pickpocket street thieves

Belly dancers

Prison Break

As Elvis Presley's "Jailhouse Rock" reverberates through the venue, guests are lined up and "frisked" for valuables by the prison wardens. Others are handcuffed and escorted to a height chart and ordered to stand for their front-on mug shot. Prison numbers are issued as guests are fingerprinted at random.

The loud clanging of iron prison gates sounds at every guest's entry into the mess hall, which is filled with white-blue fog. Sirens scream and searchlights scan the hall, occasionally spotlighting a guest prisoner who is surprised and stunned. Large screens placed at either side of the stage display *Escape from Alcatraz* and *The Shawshank Redemption*. The waitstaff, dressed in basic gray and white prison stripes, offers drinks served in tin cups and canapés arranged on cafeteria-style trays.

Indeed, the inmate guests are ready for a fun evening. This concept lends itself to a bench style of seating or the square table style. The tablecloths have black-and-white stripes and the chairs are covered with large black garbage bags and tied with yellow builder's tape with the word "Danger" printed in black.

The stage has an Alcatraz-painted backdrop and the décor set units include fake window frames, wire mesh screens, wire fencing, freestanding steel gates, and prison signage. These are displayed in specific areas of the room for effect. Al Capone and his thugs mingle and amuse while the band plays the rock music of the era, which will have guests on their feet from the moment the prison gates open.

Color Palette

Black, charcoal, and college gray with white accents

Décor and Prop Design

Painted and scenic canvas as the stage backdrop

Window bars made from dowel sticks

"Wanted" billboard with large black-and-white shots of party hosts

Fingerprinting and mug shot area with signage

Individual signage with the words "Cell Block," "The Hole,"
"Do Not Enter," "Danger: Restricted," "Security Office," "Mess Hall,"
and "Laundry"

Lengths of chains and rope, and rolls of wire netting

Damaged or second-hand steel gates used as props

Stale bread, tins of baked beans, potatoes with peelers

Cutouts of tools: hammers, shovels, picks

Prison numbers for guests

Entertainment

Warden and security guards

Alcatraz dance group

Look-alike gangsters

Tap dancers and pole dancers

Rock band

Launching the Jewel

Divine decadence. Think jewels, think luxury, think champagne, think *Lifestyles of the Rich and Famous.* This is a night when French champagne flows and everything sparkles. The waitstaff is dressed in white tailored trousers and white shirts with soft gray silk cravats. They serve Moët and Bollinger, filling the crystal flutes as guests move from showcase to display stands, viewing the fine range of jewels on display in the lavish interior of this boutique.

The white grand piano takes pride of place on the floor, and a pianist delights the guests, playing evergreen, easy-to-listen-to numbers. A violinist moves around and through the crowd, providing sophisticated entertainment appropriate to the formality of the launch.

The evening is the epitome of refinement, with all decorative elements in dazzling white, and 3-foot white ceramic urns traditionally arranged with white roses, lilies, and seasonal blooms and placed to beautify the surroundings. Positioned on glass counters, pedestals, and credenzas, the florals make a sophisticated statement.

Lighting plays an important part and specific effects enhance the ceiling, which is massed with cascading drops of fairy lights and complemented with clouds of pearl-colored balloons. Bubble machines send out a continuous flow of various-size bubbles that pop and fade into the evening with lighting effects bouncing off this décor.

Color Palette

Full white with splashes of silver

Décor and Prop Design

Freestanding floor-size candelabras

Cutouts of diamonds, sapphires, and rubies, glittered for effect

Lavish and traditional urns of white florals with white silk fabrics

Bare branches painted white, dripping with diamanté strands or glittered

Collection of stylish glass containers with candles massed

1,000 pearl white 3-inch balloons released on the floor

Clouds of pearl white balloons arranged in clusters for the ceiling

Bubble machine and soft white fog machine

3-foot ornamental champagne glasses with orchids

Half-size bottles of champagne

Entertainment

Roaming violinist

Professional pianist on a white grand piano

String quartet

Piano duet

Rock Around the Clock—the Fifties

The sound of the fifties, starring Buddy Holly and Bill Haley and His Comets, provides the music for a night of swirling skirts, cashmere sweaters, ponytails, and bobby socks. Jitterbugging gents in tight pants and leather jackets groom their slicked-back hair as they hang loose at the jukebox. The continual stream of fifties music sets the scene for a night of reminiscing about the period, with fun and frivolity as the main ingredient.

This is the party where couples can kick up their heels, don roller skates, sip on a cherry soda, twirl hula hoops, or enjoy a luscious ice cream sundae. The event harks back to a time when rock and roll ruled, and hamburgers and hot dogs were made to order at the local diner.

The bobby socks crowd finds a perfect meeting place on the brightly spotted dance floor, where intricate jitterbugging dance moves delight onlookers. The MC, dressed in a sequined jacket, directs the activities, singers, and dancers.

This setting is re-created by displaying an old-fashioned fifties Cadillac with a collection of balloons clustered throughout the venue for decoration. Jukeboxes take their place as set décor, while pinball machines provide interactive fun for guests.

Color Palette

Purple, orange, red, blue, yellow

Décor and Prop Design

Decorative cutouts reminiscent of the decade, such as guitars, ice cream sundaes, flamingos, poodles, fifties signage

Bars set in "diner style"

Tables with polka dotted cloths

Hula hoops in various sizes

Rented jukeboxes and pinball machines

Rented vintage 1950s Cadillac

Rented soda-fountain-style ice cream sundae bars

Signage for hot dogs and hamburgers

Clusters of balloons styled in arches and clouds

LP record covers

Braids, ribbons, and trims

Bags of popcorn

Polka dotted waitstaff uniforms or décor

Entertainment

> Jitterbug dancers
>
> Fifties band
>
> Waiters on roller skates
>
> Elvis Presley impersonators

Chinatown Charade

A large bronze gong signals the entry of guests as they step into a re-created and mysterious ghetto in the back alleys of Shanghai. Bursts of misted fog escape from fake grates and freestanding Chinese screens that are placed near the entrance to provide the ultimate Eastern effect.

The arts and crafts of Chinese culture are introduced as the guests and craftsmen experience interaction through the decorative displays of the doll maker and the lacquer painter. Guests move in amazement to view the culinary artistry of the noodle maker.

All male waiters wear a wraparound silk kimono over black trousers. A professional face makeup artist accents the eyes with makeup and adds the Chinese moustache. They look the part as they serve exotic cocktails.

A seated fortune-teller takes an occasional guest for a reading while an artisan, cross-legged on the floor in the dim light of a large lantern, forms delicate calligraphic symbols on scrolls of white paper. As the evening progresses, the guests are ushered past a life-size rickshaw and large Chinese dragons en route to tables. The centerpieces include silk and tissue lamé fabrics in rich red and gold with fans, miniature silk lanterns, and fortune cookies massed for effect, and many votive candles decorate the tables.

Color Palette

> Red, gold, and black

Décor and Prop Design

> Chinese umbrellas made out of silk or paper
>
> Red Chinese lanterns with gold trim and tassels
>
> Bamboo stalks painted in high-gloss red lacquer
>
> Lavish ceiling or wall draping in red and gold taffeta silk

Cutouts of dragons

Huge basketware pieces arranged in clusters

Traditional Chinese hats and red lacquered fans

Freestanding Chinese screens

Entertainment

Chinese fortune-tellers and calligraphers

Chinese masked stilt walkers

Noodle maker, doll maker, lacquer painter

Chinese dragon dancers

Team of jugglers

Carnival, South American–Style

South America—its culture, people, and celebrations—is pure inspiration for decorating or styling a venue. A ballroom transformed for this theme explodes with color and resonates with vibrancy and vitality.

To create this dynamic environment, scenic canvases cover the walls, immediately setting the atmospheric scene. Ideally, fabric lengths can be slung through and attached at the ceiling point. In addition, yards and yards of multicolored ribbons can be used. Life-size cutouts of Brazilian dancers, male and female, are included with this set décor, as well as huge paper flowers attached to pillars, stairways, mirrors, or a stage truss.

Whistles blow, maracas clack, shakers shake, and drums beat as toned but scantily clad bronzed bodies move rhythmically to dazzle. Capoeira experts wind their way around the guests, handing out masks and leis as the infectious beat of the Latin American band takes hold.

Female dancers balancing exotic headdresses on their pretty heads entice male guests to samba and rumba. Other scantily clad beauties delight as they guide guests to their designated tables. Table dressing includes a collection of tropical fruits highlighted with the addition of tropical leaves. Votive candles are placed to give added glow. The waitstaff is dressed in smart black trousers, black shirts, and very colorful cummerbunds with matching bow ties.

Color Palette

Bright greens, orange, bronze, hot pinks, purple

Décor and Prop Design

Life-size plywood cutouts of Brazilian dancers

Huge crepe paper flowers in hot colors

Huge pots of colorful flowers or plants

Palm leaves painted in hot colors

Chandeliers of floral and silk fabrics

Ribbon treatments from wall to table

Entertainment

Latin American band

Samba dance group and Brazilian drummers

Brazilian stilt walkers

Fire-eaters and jugglers

Step into the Outback

G'day mate! Welcome to outback Australia, minus the mozzies, flies, sweltering heat, and dingoes. As an authentic bush band plays in the background, guests walk into a re-creation of an Australian country town, complete with post office, outhouse, general store, and importantly, the outback pub. This Aussie pub is re-created as the decorative set for a stage used by an Aussie band playing instruments such as guitar, banjo, piano accordion, drum, washboard, and mouth organ.

The room itself is dressed with Aussie favorites: a freestanding old-fashioned water tank, a 16-foot-high windmill, a series of telegraph poles, large pots of gum trees, and bales of hay. And, of course, decorative cutouts could be added of kangaroos, parrots, cockatoos, a mock crocodile in a swamp, and stuffed koalas up the gum trees.

Against a backdrop of rich, earthy reds and burnt orange, the tables are covered with deep green burlap and dressed with swag hats, billy cans, tin cups, tea bags, chunks of coal, scatterings of wood chips, and lanterns.

The Aussie blokes serving as waitstaff are dressed in long khaki pants, khaki shirts, worker's boots, and typical Aussie straw hats (which have corks on strings hanging from the outside rim to keep the wearer free of flies and insects).

Color Palette

Beige, brown, and burnt orange

Décor and Prop Design

Huge gum trees

Backdrop of country scenery

Mock-up set of the country pub

Water tank and windmill

Cutouts of Aussie birds: cockatoo and parakeet

Plywood cutouts of koalas and kangaroos

Fencing, wire gates, and mock-up sheds

Logs, bricks, lanterns, lamps, and telegraph poles

Saddles, rugs, canvas, and water bags

Mock-up campfires or freestanding tents

Entertainment

Bush band

Crocodile hunter or sheepshearer

Performers dressed as Aussie reptiles, kangaroos, and other Australian creatures

Aboriginal dancers

Art Deco Garden Party

The palatial, patrician country home becomes the backdrop for this corporate picnic. This theme is based on the *Great Gatsby* novel and movie, set in the 1920s. Step back to a time when the flamboyant world of high society partied hard and entertained colleagues, clients, and even a few criminals in lavish style.

The marquee covers beautifully manicured lawns, where masses of big, comfy brocaded cushions are scattered for seating. Dressed in full white attire, the waitstaff hands a white rose boutonniere to the men and a white corsage to the ladies for either their shoulder or wrist.

The orchestra is made up of a piano, saxophones, cornets, trombones, and high and low drums. It entertains the Gatsby guests with songs of the 1920s and 1930s, like "It Don't Mean a Thing if It Ain't Got That Swing" and the music of songsters Billie Holiday and Ella Fitzgerald.

The high-style pillars and pedestals holding large pots of ruffle ferns and white ostrich feathers beautify the interior walls. On the ceiling of the marquee, hanging baskets of cascading ferns add style and finesse to this very distinctive affair. White vintage cars dress each corner of the interior and add to the interest for guests.

Color Palette

Full white look with soft green and aqua

Décor and Prop Design

Large pedestals with urns of cascading ferns

Soft green and aqua silk fabrics

Urns of white ostrich feathers or white seasonal blooms

Clear crystal beaded curtains to hang from wall or ceiling

Art deco posters

White boutonnieres for the men and jeweled headbands for ladies

Floral corsages and wristlets for the ladies

Clusters of white gardenias for tables

Art deco lamps for tables

Rented white piano

For pool décor, white florals on floating foam surfboards

The flower heads only of large white gerberas to float in large garden pots filled with water

Entertainment

Violin string quartet dressed in white dinner suits

Look-alike celebrities of the period

Feature artists singing the hits of the twenties and thirties

Theatrical Experience

A new film release serves as a creative idea for this night of theater and corporate dining. The elite guests walk the red carpet on their way to the pre-theater area as blue searchlights scan the sky and paparazzi flash their cameras.

Ladies in evening gowns and gents in dinner suits are entertained by the formal sounds of the string quartet. Guests are handed an entry ticket by formally dressed waiters, who serve cocktails and canapés in the pre-theater foyer. Urns of seasonal blooms adorn this area, where larger-than-life statues are on display under beautiful crystal chandeliers.

Guests are escorted to their allocated seating, and the MC on the stage welcomes all and then introduces the new release; the movie runs for one hour. The intermission begins. Guests reemerge to the pre-function area to find an innovative setup of dining stations, which become the focal point in the foyer. Guests experience a culinary journey as they select the tastings of their choice from professional chefs serving from behind the French food bar, the Japanese sushi bar, the oyster and seafood bar, and the skewered steak grill.

Following this delightful interactive interval of food and wine, guests are escorted back into the theater to reconvene for the balance of the movie. After the finale, guests flow back into the foyer to find that all food stations have been removed. In their place is a lavish buffet-style display of desserts. Coffee, conversation, and music from the pianist at the grand piano complete the evening.

Color Palette

Silver and gold

Décor and Prop Design

Pair of 8-foot-high Oscar statues

Movie posters on freestanding screens

Celebrity posters on freestanding screens

Mini Oscars and film negatives for tables

Theater programs as souvenirs

Beautiful bowls of roses

Entertainment

Paparazzi who mix and mingle

Professional MC

Movie star look-alikes

Wild, Wild West

Howdy, pardner. Y'all come on in to where horse-drawn wagons lazily make their way into dusty towns and old saloons. Painted and feathered Native Americans welcome the costumed guests. The ladies wear long skirts, frills, and lace, and the gentlemen wear checked shirts, tweed pants, and cowboy hats, along with neck scarves and holstered guns.

The Dodge City saloon is decorated as the interior of an old-time dance hall through scenic canvases, signage, and a Western-style bar, with an old-style upright piano taking pride of place. The saloon "madam" reveals cleavage and, together with her floozies, sings and dances to entertain the guests. The city sheriff endeavors to enforce law and order with the rough and tumble card players while the funeral director discreetly measures up his next potential client.

The old-time band plays the music of the era and a dramatic showdown takes place as Chief Sitting Bull arrives and the line dancers take to the floor. The mechanical bucking bull is positioned in-house to tip and spill a cowboy.

Freestanding tepees are positioned in the four corners of this transformed Wild West environment. Mock-up sets include stables, a blacksmith, a grocery store, a sheriff's office, and the O.K. Corral, with three-dimensional cattle and horses to decorate specific areas.

Tables are covered with burnt orange burlap cloth and vegetable artistry becomes a conversational piece. Small pumpkins or gourds are centered, and eggplant and red bell peppers are halved to hold small votive candles. Clusters of green beans, asparagus, and baby carrots are tied into small bundles with string or raffia and placed for effect. Additional bundles of wheat and dried twigs, reeds, and weeds can be added.

Color Palette

Brown, beige, burnt orange

Décor and Prop Design

Painted canvas of the period town

8-foot high tepees

Saddles, cart wheels, and sections of fencing

Cutouts of cowboys and Indians

Freestanding wagon

Kegs, bales, water troughs, and clusters of dried grasses

Mock-up set of the undertaker's office and the stables

Plywood cutouts of cactus (8 feet in height)

Plywood cutouts of cattle and horses

Entertainment

Town piano player

Saloon madam and her floozies

Wild West line dance group

Performing funeral director, sheriff, or town crier

Wild West whip cracker

Chief Sitting Bull

Cowboys and cowgirls on stilts

Wild Bill Hickock

The Ice Heist Fundraiser

The entrance to this gallery is decorated from ceiling to floor with lush silk swagging. On either side of the entrance doors, a very large timber chest is decorated with masses of imitation jewels, including lengthy strings of pearls and beads. They are arranged in a cascading effect, pouring out and over the top of the chest in a lavish manner.

Guests arrive in the stipulated dress code of black or white at this prestigious fundraiser where the most valued of treasures, such as old estate jewels and paintings, are to be auctioned.

To gain entry, guests are issued a numerical code to try their luck at unlocking the huge mock vaulted door. The code works at random and a burglar alarm rings through the venue. The cat burglars (aerial artists) drop from the ceiling and spill and twirl above the heads of the guests.

The element of surprise continues as the elegantly dressed waitstaff offers cocktails and canapés before seating guests for the sumptuous dinner. Following the other cat burglars, a trio of close-up magicians scouts the room with flashlights, occasionally producing fake gems and gold coins to dazzle and delight the guests. The trinkets are hidden on and under every imaginable object on their table, or secreted up their sleeves.

The distinctive room décor includes freestanding 12-foot-high pedestals massed with palms that have been painted black and white. They surround the room and are a dominant part of the décor, making a repeating and impressive statement.

The stage and ceiling are swagged with lengths of black and white silk, complementing the urns on the outer walls. Cloths, chair covers, and napkins follow the same color pattern throughout. The tabletops are bedecked and bejeweled with clusters of gems at the base of towering candelabras. Votive candles, rose petals, rock salt, and glass pebbles add to this glamorous look.

Two major features in the room are the 12-foot ice bars. They not only look like ice, but are made of ice. The talented and skilled waitstaff serves champagne on request throughout the evening.

Color Palette

Black and white

Décor and Prop Design

Lavish silk draping

Timber chests spilling with colorful gems

Huge cutouts of diamonds, sapphires, and rubies

Pedestals or columns dressed with fabrics and flowers

Entertainment

Professional MC

Roaming jazz violinists

Ballroom dancers

Aerial artists dressed as cat burglars

Trio of magicians

Oasis Sanctuary

Take yourself off to the desert and live it up in an oasis of tropical palms, fabulous food, and balmy Middle Eastern music.

A snake charmer plays his flute as he entices his pet cobra out of a basket to greet guests. The walkway entrance is lined with rows of large fresh potted palms. At the base of each pot, spices spill from sacks as a décor accent. Guests remove their shoes, are given slip-on scuffs, and are led by Bedouins in costume and headdress. They follow man-made sand tracks leading from the entrance to the venue. The camel and its keeper are present to meet and greet.

On entering, the guests see the marquee ceiling billowing with yards of colorful fabrics and a variety of large hanging silk lanterns glowing with warm light. This mimics the atmosphere of the Bedouin tent under a Middle Eastern night sky. Palms, date fronds, baskets of overflowing foliage, and huge bowls of bananas are clustered and scattered throughout.

Persian carpets are featured and can be either hung from side walls, suspended from the ceiling, or laid on the floor with masses of big, colorful cushions scattered on top to provide guests with seating for informal dining. A palette of exotic foods of the East is presented for guests' enjoyment along with the folk music and dancing.

Color Palette

Soft green, moss green, and caramel shadings

Décor and Prop Design

Tropical palms in varying heights

Huge cutouts of palms

Huge cutouts of life-size camels

Eastern floor carpets

Masses of big silk cushions

Chiffon draping

Floor-size ceramic pots

8-foot-high Eastern pillars

Entertainment

Belly dancers

Snake charmers

Camel keeper

Persian jugglers

Walk Like an Egyptian

The spectacle of Egypt offers a dose of fantasy, lively music, amazing costumes, and fine wines, and it provides the perfect ambience for a colorful and enjoyable evening. The Bangles' "Walk Like an Egyptian" plays continuously as guests arrive and are shown into the Arabic lounge bar. Waitresses don Cleopatra wigs, long caftans, heavy eye makeup, and gold sandals. Waiters wear loincloths and Egyptian headdresses as they serve guests in true Egyptian style.

This gala event is designed to make Cleopatra go weak at the knees! Hieroglyphic panels adorn the walls as guests are ushered through a huge replica pyramid fringed by palm trees and sand. Mummies peer out from open sarcophagi, watching guests' every move. Mini sphinx models are scattered around the venue.

Symbolic images include the god Anubis and an Egyptian barge, and decorative elements include typical geometric braids, pottery, and trims. The pyramids, the tombs, and huge limestone blocks are highly visible. Mummified figures further support this concept.

The royal archers in full dress gallantly escort guests to their beautifully set table, which is massed with a series of rose posies in colors of burnt orange and rich reds. Tables can be lavishly dressed with a collection of fresh flowers, red apples, brown pears, green bananas, purple passion fruit, and bunches of grapes to evoke ancient Egypt and represent its culture.

Color Palette

Rich maroons and royal blues

Décor and Prop Design

Scenic backdrop of pyramids

Walkway of pillars dressed with fabric swagging

7-foot-high fabric flame pedestals

Decorative three-dimensional mummy or mummies

Collection of basketware and pots

Nubian slave urns

Leaf-motif and patterned braids

Garlands of flowers

Life-size Tutankhamen mask

Large fiberglass "limestone" bricks

Columns and decorative-patterned tops

Entertainment

Court jesters or magicians

Egyptian belly dancers

Antony and Cleopatra look-alikes

Case Study: The Variety Club's Children's Charity Annual Christmas Party

This case study has been provided courtesy of Glen Lehman, CSEP, of Lehman and Associates, Sydney.

This charity party for a leading not-for-profit organization is held annually and devoted to the welfare of children. This case study illuminates some of the challenges the event planner faces when working on a very large event, especially one that involves children and volunteers.

The Variety Club raises $250,000 each year to cover the costs of this ambitious affair for 5,000 mentally and physically disabled children. For many of these children, the Variety Christmas Party is the only festive event they experience during the Christmas season due to their circumstances. The goal is to make every one of these children feel special.

This event is staged in five adjoining halls of the Sydney Convention and Exhibition Centre each year. The layout of this venue, with one hall opening into the next one, is common in convention centers (see the CAD plan below).

This event carries the challenge of having 2,500 caretakers present with the children. In addition,

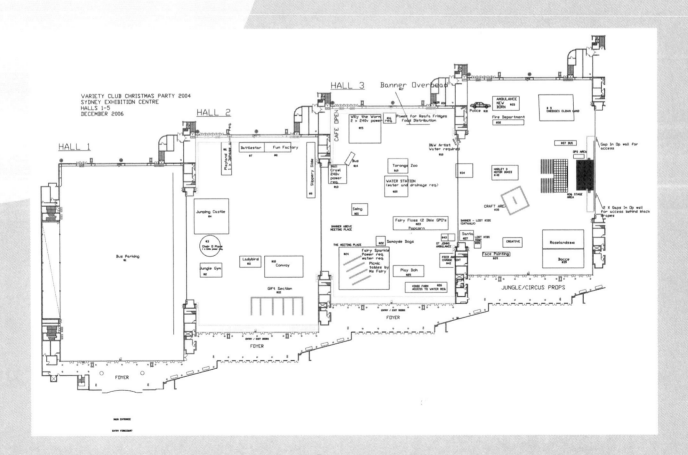

more than 500 Variety Club volunteers are on hand to help out where needed, each dressed in the Variety Club's distinctive red T-shirt. There is a strong emphasis on creative entertainment and gift giving during this event.

On arrival, the children are greeted by a striking Christmas Nativity scene. Throughout the venue, they enjoy decorated Christmas trees, fiberglass reindeer, oversize gift boxes, and masses of Christmas lights. Many other distinctive elements, carefully chosen each year, add to the holiday atmosphere.

Street theater characters are dressed in bright costumes and move around the venue entertaining the children. Vibrant background music keeps the party humming. Other highlights of the day include the arrival of Santa, carnival rides, a baby animal farm, Samoyed dogs, cartoonists, caricatures, circus acts, face painting, cotton candy, pony rides, table tennis, and a Play-Doh table. The main stage program includes high-profile entertainers who donate their time to the cause.

The following list shows the decorative components and entertainment requirements that were positioned on the floor plan for the 2007 party.

STAGE ENTERTAINMENT

MC

Brent Street Kids

Dorothy and Friends

Go Seek Band

Super Hubert performer

Elly May Barnes

Circus acts

Langshaw Dancity

Rod Radley Group

Various music bands

FLOOR ENTERTAINMENT AND CHILD ASSISTANCE STATIONS

Amusement Services

Arnotts All That Jatz

Auburn Police

Cartoonist Association

Bearsville

Caricatures

Child care area

Circus trio act

Costume characters

Face painting and cotton candy

Food distribution

Football Australia x 2

Harley motorcycles x 8

Kids' zoo

Liberty Swing x 2

Lost children

Meet and greet / meeting place

NSW Rural Fire Service

Nuskin

Play-Doh

Pony rides (Kindifarm)

Presents

Santa

Scholastic Australia

St. George Zoomobile

St. John Ambulance

Table tennis x 2

Ten Pin City

Water station

BACKSTAGE

Celebrity corner

Hospitality

Transport

Volunteers

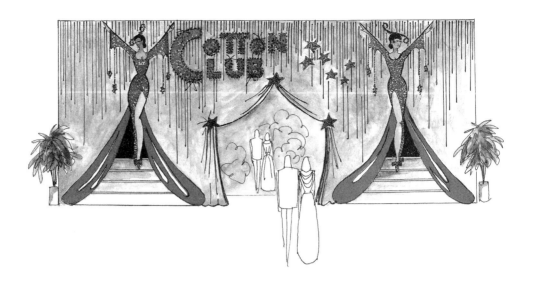

Research the Past Decades

The following section is primarily about the fashions, styles, and history of times gone by—and some of you may be wondering what this information has to do with event planning. The answer, in short, is everything.

Fashion, style, and history are at the heart of every theme, not only decade-specific themes. History provides a brilliant canvas for us to draw upon, while the future challenges our daring and imagination. How you interpret the past for your own event planning today will depend on your own style, but fashion and history are, and forever will be, the springboard to creativity. Our awareness of past decades enriches our knowledge and expands our horizons, allowing us to develop ideas that can be used when designing all kinds of events.

How fortunate we are to have access to the Internet, which contributes to the success of our work by enabling us to readily locate information and research topics. Refer to the book recommendations on page 223 and use Google searches to start you on your way. You could further expand your ideas by researching typography relevant to an era, perhaps even architecture and furniture design. Your findings on typography can be used when designing invitations, menus, signage, and promotional materials for the event.

I am providing examples of facts from each decade that you may find helpful in stimulating your imagination. I often find that immersing myself in the history, facts, and social trends of the time helps me create a more colorful image of that period. It's amazing how sometimes a dry fact can inspire a unique décor idea. Little cards at each place setting containing facts make for fun conversation, and a menu with prices of the time would have a similar effect.

The Twenties

Vogue magazine struck gold when the first edition of French *Vogue* appeared in 1920. The magazine's first fashion shoot featured a collection of Parisian dresses worn by models in November 1920. At that time, it was hard to differentiate between designers, so the magazine decided to run a competition to identify the most famous.

The prize was 100 guineas and it was rare indeed that cash was even mentioned in those days! Price tags were never printed in *Vogue*. Economy was a dirty word, and certainly one not used in that particularly extravagant decade.

Fashion then was about very basic elements: fabric, color, length, and shape. Parisians and other international socialites were drawn to short skirts, bobbed hair, fur and pearls, lace, and lamé. Plunging necklines were the thing, along with plummeting backlines, and anything in velvet or satin was adored. Of course, the pet du jour was the greyhound. No handbag-size canine companions for the ladies of the daring twenties!

The female body shape was stylishly boyish, and straight, skimpy shifts became the template for this decade. Add a feathered fan (for flirting, of course) and the ultimate, smoldering fashion accent—the long bejeweled cigarette holder—and you'd be the height of fashion, able to take your place at any social event.

Perfume was produced for a specific type of woman. Blondes had their own perfume or scent, as did brunettes, redheads, and auburns. These sultry aromas were designed around the images of the day, which varied somewhat from today's concepts of women. Back then, for example, blondes were seen as cool and somewhat calculating, as opposed to the fluffy, playful image of today. Passion was seen as a brunette thing, with that trait escalating as the tone deepened, blowing out to downright wild for any redheads.

Movies had entered an exciting new phase: they could be heard as well as seen. The talkies had hit town! And while they were treated as the eighth wonder of the world, no one really foresaw the amazing effect that movies with speech would have on society, nor how they would shape the world. Coco Chanel wondered where the innovative picture show was moving due to the continued, fast development of the cinema world. Within a relatively short time, the world would change and not only would art imitate life, but life would imitate art. And what you couldn't learn about fashion, culture, and social expectations anywhere else, you could learn from the movies and emulate.

Such was the success of this new medium that the powers that be saw fit to offer awards for the best of the best, and thus the Academy Awards were born. That meant the birth of a certain tall, golden, muscled image named Oscar.

Facts of the Twenties

The average annual earnings in the United States was $1,236.

Gangland crime included murder, swindles, and racketeering.

It took 13 days to reach California from New York by car.

Dance marathons were the rage.

Dance crazes included the Charleston, black bottom, and shimmy.

Harry Houdini was the great escape artist.

Movies
Movies of this decade include:

- *Dr. Jekyll and Mr. Hyde*
- *The Great Gatsby*
- *Huckleberry Finn*
- *Pandora's Box*
- *Robin Hood*

Broadway was another wild success and reached an all-time peak, so it doesn't hurt to revisit the shows of that time for inspiration. George Gershwin was a hot property and Fred Astaire was tapping up a storm in *Funny Face.*

The twenties also heralded the birth of radio networks, which again turned another medium on its ear—music and entertainment! Austere, authoritative voices were cast aside and the guys and dolls of the twenties were bopping out to brash young crooners like Bing Crosby.

This decade was also recognized as the period of the vamp. Chicago's Cotton Club was the place to be seen if booze and gambling were your thing. The Cotton Club, with its sly grog, sexy saxophones, and illegal gambling, remains a favorite theme, supporting the theory that we can draw much color, atmosphere, and fun from the past.

The Thirties

After the opulence of the twenties, the thirties was a much more frugal and austere time. By this decade, Americans had suffered the Wall Street crash and the Great Depression was in full thrust. Life was tough and unemployment was escalating worldwide. Food coupons were the currency of the day, and lines to swap a coupon for a precious loaf of bread or lump of lard stretched a mile long.

Yet Hollywood reigned. Poised for world domination, Hollywood provided the only relief in a dark world. It was the escape of the masses: for a couple of hours people could remove themselves from drudgery and heartache and pretend they were the stars up on that silver screen, pretend that they too had riches and fine food and sang and danced their lives away. Life on the screen provided hope. It was the ultimate dream.

Film continued to dominate everything, including, of course, fashion. And Hollywood continued to pull off the ultimate seduction; the world was watching and absorbing its every nuance. If Hollywood did it, wore it, or advocated it, America, and then the world, wanted it.

Eyes turned back to Paris, though, which cemented Chanel's fashion dominance when she changed the direction of couture by changing the fabric and line. The straight styles of the twenties gave way to the bias-cut gowns of the thirties. And both sides of the Atlantic continued to distract the world with the greatest illusion of all: that life was carefree and that the thundering echo of an army marching forth was just a figment of the imagination.

On the fashion front, Paris met Hollywood when Chanel was contracted by MGM to design costumes for its starlets. And she wasn't the only one headed to California.

"Go west, young man" (and take your family, too!) became the catchphrase. People saw California as the Promised Land, no doubt inspired by the Hollywood myth. In the movies, no one in California was out of work or hungry. California was the place to go. So people packed up their families, tied their meager possessions onto the top of their cars and trucks, and set forth on the greatest adventure of their lives, seeking work in the fields, mines, and cities of the vast West.

But no matter where you were, east, west, or in the middle, surrounded by the Pacific, Atlantic, or Indian Ocean, survival became the focus. Thoughts of advancement were laid aside as just getting through the day, feeding the family, and keeping mind and spirit healthy became the toughest battle of all. Through it all, Americans and the democracy they had fought hard for stood firm.

That said, it was still a time of change, although mostly in attitude. With money in short supply or nonexistent, parents were unable to provide children with clothes or books. More and more children stopped going to school. The government had to step in and the result was the introduction of a severely shortened school term. Teachers' salaries were cut as well.

But this was an age where parents wanted more for their children; they wanted them educated; they wanted them to be able to read. Some even bartered wood for classroom potbellied stoves in return for tuition.

Yet, on the entertainment front, the sun was still shining in Hollywood. No dark gloomy clouds there. At least not on the screen, which became more and more powerful. Gingers Rogers made her first appearance and a star was born. Cole Porter's music was huge, and the Ziegfeld Follies dazzled audiences with its risqué costumes and glittering sequins. And it was the first time the words *sex appeal* made an appearance in public!

The thirties were to become known as the Golden Age of Hollywood, and with good reason. Movies rolled off the reels so fast it would make your head turn, and the depressed audiences of the thirties loved them. They lived for them. Names like Clark Gable, Bob Hope, Greta Garbo, and Bette Davis were household names. And a young man with big dreams and an even bigger imagination stirred people's hearts and lives and began the work that would make him a legend for generations to come: Walt Disney had arrived and so had the first full-length animated film, *Snow White and the Seven Dwarves*. The year was 1937.

Everyday fashion was pretty grim, but those on the screen still did it with style. The focus was again on fabric: high collars were a hit. Garbo was rarely seen without her fox scarf or neck warmer. Tulles, silks, and full-skirted organza gowns swirled across gleaming dance floors. And who could forget Dietrich and the feathered boa she introduced with such panache? Buttons were big, but the zipper became the talk of the country.

Facts of the Thirties

The average annual salary in the United States was $1,368.

Unemployment rose by 25 percent as the decade wore on.

Milk was 14 cents for half a gallon. Bread was 9 cents a loaf.

You could get a steak for 42 cents.

Nightlife included dancing to the big bands of the time: Glenn Miller, Benny Goodman, and Tommy Dorsey.

Hats were mandatory for men.

Eighty percent of the population owned radio sets.

Television made its debut in 1939.

World War II disrupted the world as people knew it.

Movies
These were the most popular movies of the time:

- *Morocco*
- *Shanghai Express*
- *Tarzan, the Ape Man*
- *The Wizard of Oz*

The Forties

The world was at war. London crumbled, Paris was fighting for its spirit, and the rest of Europe was a dark, cold place. Fashion, once again, echoed the times: authoritarian and utilitarian.

Industry wasn't the only thing frozen—so was imagination, as the world looked on in horror. People were fighting for their lives; united, they did their bit, whether it was on the front line or behind the scenes.

These were serious times and fashion reflected that. Gone were the decadence and opulence of decades past, and in their place were khaki, uniforms, and shoulder pads. Shoes were practical and sturdy, but there was one touch of femininity that women clung to: the silk stocking. Twelve denier stockings, the finest silk stockings available, arrived, complete with back seams.

The one positive was that the increased production necessary to maintain a war helped pull America out of the Great Depression. But with that turn of events came one of the greatest changes of the 20th century: for the first time in America, many able-bodied woman went to work. Women who had been conditioned to stay at home to keep house and raise families suddenly found themselves the equals of their male counterparts. Female independence was raising its head, and women took to it with relish. They did it to the seductive sounds of Glenn Miller and his boys.

As the war continued, however, fashion became even more authoritarian and even masculine. Rationing meant that most things were in short supply, so recycling was commonplace. No matter what the fabric, it was saved for a future use. Shoes made reappearances covered in different fabrics and colors, though due to the short supply of dyes, the colors were dull and solemn. Hats were remodeled, and the little black dress became the staple of every wardrobe, pulled out for every formal occasion, be it a wedding or a funeral.

It was a time when you made do. There were no frills and pretty lace, and with most supplies hard or impossible to get—including items as basic as pins, thread, elastic, buttons, and paper—it wasn't surprising that many ingenious young women took to drawing a stripe down the backs of their legs (with eyebrow pencil) to make it seem like they were wearing seamed nylons.

The end of the war brought a fashion shift. Couture celebrated with the reintroduction of lavish fabrics and full skirts, and Christian Dior led the charge.

Rhythm and blues grew out of the big band era. Bing was still around, but there were several other talents knocking on his door—names like Dinah Shore and Perry Como, as well as Mr. Frank Sinatra, the Chairman of the Board himself, led the hit parades of the time.

Movies had taken a bit of a beating as well, and while they were still made, they reflected darker times than they had thus far. The stars that still held the hearts of the

Facts of the Forties

Minimum wage in the United States was 43 cents per hour.

Fifty-five percent of homes had indoor plumbing.

Refrigeration led to the invention of the frozen dinner.

Jitterbugging made its appearance.

The average home was a one-level ranch-style house.

The New York skyscrapers aimed to be the biggest and best.

Computers were developed.

Commercial TV became available with 13 stations.

Movies
These were the hottest movies of the forties:

- *Casablanca*
- *Easter Parade*
- *Meet Me in St. Louis*
- *On the Town*
- *Road to Singapore*
- *Ziegfeld Follies*

people of the forties included heartthrobs like Gary Cooper, Humphrey Bogart, and Cary Grant, and stars such as Katharine Hepburn, Bette Davis, and, of course, the hot sirens who would go on to sizzle on screens and make headlines and hearts beat faster: Marilyn Monroe, Lana Turner, Rita Hayworth, and Elizabeth Taylor.

The Fifties

The end of World War II was like a new beginning for America. Millions of men and women returned home and tried to pick up their lives where they had left off before they'd been so rudely interrupted.

Across the world the baby boom was in full swing, and with renewed enthusiasm, energy, and confidence, industry recharged. Peacetime needs had to be met, and industry was primed to meet the demand. With demand for previously unavailable goods growing, American companies expanded to supply those needs and more wealth was generated.

Women rediscovered femininity. Dresses were flattering and figure hugging, some with full skirts and tight bodices, others streamlined. Hats and gloves became *the* fashion accessory and lifted the most inexpensive dress to another level.

Entertaining at home was seen as very chic, and house-proud women were interested in stylish decorating ideas and beginning to be more adventurous with their cuisine. No doubt, as the guests nibbled cheese and pickled onions off toothpicks plucked from an orange sitting on a decorative platter, they hummed along to Frankie Avalon and Dean Martin, those brash young singers of the time.

It was a time to celebrate being a woman, and women of the time took their cues from stars like Debbie Reynolds, Marilyn Monroe, and Elizabeth Taylor. And the bikini gained public favor. Breasts were something to be proud of, and padded bras enhanced what the gene pool didn't provide. For those who didn't need the extra help, extra-support bras were now available, which was great because perky was the style and with the tight bodices of the time, that was a good thing. Again, fashion was dictated by a combination of Paris and Hollywood.

This was also the time that dieting became a national pastime. Was it Zsa Zsa Gabor who said, "You can never be too rich or too thin"? Nowadays she could add, "or too young," because it was in the fifties that people first started railing against the passage of time and the effect that it had on their bodies.

Modern French design influenced home décor, and the throwaway age had its birth in this decade. For the first time, young people were not starting life with Mom and Dad but were venturing out on their own—in their own homes and with their own modern-styled, cheaper furniture, which within a decade or two would be tossed and replaced with pieces reflecting the next fads in shape and color.

Color made a comeback, and light, bright, and vivid colors graced people's walls

Facts of the Fifties

The population of the United States was now 140,880,000.

The male-to-female ratio in the labor force was five to two.

The Immigration and Naturalization Act was signed.

Fighting ended in Korea.

Movies
These were the most memorable movies of the time:

- *High Noon*
- *The King and I*
- *Rebel Without a Cause*
- *The Searchers*
- *Singin' in the Rain*
- *Some Like It Hot*
- *Sunset Boulevard*

and bodies. Fluorescents made their debut, and who could forget the lime, hot pink, and orange socks worn by the brash young men of the time? Along, of course, with their slick hair, dripping with oil, and their white T-shirts and leather jackets. You can't do any better than Richie and the Fonz from *Happy Days* or Danny from *Grease* for inspiration for this time.

Technology influenced fabrics, and synthetics were beginning to make a statement. And denim moved off the farm and took over the youth culture. What an amazing move that was! Today, half our closets would be empty if we removed all the denim.

Still, in fashion Dior remained the law and promoted the flounced, full skirt complete with roped petticoats. To celebrate the fact that fabrics were now freely available, detail was reintroduced, whether it be in trim work or pleated sleeves or pockets. Hemlines were coyly just below knee length, and again affected by the availability and variety of fabric as well as the Dior influence.

Age differences started to dissolve, but not to the extent that they did in the sixties and seventies. Still, the ageless society that we would become had its roots here. This was where the adage "you're only as old as you feel" was first heard.

It was also the time of the twin set (usually worn with pearls), and mix and match was introduced into fashion, thus doubling a wardrobe with carefully planned purchases. Seductive black veiling draped over the eyes enhanced headwear, and long white gloves were a must. Think Audrey Hepburn.

Pierre Cardin entered the scene in 1945 and became Christian Dior's head designer in 1947. Coco Chanel adopted a very French attitude when she discovered that her designs were being copied. She threw her hands in the air and declared that "imitation was the sincerest form of flattery."

The Sixties

The sixties was the age of the flower children, the hippie movement, the Vietnam War, and the sexual revolution, and also of LSD, Elvis, and the Beatles. Mrs. Robinson sent eyebrows raising and tongues clucking—and made Dustin Hoffman a star. It was the decade when Jackie Bouvier Kennedy breathed fresh air into the very traditional White House.

Sex, drugs, rock and roll, and the United States' youngest-ever president, JFK. It was all happening.

The first of the children of the baby boomers had hit the teen years and young adulthood, and they were making their presence felt. "Free love" was their mantra and "Make love, not war" was their rallying call. There probably hasn't been a decade in history of such dramatic change as the sixties.

It was a time when the cultures of the Western world were tipped on their ears and shaken vigorously. Cobwebs were disturbed that never again were allowed to form, and the "establishment" was heard groaning deep into the decade.

The form-fitting bras and stretch underwear that molded the figure that the women of the fifties were so proud of were burned by their rebellious daughters, who were spurred on by the new generation of males who believed in and supported female equality.

And young men and women proved that youth power would never again be ignored when, as a result of the revolution they instigated peacefully, changes were made in every facet of life, from government and laws to entertainment and values—even the Vatican made changes.

The birth control pill was introduced (well, something had to happen with all that free love), and that, too, changed the structure of society. Women were demanding and relishing their newfound freedom as the fear of pregnancy was lifted, but as the pendulum settled, infidelity and the divorce rate rose.

Fashion went to extremes. The hemline rose and fell and rose again. The mini and the maxi were interchangeable, and psychedelic patterns and outrageous colors were all the rage, but the idea was that you were free to strut your own style.

Hair was big and headbands in matching fabrics were a hit. For guys, the crew cut was prominent. Earrings were huge, and heavy black eyeliner (kohl) made its mark and never looked back. The look was completed with white iridescent lipstick and matching nail polish. The styles were sleek or flowing, and despite the carefree attitudes of the day, grooming was still a big thing.

It was a time when teenagers had opinions they wanted heard, cosmetics were used as never before, and the look was haughty. Models worked in boutiques and started to become icons in their own right.

It was a time of unisex fashion—one style suited all genders—and second-hand clothing became a fashion statement. The mini continued to rise until women ended up with what were affectionately called "bum freezers," which covered almost nothing. Celebrities, models, and movie stars held the world enthralled as royalty lost some of its fascination factor in favor of more interesting subjects.

In terms of social changes, the summer of 1967 was known as the Summer of Love, but while the sixties was a time of great change and positive influences, it was also a time of social decline. Crime rates soared and communes and sects appeared—some of them wholesome, some of them not. Mystic religions gained favor with young people, and the sixties also became the decade of protest.

Castro was in charge of Cuba, and Americans broke off diplomatic relations and continued their race for space with the Russians. Tragically, America lost John F. Kennedy in 1963, and the world, not just the country, mourned. Johnson took the

Facts of the Sixties

The population of the United States rose to 177,830,000.

The average annual salary in the United States was $5,174.

Chubby Checker introduced the twist.

Go-go girls danced on stages in birdcages.

The Pulitzer Prize–winning novel *To Kill a Mockingbird* described racial turmoil.

Movies
These are the most remembered movies of that time:

- *Bonnie and Clyde*
- *Butch Cassidy and the Sundance Kid*
- *Funny Girl*
- *A Hard Day's Night*
- *Hello, Dolly!*
- *West Side Story*

reins. But in 1969, it was all celebration when Neil Armstrong and Buzz Aldrin first walked on the moon. That was some moon walk!

The sixties was a great decade for musicals, and Broadway was bursting at the seams, which caused the off-Broadway theater to develop. Some of the shows included *Camelot, Hello, Dolly! Oliver! Man of La Mancha*, and *Funny Girl*.

The Seventies

Many of the events of the sixties, including war and social changes, continued on into the seventies. American culture flourished, and there was now a heightened interest in the environment and space exploration.

Hair was one of the most popular musicals on Broadway, and people flocked to see the naked actors cavorting on stage in a psychedelic tribute to the sixties. Jesus Christ was declared a superstar, and we all bopped along to the music.

Fashion saw such things as the huge straw hat, the halter neckline, Indian silk prints with tassels and embroidery, and the platform shoe. How high could the platform go? How high would it go? That was the worry of the day. Yet women slavishly followed the fashion and made it a huge hit.

It became a decade of flashing lights and feverish sounds. *Saturday Night Fever* burst onto the scene with a lot of blue language to boot. Rock and roll had cemented itself, and the music on the radio could never be turned back. This decade saw the breakup of the Beatles and the death of Elvis, which robbed rock of two major influences.

Rock and roll streamed into various styles. People listened to soft rock, hard rock, county rock, folk rock, and shock rock. But none of the styles could touch disco, which gave rise to dance moves such as the hustle and the bump.

Three presidents sat in the Oval Office during the seventies, and it was a time of political turmoil, with Watergate and the continuation of the Vietnam War threatening to split the nation. More women entered politics than ever before, and divorce was higher than at any other time, leaving many women as the sole breadwinners and caretakers of the children.

The Eighties

Who can forget high-fronted hair, balloon skirts, and shoulder pads? The eighties is identified with the "me generation" of status seekers. Billionaires abounded during the age of the leveraged buyouts and mega-mergers. Donald Trump and Leona Helmsley headed the list of this new breed of self-made people, and people followed their iconic rises and falls with awe.

Facts of the Seventies

The U.S. population was recorded at 204,879,000.

The average annual salary in the United States was $7,564.

Milk cost 33 cents per pint. Bread was 24 cents.

You could buy a steak for $4.30.

Floppy discs and bar codes were introduced.

The Beatles broke up.

The World Trade Center was completed.

Movies
These were the biggest movies of the seventies:

- *Cabaret*
- *Close Encounters of the Third Kind*
- *Escape from Alcatraz*
- *Grease*
- *The Godfather*
- *Jaws*
- *Stars Wars*

Money was simply a commodity; the new fast-trackers made it and lost it with ease and then started all over again. It was the can-do era. Everyone had to have everything. Binge buying and credit card debt rose as a result.

Technology had begun its upward surge, and it seemed there were no limits. Privacy was at an all-time low. Camcorders were on everybody's Christmas list, talk shows became part of people's lives, and everyone wanted to bare all.

President Regan declared war on drugs, and some of the saddest times came when many adored entertainers succumbed to the new black death: AIDS. The American Constitution celebrated its 200th birthday.

Nancy Regan's elegance and Princess Di's unfailing sense of style stimulated a turn away from the wilder fashions of the seventies. Women wanted more style and suits with big shoulders; the power suit made a return, as did satins and opulent fabrics.

Denim was important as a fashion statement, and the mini slipped back into contention. Anne Klein, Donna Karan, and Calvin Klein ruled the American catwalks.

The CD revolutionized the music world. Dances were uninhibited and sensual or wild and energetic. Slam dancing and break dancing were a few of the trends people followed or watched on the new MTV channel. Rap and hip-hop made their mark and stayed on. Artists like MC Hammer and Vanilla Ice led the charge.

People could now stay at home and have the (almost) latest movies come to them. And they did. In 1981, VCR sales rose by 72 percent in one year. And by 1989, 60 percent of all American households were paying for cable TV. On Broadway, theater lovers enjoyed the new sensation of Andrew Lloyd Webber with *Cats*, *Starlight Express*, and the *Phantom of the Opera*. It was also the time for TV sitcoms, with *The Golden Girls*, *The Cosby Show*, and *Roseanne*, and who can forget dramas like *Dallas* and *Dynasty*?

The Nineties

The nineties have been called the merger era. Health care, gun control, and social security led the headlines in government sections for most of this time.

Sex and violence dominated the media. O. J. Simpson made people question the judicial system and search their hearts. The Oklahoma City federal building bombing and 14 incidents of school shootings made Americans wonder whether society had gone mad.

Despite this, the economy was booming, and the stock market reached an all-time high, thanks in no small part to burgeoning electronic advances. This was the age of the silicon chip billionaires. Smart kids came up with brilliant ideas and the world imploded, never to be the same again.

Why? The World Wide Web. It changed the way the world communicated and made the world ever smaller—it was now merely a global village. In 1994, 3 million

Facts of the Eighties

Lady Diana Spencer married Prince Charles.

Ronald Reagan became the 40th president of the United States.

MTV was launched on cable television.

The *Exxon Valdez* oil spill shocked the world.

Movies
The movies we loved most in that decade were:

- *Back to the Future*
- *E.T.*
- *Fatal Attraction*
- *Good Morning, Vietnam*
- *Out of Africa*
- *Platoon*
- *Tootsie*

people were online. By 1998, that figure had risen to 100 million. It was a true phenomenon. Bill Gates became a household name, and Microsoft continued its dominance of the world's computing economy.

The fashion model was now as much of a celebrity as any movie star. However, fashion in the nineties was a mixed bag. It was a time of resurrection, and fashions of the sixties and seventies were again at the forefront. Flares, platform shoes, and stretch leggings were all must-have pieces for a woman's wardrobe.

Princess Diana graced the cover of *Vogue* in 1991, wearing her black polo neck sweater and tousled hair. A new look for the royals. Sadly, before the decade was out, the world would lose her, and it fell into a deep mourning that rocked the royal House of Windsor with its intensity.

And who could forget Liz Hurley and that amazing Versace safety pin dress? If you've got it . . .

In politics, George Bush Sr. made a one-term appearance in the White House (1989–1993), and then came the most charismatic president since young JFK: President Bill Clinton (1993–2001).

People met and fell in love with Tiger Woods, the golfing phenomenon. And they watched the meteoric rise of two television stars who went on to dominate their respective slots: Oprah Winfrey, who became the queen of daytime television, and David Letterman, who owned the late-night slot.

Women made strides in business, and a lady by the name of Bobbi McCaughey gave birth to the first set of surviving septuplets. That's seven, in case you're wondering!

Televisions were found in 99 percent of U.S. homes, and the average time spent in front of the box was a massive seven hours per day! Viewers found out more than they really wanted to know about *Sex and the City*. And they made *Friends* with six lovable, sassy young people who became part of their lives. Every young single wanted to be them, or have friends like that.

The music world reeled with the advent of the rewritable CD, and copyright issues exploded. Music people were buying included the new sounds of grunge and techno-hip-hop, with the former made popular by bands such as Nirvana, Pearl Jam, and Soundgarden. Hip-hop experienced a revolution as many underground artists made their way to the surface. And groups like Massive Attack and Public Enemy surged in popularity.

Megaplex movie theaters were born, some boasting as many as 24 screens under one roof. Music stations diversified into niche markets, as they specialized their programming rather than playing a mix, and this trend gave rise to country music stations, rock stations, dance stations, jazz stations, and talk-back stations. Andrew Lloyd Webber continued his domination of the theater with his outstanding productions, such as *Sunset Boulevard*.

Facts of the Nineties

Seinfeld, a realistic television sitcom, was born.

A worldwide financial crisis erupted.

The U.S. federal minimum wage was increased to $5.15 an hour.

The stock market reached an all-time high.

Movies
So what were people watching on all those screens?

- *American Beauty*
- *Braveheart*
- *Dances with Wolves*
- *The English Patient*
- *Schindler's List*
- *Shakespeare in Love*
- *Silence of the Lambs*
- *Titanic*

The 2000s

The 2000s (also the "naughties" or "uh-ohs,") was a decade of turbulence. Globalization, terrorism, global warming, the global financial crisis, and the war on terror are all terms that can be considered synonymous with this decade. National borders became less and less meaningful as global linkages were strengthened and goods, services, technology, culture, and information were transported around the globe.

Some of the worst and most destructive natural disasters also occurred in this decade. Tsunamis, earthquakes, bushfires, cyclones, droughts, and floods all made their impact on the 2000s. On December 26, 2004, the biggest and most destructive tsunami, the 2004 Indian Ocean Tsunami (also known as the Boxing Day Tsunami, the Asian Tsunami, or the Indonesian Tsunami), crashed into coastal areas of Southeast Asia, causing massive damage to human life.

Hurricane Katrina nearly flattened New Orleans in 2005 and killed at the very least 1,836 people. Many people lost their homes, and an estimated $81 billion in damage was caused. On Saturday, February 7, 2009, bushfires tore through the state of Victoria in Australia, killing 173 people, injuring 500 people, and destroying more than 5,000 homes.

On the political scene, the biggest news of the decade was the election of Barack Obama, who became the first African American president in U.S. history.

Of all the decades, the 2000s saw the highest increase in technological innovation and use. There was a huge boost in the number of people with computers in their home, as well as the number of people connected to the Internet and owning mobile phones. Google, iPhone, blogs, and texting were common terms for anyone living within this decade.

Fashion in the 2000s was somewhat varied, combining trends from the forties, fifties, sixties, and eighties. Think skinny-leg jeans, Ugg boots, hoodies, boho, leggings, washed denim, and trucker hats.

The music of the 2000s changed very little from the previous decade. Pop, hip-hop, contemporary R&B, new wave, and alternative rock dominated this decade and gave rise to many big names. Individual artists of the "naughties" include Eminem, who was the highest-selling artist of the decade, Britney Spears, and Beyoncé. Group artists include the Killers, Coldplay, and the Kings of Leon. Perhaps the biggest news in the music industry was the death of Michael Jackson, the King of Pop, in 2009.

The 2000s saw the development of new technologies for film production and screening. Think blockbuster movies with innovative special effects, such as *The Lord of the Rings* and *Pirates of the Caribbean*, or even the 3-D film *Avatar*. In addition, the decade was known for computer-generated animation, as in *Finding Nemo* and *Ice*

Facts of the 2000s

Approximately 2.1 billion people went online worldwide.

The Twin Towers in New York fell under terrorist attack.

The space shuttle *Columbia* exploded on reentry to Earth's atmosphere.

President Barack Obama was elected to office.

Movies
Well-loved movies from this decade include:

- *Avatar*
- *The Dark Knight*
- *Gladiator*
- *Harry Potter* series
- *The Hurt Locker*
- *The Lord of the Rings* trilogy
- *The Matrix*
- *Pirates of the Caribbean* series
- *Shrek*

Age. Documentary films raising awareness of current problems, such as *Bowling for Columbine* and *An Inconvenient Truth*, also became extremely popular.

Video games became all the rage during this decade. Games and game consoles became more interactive and graphics became more realistic. Games included story-lines that were entertaining to play as well as to watch. PlayStation 2 was released in the early 2000s and became the best-selling console of all time. Popular games of this decade included *Grand Theft Auto, World of Warcraft, Call of Duty,* and *Halo.*

I hope you found some inspiration in this section. I've always found that in order to pull off a successful period-themed event, I need to know some of the history and characteristic events as a starting point. Go and do your own research to add to this brief overview. Today, we have the Google search engine to help us gather information about past historical events and do research to help us plan for future special events. Take advantage of the Internet if you wish to discover more details on any particular decade or time.

Burst into Weddings

EVENT PLANNERS TODAY ARE ALWAYS LOOKING FOR NEW streams of income to lift their business, and one sure way to recession-proof your enterprise is to expand into the wedding market. The wedding coordinator was pushed into the limelight after the successes of movies such as *Father of the Bride* and *The Wedding Planner,* and more recently, reality television shows such as *Whose Wedding Is It Anyway?* have also helped the cause.

Not all weddings are on the scale of those depicted in the movies, but the movies certainly helped reinforce people's understanding of just how much has to be done when planning any wedding, whether it be intimate or on a grand scale.

The Wedding Market: An Overview

No matter how you look at it, planning a wedding is like putting together a jigsaw puzzle of mammoth proportions. Add to the mix bundles of nerves, financial stress, arguments, tension, fear, insecurity, and the hopes and dreams of a lifetime, and what you are left with is a many-headed monster with needs, tastes, emotions, egos, and budgetary concerns all pulling in different directions.

This is where the wedding coordinator comes to the rescue. Everyone loves a good wedding, but few people are able to plan one without bloodshed or at least the threat of it. A coordinator can step in and take all the worry off the shoulders of the people who are supposed to be enjoying the event.

It seems that the wedding of today has a tendency to veer into one of the following two directions: a wedding that has a pared-down guest list and higher-quality food, wine, and flowers; or a wedding that sacrifices quality here and there in order to include more guests.

Of course, for every rule there is an exception, and it's true that some weddings do have the budget to allow for the first choice in everything, from guest numbers, choice of venue, and style of wedding to the cost of the bridal fashion selected. But such events are not common these days.

Another fact about today's weddings is that brides and grooms are quite concerned about the details of the wedding and want to be involved at every turn, unlike the old days, when parents did almost everything and made most of the decisions, leaving the happy couple to simply turn up. Another big change from the weddings of yester-year is that brides and grooms are usually the ones footing the bill.

As far as the planner is concerned, a wedding requires just as much attention as the biggest corporate event. On a personal level for the planner, a wedding can be more stressful than other events, as emotions usually run high when you're dealing with an occasion that a couple genuinely hopes will be a once-in-a-lifetime event. With that in mind, they're not just looking to have a wedding—they're looking to have a day so special that it will lay down romantic memories they will cherish over a lifetime.

One of the tricky things with weddings is that invariably the couple wants "something different." They want something that others haven't had; they want their event to stand out, to be the best. In this day and age, that request is becoming increasingly more common, and ever more difficult to fulfill.

This is the ultimate challenge for the coordinator. For some pointers on how to achieve this outcome, see page 207, where traditions from other cultures are outlined. These traditions can give you ideas to incorporate during special moments on the day of the wedding, or even provide an inspiration for the whole wedding concept.

Today's brides and grooms are tech-savvy and often request that you incorporate (or welcome your suggestions for) a number of state-of-the art technological elements on their wedding day, such as extravagant lighting, sound, visual effects, or special effects.

For the couples who insist on something even more special, it is always necessary to keep in mind (and to remind the couple) that custom work to individualize a wedding requires a bigger budget. There is no doubt that every client wants a customized wedding, but not every client can afford it. As cold-hearted as it sounds, you are in the business for reasons that are twofold: Yes, you want to make the bride's dreams come true. Who wouldn't? But you also have to make money. You have a business to support and staff to pay. You have responsibilities. So, while it is your job to try to fulfill the couple's requests within their budget, there will be times when it simply can't be done.

This is the tough part, and finding the balance between keeping the couple happy and satisfied and still making a profit is the key to success for the wedding coordinator.

The table setting generally calls for lots of discussion. Keep in mind that luxurious linens and chair covers are a must for a wedding, whether it be a mega-wedding or a small, intimate affair. It's wise for the coordinator to create two prototype styles and layouts for viewing. The goal is for the client to make solid choices from these prototypes from the samples that would be shown. Once the style is selected, it can be costed accurately.

The food service can be styled in a creative way, and often a very upscale buffet can surpass the basic sit-down, three-course meal. The consideration here is that a buffet table is a more affordable option, but guests would almost always prefer to sit down and converse comfortably.

The couples of today are willing to accept nontraditional menus and ways of serving food. One way to introduce a creative menu in a nontraditional manner is to stage food stations around the ballroom or tent (marquee), with each station boasting a different variety of food. This setup adds a buzz and brings a sophisticated flair to the event.

Within the tent, conversational areas can be created by bringing in rental lounges, so that guests have a place to converse with one another in a more cozy and relaxed atmosphere.

Extend Your Business to Attract the Wedding Market

One of the great things about weddings is that we'll never run out of them. As long as there are people, there will be weddings. Like funerals, they are something we can count on—it's a natural instinct, propelled by tradition, for two people to want to join forces and set up a life together. And more often than not, at least one of these two people is going to want a wedding. The business is there—you just have to attract it to your company.

Five Steps to Becoming a Wedding Coordinator

1. *Create a Wedding-Friendly Office Environment*

   One of the first things you must do is look at your place of business. Ideally, if space permits, allocate an area or separate office specifically for meetings and planning pertaining to weddings. Meetings with the bride and groom, parents, or bridesmaids will be necessary, and if they can visit you in your studio, you will find that it facilitates the closing of the sale. Each bride and groom must feel like they are your most important client. When you meet with them, they do not want to be disturbed by staff coming to you with questions, by a phone that rings continuously, or by any distracting business problems that you need to handle. The wedding market is very competitive and these clients require very special attention and care.

The area needs to be quiet and free from disruptions and the usual clatter of your employees preparing for another event. It also needs to be a phone-free zone. Your employees should understand that when there is a meeting taking place in this room, there are to be no interruptions.

Lighting: A Case Study

The following information has been provided courtesy of Jeremy Koch, lighting designer and director of Innovative Production Services in Botany, Sydney.

"A wedding is a very special day for two people. Everything has to be just right, from the food and wine to the entertainment and décor. It's all part of creating an atmosphere that will be etched in the memories of all that attend that very special event. This atmosphere relies heavily on the very important component of lighting. It can transform a cold sterile room into a friendly environment and give life to an otherwise plain room.

Lena came to me with the brief description of a wedding for a high-profile client to be held at a beautiful venue, Doltone House in Sydney. The wedding was to be sophisticated and elegant—in simple terms: absolutely beautiful. Fortunately, the bride was a big fan of spectacular florals, and Lena is a big fan of lighting. At the venue site inspection, we discovered that the venue included a vast pillar-free space, featured beautiful wooden beams throughout, and had workable wall and carpet colors.

I knew Lena's flowers would be a standout and that her exciting design concept would bring a new layer and dimension to this occasion. The lighting had to be nothing short of spectacular. For the floral designs, Lena had the following vision: The two-part design would consist of ceiling pieces and tabletops. Large circular wreaths of roses would be suspended above the center of each table above the guests' heads, and lush rose-based designs placed on the tables themselves would repeat the circular shape; their heights would be 12 inches or less, so as not to interfere visually with conversation across the table.

We faced the following technical challenges regarding the ceiling elements:

1. Hanging the flower pieces with pinpoint accuracy over the center of each table

2. Designing the equipment to hold the 30-odd pieces

3. Avoiding any unsightly rigging

4. Lighting the suspended pieces and the room itself

The wedding meeting room should also ideally be furnished tastefully and should boast shelving showcasing some of your wedding designs and ideas.

The family members may not all be in attendance at the same time at these meetings, but at one time or another, it is inevitable that they will become part of these meetings. Planning a wedding does involve family on both the bride and groom's sides; in fact, you could find yourself dealing with a whole group of people who all envision the finished product in a different light, which is one way that weddings differ from corporate events. A corporate client may have a committee of several people involved in organizing an event at hand, but these people tend to have a unified vision that they have agreed upon before consulting with the event planner. Remember: if they like you, they will buy from you.

5. Obtaining a formal approval from the venue's engineer to complete the ceiling work

The first thing that came to mind as a solution was using a truss grid throughout the ceiling space. Normally, in a venue like this, a standard truss won't work due to legal rigging restrictions in the building, but we designed a small and lightweight truss and suspended it above the heads of the guests. It was a multipiece construction and we erected it bit by bit. Importantly, we managed to avoid the ugly look of motors or chain blocks. We were able to achieve the goal of using technical equipment in a way that would give the ceiling an extremely clean look.

In terms of lighting, I decided to 'top light' the ceiling flowers for additional visual effect using chrome PAR 56 fixtures, which could be mounted on the truss at the desired angle due to their lightness. This solution allowed me to get the angles of light projection just right so that the light not only put a beautiful glow on the arrangement but also spilled through the center of the ceiling wreath onto the tabletop itself for effect.

Again, by having infinite rigging locations for the purposes required, a minimal number of fixtures could be used. However, we added special lights to highlight the bridal table, cake table, and other room features, and, surprisingly, the ceiling rigging became almost imperceptible as all cables were taped and perfectly matched in color. We also introduced intelligent lighting with small, moving mirror lights providing other design effects, and we had additional lighting movement for the dancing later in the evening.

The color of the lighting was critical. The lighting needed to exude elegance and style, so we chose the dark pink shade of Lee 111 coupled with PAR 56 lamps. The effect proved to be subtle, not overpowering. The lighting added warmth, complementing the chocolate tones of the interior.

In the end, the engineer approved the setup, Lena thought we met the expectations, and, most important, the bride, groom, and their families were absolutely enthralled. See color plates, Figure 36, to see the end result of our work."

Never forget that while the wedding of the two people in front of you may represent the 100th wedding you've planned, for them it is their first together and what they hope will be their last. They need to know they have your complete attention, and that their wedding is the most important one you've ever done. And it will be because it is the one you are planning at that moment.

2. *Create a Wedding Library*

You will require a collection of bridal books and the most current bridal magazines. Invest heavily in this area. Buy books on wedding etiquette, church and reception décor, wedding cakes, bridal sprays, and floral accessories. See Select Resources (page 223) for the books I recommend on this topic.

3. *Become Educated*

Acquaint yourself with the different cultural aspects of wedding traditions (see page 207). Don't limit yourself to just one narrow niche; become known as the wedding planner who has all the answers. The client and the client's entourage will look to you for guidance. You need to know the etiquette of every aspect of weddings and all the celebrations that precede and follow them.

You need to be educated and up-to-date on the latest trends and fashions. You can't bluff your way through; you must know what you're talking about. Informed answers will immediately instill a sense of confidence in your clients, and that will be half the battle.

4. *Create a Wedding Design Team*

The next step is to develop the team you wish to use for weddings. You will require the following specialized service providers to partner with:

(a) Photographer

(b) Travel and limousine service

(c) Wedding cake specialist

(d) Floral designer

(e) Caterer for off-site locations

(f) Rental company for off-site venues

(g) Balloon specialist, if requested

(h) Lighting designer

(i) Sound specialist

(j) Video specialist

(k) Table linen suppliers

In addition, you will need a list of various performers and musicians you can suggest to the couple. Also, quite often, some couples, especially for very formal weddings, may wish to employ a professional master of ceremonies (MC), so be prepared with a list of suitable candidates.

You may have some of these experts working within your own establishment; otherwise, source and select partners who are totally reliable and committed to excellence. It is imperative that you choose people who take pride in the services and products they supply. If one of them isn't professional, it will reflect poorly on you. Make your choices carefully.

Before making any bookings, take the time to review the products of different contractors you are considering. You will need those that specialize in rentals of tents (marquees), tables, chairs, and luxury linens. The vendors you selected as good candidates will supply you with a collection of photos that you can refer to during your meetings with the client. Remember: when the future bride, groom, and parents visit you, they want to see, they want to touch.

5. *Create Exposure: Be Seen, Be Heard*

Your company needs to be seen. You may have made yourself the best, but unless people know you exist, it really doesn't matter.

Exposure can be achieved through advertisements of your services in bridal magazines or your local newspaper. And don't forget to invest time into marketing your company on the Web. An initial financial outlay is necessary if you wish to extend into the wedding revenue stream.

Remember that since weddings are booked at least six months in advance, often much longer, you can't expect to start building a reputation overnight. Once your bookings start, it can take another 12 months for a momentum to gather and for people to start talking about you.

There is another good method of creating exposure that is less expensive and will pay off. Review local and surrounding newspapers and find the engagement section of the papers. Record the names and addresses of the couples and send them a card of congratulations, enclosing your promotional materials and an invitation to visit your showroom or office. Let these potential clients know that on presenting the invitation at your studio, they will receive a complimentary bottle of champagne.

Bridal exhibitions are a great idea to bring instant exposure to a wedding planner. They require a special setup: The table should be positioned with one chair for you and two or three chairs on the opposite side of the desk for meeting with a couple. Additional staff must be available on the premises to field general inquiries while you are immersed with one couple at a time. You need to be able to focus on the couple and not worry about others waiting. I always display a beautiful bowl of fresh flowers centrally, as well

Black-and-White Wedding: A Case Study

The following case study has been provided courtesy of Sean DeFreitas of Designs by Sean, a company based in Dania, Florida.

"For this one-of-a-kind wedding, the bride and groom wanted a romantic and sophisticated theme. We decided on black and white, with the slightest accents of green, as the event colors, and the couple instantly fell in love with a black silk fabric that featured white ivy-patterned embroidery accents. This pattern became the foundation for the entire event concept. Phalaenopsis orchids, favorites of the bride, were used in abundance throughout the room, cascading from glass urns on the place card table and within a custom-created white-wood bar.

The room where the ceremony took place featured a billowing, white drape around the perimeter of the room, which was illuminated by soft white light. The couple exchanged vows underneath an arbor of white branches and white orchids, roses, and hydrangeas. A crystal chandelier suspended overhead provided romantic light for the area.

To create a blank palette for the décor, we carpeted over the existing hotel floral-butterfly-motif carpet-

ing and installed crisp white carpeting throughout the ballrooms and the cocktail reception room. The cocktail reception area was made to look chic, contemporary, and sleek. Here, we also used a 6-foot-wide black carpet border.

The ballroom was a magical setting for dinner. The walls were concealed by white drapery that gathered elegantly and, up-lit by soft light that filtered through the material, created a striking effect along the walls. At the center of the room, an elaborate seafood buffet was set up atop carved-ice-filled towers and trays. An impressive ice urn overflowed with more phalaenopsis orchids.

A main stage was set at the front of the room and showcased elaborate urns with blossoming branches and white florals. In front of the stage, a custom dance floor was placed, designed in white with a black-ivy border to complement the dining table linens.

Two different dining table designs were incorporated into the room. The first design featured rectangular tables covered in the signature black-silk linens with white ivy-patterned embroidery accents. At the center of each table, white trees were adorned as books, photos, and wedding accessories, such as headpieces, garters, and lace handkerchiefs. This marketing method is simple to arrange but smart in appearance, and it usually works. It gives you the opportunity to obtain for follow-up the names, addresses, and contact information of couples who are in the market for a wedding coordinator.

Pre-plan Meetings with Clients

When clients come to the first meeting with the wedding coordinator, it is important to record their contact information, gather basic information about the event, and

vith flowers, crystals, and hanging candles. Along he length of the tables, crystal candlesticks, votive andles, and crystal stands surrounded by orchids nd roses completed the look.

The second table design featured square tables ith an opening in the center to permit placement of enterpieces inside the tables. Lucite tops were placed ver the cutouts to create a seamless look on the table urfaces. These tables were covered in custom white lk table linens with black ivy-patterned embroidery ccents. The centerpieces began "inside" the tables as n arrangement of white florals, which created a stun- ing visual effect beneath the Lucite tops. Tall glass essels extended above the tables and were filled with ascading white orchids and crystals. Crystal candle- ticks provided ambient candlelight to the tabletops.

Entertainment was provided by a pianist at a black rand piano, and guests had the opportunity to relax n sleek white leather lounge furniture set throughout ne space.

Just when guests thought the night was coming • an end, we revealed a surprise: an after-party in a ortion of the ballroom that was previously concealed by a wall of drape. As the drape parted and the after-party lighting illuminated the space, the DJ began spinning and guests flocked onto a custom zebra-print dance floor. To access this area, guests passed through an entrance flanked by two 6-foot-tall shimmering crystal chandeliers. Inside the after-party area, gray carpeting covered the floor, and the perimeter of the room was draped in gray flowing fabric, creating the perfect palette for elaborate lighting designs in purple and pink tones. Groupings of white sofas and chairs mixed with cool accent tables were set around the room, and 16-foot-long, bar-height metal tables with cool black-and-white acrylic stools provided addi- tional seating.

Guests partied until past 3 a.m., not wanting the amazing night to come to an end. It was a night filled with romance, elegance, and sophistication with a touch of drama and surprise that the guests will not forget soon."

For photos from this spectacular event, see color plates, Figures 38 and 39.

interview them on their vision for the various components of their wedding. The following templates will help you gather the information you require to proceed with organization.

Remember that before the wedding coordinator can really begin work, the following items must be established:

- Reception and church venues

- Guest count, as close to final as possible

- Proposed event date and whether there is flexibility with it

- Client's wedding budget

The Client Information Sheet: A Template

Basic Event Information

Type of Information	Notes
Client name:	
Client contact details:	
Event date:	
Number of guests:	
Style of wedding:	
Church or ceremony contact:	
Church or ceremony address:	
Church or ceremony phone:	
Reception venue contact:	
Reception venue address:	
Reception venue phone:	
Bride contact:	
Bride's mother contact:	
Groom contact:	
Other contacts:	

The Client's Requirements Sheet: A Sample

The document below can be used by the wedding coordinator early in the planning process to ascertain the client's requirements and needs. It will allow for an initial cost projection and is subject to revisions. The next step is meeting with the client again to discuss the budget. At this stage, the client will either accept the projected budget—in which case a more detailed proposal can be created—or not, in which case a discussion must take place as to what can be achieved within the client's budget.

1. Home Décor	4 arrangements
2. Church	2 pedestals outside doors
	2 pedestals inside doors
	70 church pews
	4 large altar arrangements
	Petal aisle carpet
	1 large arrangement on signing table
3. Venue Pre-function	2 huge urns at the doors
4. Ballroom Décor	30 centerpieces for tables
	30-foot bridal design with flowers
	30-foot floral skirt
	Handrail decorated with fabrics and flowers
	6 fresh trees or foliage
	50 sets small white fairy lights
	10 topiary trees
	200 yards fabric swagging
5. Stage Dressing and Wall Drapes	Blackout required for the four walls of the venue, which includes back of stage
6. Table Linens	30 square floor-length tablecloths for guest tables
	30 square sheer overlay cloths
	300 napkins to buy or rent
	1 additional long rectangular cloth to cover the bridal table
	300 chair covers and trims
7. Centerpieces	20 candelabras with flowers
	10 glass vases with flowers
8. Cake Table / Gift Table	Tablecloths required *(continued)*

9.	**Bridal Bouquet**	Bouquet(s) for bride to be styled
10.	**Wedding Party Bouquets**	3 florals for bridesmaids to be styled
11.	**Light, Sound, and Special Effects**	24 small white fairy light chandelier drops
		Light color change at dance time
		Target lighting
		Lighting style to be designed
12.	**Communications**	Radio headsets for team; number required
13.	**Accommodations**	Number if required for guests
14.	**Breakout Rooms**	Number if required
15.	**Crew Meals**	The number of crew members and the menu
16.	**Piano**	Rental required
17.	**Bridal Cars**	To be dressed

Allow me to reiterate the importance of this document:

1. It clearly lists every element required for the event, and therefore nothing will be missed when preparing the budget.

2. It includes all the products and materials that will be needed for the job.

3. It specifies the requirements for the team involved in putting the event together.

Wedding Customs and Traditions in Various Cultures

Just as contemporary culture takes much of its food, furnishings, and flavor from other cultures, many couples now look to other cultures for inspiration when the time comes to plan their wedding. For the event planner, marriage traditions around the world are a rich vein of creativity that will add novelty and spark to any wedding.

Use the following examples of wedding traditions as a departure point for adding color and intrigue to your concept. Many modern brides and grooms in Western societies might have their roots in various cultures, yet they might not be aware of the long-standing traditions that their grandparents or great-grandparents may have observed at their own weddings. Couples often embrace some of these historic features as a way of showing their respect for the enduring meaning of the wedding ceremony as a pivotal event in society and in their lives.

A common feature of weddings throughout the world is the notion of celebration. After the wedding vows and rings are exchanged, it's time to party. Dancing, singing, loud music, and, of course, great food are all high on the agenda.

North American

- The couple commonly write their own wedding vows, in words that express a meaningful declaration of their mutual love and respect.

- An aspiring groom often asks the father of the bride to consent to the marriage as a sign of respect and to receive a confirmation of the bride's family's acceptance of his intentions.

- The wedding ceremony can be an extravagant affair, especially for affluent couples who wed under the social spotlight. More traditional home weddings are also common and can be just as much fun and just as special.

- Rice is tossed at the newlyweds as they leave the marriage ceremony as a symbol of fertility.

- During the reception, the groom removes his new wife's garter and tosses it to the bachelors, while the bride tosses her bouquet to the unmarried women. Custom says that whoever catches either will be the next to marry.

- A couple might express their preference for gifts at a department store's bridal registry, enabling guests to choose items without fear of duplicates or of offering something unsuitable.

- Most wedding ceremonies have a religious setting, often with a matron of honor, bridesmaids, a best man, groomsmen, flower girls, pageboys or a ring bearer, ushers to seat guests, music, photographers, and a video technician.

Spanish and Mexican

- Orange blossoms, symbolizing happiness and fulfillment, are a feature of the Spanish wedding and are often used in bouquets, wreathes, or tiaras.

- In both Spain and Mexico, the groom presents 13 coins to his bride in a special bag, box, or tray, as a token of his enduring love. The coins are blessed by the priest during the ceremony and kept as part of the family's heritage.

- At a Mexican wedding reception, guests form a heart shape around the wedding couple as they take to the floor for their first dance as husband and wife.

- A candy-filled papier-mâché piñata, often heart shaped, provides fun for the children at a Mexican wedding, who take turns swinging at it with a stick until it breaks, showering them with candy.

Jewish

- Traditional Jewish couples sign a marriage contract called the *ketubah*, which pledges the two people to each other legally for long-term support and commitment, both financially and emotionally. This agreement also outlines the expectations and the duties of each within the marriage framework.

- The rabbi, groom, groomsmen, and male guests wear white yarmulkes.

- The wedding ring is a simple band, neither engraved nor decorated.

- On the wedding day, both sets of parents escort the bride and groom, respectively, down the aisle.

- The ceremony is held inside the synagogue under a specially built canopy called a chuppah, which symbolizes the home that the couple will build together, God's attendance, safe haven, and protection.

- After exchanging the vows, seven marriage blessings are read out by the rabbi. The couple exchange wedding rings and circle together around the canopy. The couple is then offered a glass of wine. The newlyweds are left alone immediately after the ceremony, so they can have an opportunity to appreciate each other.

- Jewish traditional wedding celebrations are happy occasions with a focus on traditional dance, music, and songs. A dance called the hora is a major component of the celebrations, when the bride and groom are hoisted on chairs and proclaimed the king and queen of the night.

Indian

- The bride and groom do not see each other for several days before the wedding.

- As part of the marriage ceremony, the bride's parents wash the couple's feet with milk and water as a purifying ritual.

- On the evening before the wedding, the bride's hands and feet are painted with henna, in paisley or medallion patterns.

- An Indian groom arrives at the wedding ceremony on a white horse accompanied by a uniformed band. He wears a turban with a veil of flowers streaming down in front of his face to protect him from evil.

- Indian brides traditionally wear pink or red saris on their wedding day, and as much jewelry as possible.

- Marigold flowers are used in abundance as décor and strung together in garlands.

- During the ceremony, the couple hold grains of rice, oats, and green leaves in their hands, which signify wealth, good health, and happiness.

- Sweets, eggs, and money play symbolic roles in every Indian wedding ceremony.

- After the wedding vows, the groom's father or brother showers flower petals on the newlyweds. He then holds a coconut over the bride and groom's heads and circles it around them three times for good luck.

Japanese

- Wedding ceremonies are traditionally held at Shinto shrines.

- Japanese grooms wear black kimonos to their wedding ceremony.

- The tradition-minded Japanese bride wears a white silk kimono embroidered with purple iris.

- The Japanese bride's face is painted pure white on her wedding day to proclaim her maiden status. As well as a white kimono, she wears an elaborate headpiece covered with ornaments to ensure good luck.

A Grand Long Island Wedding: A Case Study

The following case study has been provided courtesy of Tim Lundy, CSEP, of Distinctive Design Events, a company based in Atlanta, Georgia.

"The bride, raised in the South and living in New York City, wanted her wedding to be a fun destination experience where her guests could experience the flavor of New York City. Her mother envisioned an elegantly detailed affair held in a unique, grand setting.

Three main objectives drove the event's production and design:

1. Orchestrate a destination weekend in New York City for 200-plus guests, providing round-trip transportation from the city to Long Island for the wedding for all.

   - Reserve accommodations at four hotels around Grand Central Station.

   - Provide save-the-date cards with hotel and activities information and a weekend itinerary.

2. As for the theme, combine the grandeur of a French château–style venue with subtle Gatsby-esque influences of the 1920s era and a touch of Southern tradition.

   - Use florals representative of the 1920s and the American South.

   - Create a "jazz and cigar" after-party.

   - Pay attention to elegant details in the choices of china, crystal, table linens, and so on.

3. Create a memorable experience for the guests, incorporating the fun, whimsical personalities of the couple with good food, exquisite décor, and spectacular lighting.

   - The bride and groom will initiate the wedding party as they dance through a stroll line.

   - Provide a martini bar for the after-party.

Oheka Castle, built in 1919, was the scene of lavish parties indicative of the opulence of the 1920s and was chosen as the wedding venue. We decided on a subtle Gatsby theme to fit both the site and the vibrant personalities of the couple.

On a gilded table in the grand foyer we placed a stunning arrangement of live phalaenopsis orchids wrapped in fresh creek moss sitting atop wheatgrass. The arrangement was flanked by live English thyme, rosemary, and tarragon plants placed in old, weathered terra-cotta pots. Silver trumpet vases filled with fresh PG hydrangeas, sedums, and green cymbidium orchids finished the botanical design for this greeting table.

Upon arrival at Oheka, the guests were offered champagne and directed to the formal garden with reflecting ponds adorned with boxwood, where the

- After drinking nine tiny cups of sake, the couple is considered to be joined. The families of the bride and groom also drink sake, and the fathers introduce other family members to guests. For the wedding reception, the bride changes into a red kimono, and later she may change into a Western dress. The reception features games and karaoke, and wedding guests may offer cash in sealed and decorated envelopes.

ceremony was to take place in the evening. Lush foliage garlands swagged the center aisle leading to a wrought-iron, domed arbor decorated with cascading vines of hops, ivy, green orchids, and green anthuriums. Two large floral bouquets graced the entrance to the seating area.

The bridesmaids carried bouquets of green cymbidiums, dendrobiums, Kyoto roses, Fuji mums, lisianthus, hypericums, and herbs in monochromatic shades of green. The florals added a pop of fresh color to the attendants' cocoa brown gowns. The mothers carried cattleya orchids on stems wrapped in fabric ribbon.

Each dinner table represented either a phrase or a person from the 1920s, such as "Bee's Knees," "Jeepers Creepers," "Al Capone," and others. The couple wrote individual descriptions for every table, creating another element of fun and interest.

Nineteenth century–styled silver epergnes overflowed with lush arrangements of lilies, roses, orchids, berries, and French stock, with pavé florals at the base of the flower trumpets. Other elements of décor included mirrored balls, sparkling ornaments, crystal votive holders, and glass containers of alabaster-white pillar candles. The tables were set with Vanessa gold china, Dublin Irish crystal water glasses, Vino Noble lead crystal wine goblets, and Manhattan silver flatware for that genuine, opulent Gatsby-esque look.

Bugle bead–encrusted chocolate organza overlays were draped over ivory damask linens. The menus were inserted into folded hemstitched napkins made of white Irish linen and the place card was an added accent. The cake table was covered with delicate linen made of ivory damask fabric embroidered with silver beads and threads.

Since the entrées were ordered tableside, the bride and groom shared with guests their personal opinions of the food selections by providing menu review cards. For the cover of these cards, our graphic artist created stylized renderings, printed in sepia tones. Entrée options included miso-glazed Chilean sea bass, American lamb chops, and pan-seared chicken breast. There was also a dessert bar and wedding cake adorned with hand-formed gum paste orchids.

At midnight, guests were invited to a "jazz and cigar" party in the library, complete with a martini bar and more food. A matchbook-style booklet featured the names of martinis being served and a recipe for the couple's favorite chocolate martini (which we named "The Great Barge-tini").

Advance site visits to Long Island gave us, the event planners, the opportunity to complete a SWOT analysis on challenges and risk-management issues. This step allowed us to anticipate problems and create solutions so that no guest would suffer on the day of the event. The clients were thrilled with the end result, and future repeat business was guaranteed."

Chinese

- A gift of a whole roasted pig is presented by the groom's family to the bride's family.

- The traditional wedding gown is bright red, a symbol of good luck.

- A formal bridal gown might be embroidered with chrysanthemums, peonies, and golden phoenixes, symbols of wealth and good fortune.

- The groom might wear a black silk coat worn over a robe embroidered with a dragon.

- Firecrackers ward off evil spirits

The wedding traditions of other cultures are a fascinating subject, with a wealth of variations that can help to elevate any wedding with special, individual touches that make it memorable for all. One constant is the exchange of rings at the conclusion of the ceremony. The ring is a perfect symbol for what a wedding means—a perfect, solid circle with neither beginning nor end, symbolizing enduring love.

This is what weddings are about, and if you adopt a healthy attitude to service and a professional approach to the actual event, you will orchestrate a special day for the bride, groom, and their families and friends.

Appendix:
Understanding Our Clients and
Staff Better: *Four Behavioral Styles*

The following information has been supplied courtesy of Trevor O'Sullivan, general manager of DTS International, Darlinghurst, Australia, who specializes in sourcing and applying human performance technology that helps businesses select, develop, and manage people more effectively.

Managing relationships is a necessary and vital skill in the extremely people-oriented events field. Working with people of different backgrounds and personalities, with diverse strengths and weaknesses, can be challenging and complex. Learning to adapt your behavioral style to the personalities around you can be a lifesaver.

The model of human behavior known as DISC, which stands for dominance, influence, steadiness, and compliance, is a tool for identifying and effectively handling different types of people. The purpose of this tool is to make the behavioral adaptation process we go through naturally when working and interacting with others happen faster, with more fluidity, and with less guesswork, leading to increased communication, better rapport, mutual trust, and better cooperation.

The DISC model is simple and easy to learn. It examines solely a person's behavioral style, that is, a person's way of doing things, also described as someone's communication style. One person you meet might be talkative, sociable, and loud, while the next might be quiet, shy, and methodical. These behavioral quirks can make clicking with someone similar to you feel like a breeze, but for people who are not similar to you, communication can be tricky, challenging, and even exhausting at times.

Even though we are all infinitely diverse in our mix of intelligence, talent, values, beliefs, and life experience, in terms of behavior, there are four common patterns that are universally shared. These four "styles" have become known as the DISC model of human behavior.

At a glance, the DISC acronym stands for the following four behavioral characteristics:

Dominance:	How you approach problems and challenges
Influence:	How you interact with and attempt to influence people
Steadiness:	How you respond to the pace of the environment
Compliance:	How you respond to rules and regulations set by others

All people exhibit some behavior in each dimension; however, most people naturally prefer just one or two over the others. This preference is typically established at a very young age and will usually remain consistent throughout the course of life. Some people, for instance, have a strong natural preference in the D dimension and will tend to exhibit behavior that is direct, decisive, and assertive. Other people have a strong natural preference in the S dimension (the opposite of D) and will tend to be more reserved, indirect, and passive. Ds and Ss live in completely different "communication universes" and are galaxies apart in terms of how you should go about interacting with them.

Think of it like landing on a planet on which there live only four native tribes, each with a distinctly separate language and acceptable customs. But doing a particular thing that is celebrated in the D land may be perceived as a criminal act in the S land. Only by spending time with each of the tribes, carefully observing them, and then taking steps to act in a similar way, will you be embraced by the people of each tribe as one of their own.

It may sound simplistic at first, but it has been proven that adapting one's behavior to suit another's primary style will dramatically enhance the ability to communicate with them.

To reveal exactly why this is the case, let us consider the four styles and what they mean in more detail. As we go, try to think about which style sounds most like you, as well as which is least like you. Understanding your own style is the first, crucial step toward becoming a more effective relationship builder.

Dominance

The higher a person scores on the dominance scale, the more determined and aggressive that person is in responding to challenges.

Words descriptive of the D style include

Driving	Forceful
Competitive	Independent
Ambitious	Determined

Decisive	Stubborn
Pioneering	Aggressive
Strong willed	Goal oriented

People high on the D scale are chiefly concerned with getting results. They love to win and hate to lose. They prefer giving orders as opposed to taking them. They can be very frank and direct in expressing themselves and sometimes might be overly blunt or bossy. Ds are very good at getting the job done, but might rub people the wrong way by putting action before diplomacy. They like to attack life head-on, make prompt decisions, and get things done sooner rather than later. Their motto is "shoot first, ask questions later." Ds have a tendency to be impatient with anything that dithers too slowly or holds up the decision-making process. They are prone to losing their temper if they are impeded and cannot get the results they want quickly.

Obviously, having some high Ds around is a very good thing. On the other hand, having all Ds might lead to conflict: too many chiefs and not enough Indians.

Influence

The influence scale measures the way in which a person tries to influence and persuade others. People who measure high on the I scale tend to influence others by verbal skills and warmth.

Words descriptive of the I style include

Talkative	Persuasive
Demonstrative	Polished
Magnetic	Trusting
Enthusiastic	Sociable
Optimistic	Friendly

Bright, bubbly, sunny, and optimistic, Is love meeting new people and tend to have and make many friends wherever they go. They want to draw people into their world, share their stories, and express their thoughts to them on a wide range of topics.

Unlike Ds, they usually prefer to engage in small talk before getting straight to business. They get into long discussions about what they did in their personal and professional life. They are quick to trust and desire lots of quality social time.

For Is, people are at the center of the world, and for this reason they are naturally inclined toward work that involves networking, sales, and promotion. However, don't expect them to sit for hours and attend to highly detailed work. Like a grasshopper, they won't be in one place for very long.

They have many interests that attract their attention but often lack the time to devote to these pursuits. A room full of Is will have a wonderful time, but if they're not careful, they may not accomplish very much.

Steadiness

The steadiness score measures the capacity to adapt to changes in the environment. People high on the S scale dislike quick or sudden changes.

Words descriptive of the S style are

Patient	Deliberate
Passive	Stable
Predictable	Loyal
Consistent	Relaxed
Reliable	Dependable
Steady	Modest

S is the most commonly found style. Ss are the ones who make the world go round. Unlike the Is, who may be described as the show horses, Ss are the plow horses. They are the foot soldiers of the working army. They follow orders, but might be hesitant to stand up and voice their opinions, particularly if doing so will rock the boat.

Although Ss are less open and trusting than Is, once they develop relationships, they are reluctant to part with them. Ss are very loyal and tend to stay with the same business or circulate with the same people for a long time, unless they feel that they have been abused or betrayed.

Ss do not become as restless or bored with routine work as do Ds and Is. They can be counted on to show up for work, and when there, they will work at a steady pace all day. On the other hand, they are less assertive, which may, at times, prevent them from getting what they want.

Compliance

This style is characterized by the desire for order, precision, and accuracy. Cs prefer to follow rules and procedures rather than part with them.

People high on the C scale may be described as

Worrisome	Neat
Careful	Systematic
Dependent	Conservative
Cautious	Precise
Conventional	Perfectionistic
Exacting	

Cs are content to do routine or procedural work. They will generally do so with a strong desire for accuracy and precision. They are rule followers rather than rule breakers and prefer to accept authority rather than rebel against it. They prefer taking orders to giving orders, but they are quite sensitive and do not respond well to confrontation or criticism of their work.

You can identify Cs by their insistence on taking time over decisions: they get as much information as possible beforehand, carefully weigh the advantages and disadvantages, and limit the risk as far as possible before making up their minds.

Their innate love of precision means they are often accountants, engineers, scientists, or bankers and are found in other occupations where following established procedures in an accurate and exacting manner is desirable.

Working with the Four Behavioral Types

As you read the pointers below, consider how you might use the DISC theory to help you in business relationships. For example, how would you approach a D client versus an S client? Why might your I salespeople have greater difficulty in dealing with C prospects?

If you understand the behavioral styles of your clients, you can give them the treatment and service they expect. If you understand the behavioral styles of your employees, you can give them effective training and avoid putting round pegs in square holes.

Dominance

When you have D types on staff or you recognize the type in some of your clients, remember that Ds have an inherent desire to get results immediately. You will need to pay close attention to managing their temper when things don't go according to plan. Encourage your D employees to become more aware of the impact of their work style, particularly when they are working with those who want to go at a slower pace. It may also be necessary to look at any friction that is caused as a result of their being too direct and forceful when dealing with other team members.

When delegating to Ds, make your instructions short, specific, and to the point. Beware of wasting their time; they won't be impressed by an avalanche of useless details. They don't need to know every fact there is to know about a person, place, product, or situation. Simply try to hone in on the primary objectives for the Ds. You may wish to provide a summary of key points and offer these in bullet-point style, particularly if delegating through e-mail. Clearly express the goal, but provide options and allow them freedom to achieve results in their own way.

When giving Ds a compliment, focus on how that person stands out from the competition. Ds like to stand tall, on their own two feet, and to know that they can surmount any obstacle in their path. They have high ego strength, which means trophies, awards, and impressive titles will be very flattering to them, the bigger the better.

Allow correction to be constructive. Frame the conversation around how the change will make the Ds more efficient. Ds have a tendency to take on too much, too fast, too soon and want to have it all done their way. They wish to fly solo and with the afterburners on maximum. They may need a copilot to show them how delegating some of their workload can lead to better, more efficient results—thus getting them to their target in less time. Put in place systems that will give Ds greater freedom and autonomy in their work but without having to do everything their way.

Ds have an inherent need for control over their environment. Loss of control will cause them stress. However, giving them too much control can mean the Ds will always get their way and only hear what they want to hear. In extreme circumstances, this situation can lead Ds in managerial positions to adopt a dictatorial management style, stifling morale, productivity, and creativity.

Have conversations with Ds geared toward identifying and utilizing the strengths of others on the team. Be confident when putting forth your ideas; Ds will pick up on doubt and uncertainty. Stand firm, but never talk down to Ds. They like to feel they are in charge and will not be made to take orders from anyone if they can help it.

A common way for Ds to relieve stress is physical activity. Provide them with the opportunity to go for a walk or run, go swimming, or work out at the gym. Ds build up steam very quickly so it is important to allow for an appropriate outlet for it (one that doesn't involve the steam coming out their ears!).

Influence

When working with I types, be warm and friendly with them in conversation—avoid being cold or too impersonal.

They like feedback from their managers on how they are doing. It may feel like a feed of "breaking news" bulletins for even mundane events, but it's important to remember that they wish to remain in the loop at all times. When giving them feedback on performance, begin by recognizing aspects of their work that have recently impressed you, before moving straight into areas that need to be developed.

Regular social interaction is important for Is. Their goal is to have and make many friends, so provide opportunities for this, within reason.

When delegating to Is, provide a proven model, or framework, to help them go about the task at hand. Otherwise they may go on instinct and jump in before they are fully prepared and ready. Help Is prioritize tasks in order of importance and urgency, but keep things simple. They are full of energy and their enthusiasm can help

Selling More to the Four Types

Ds Are Looking for
Results

- Be confident. Don't be intimidated.
- Disagree with facts, not with the person.
- Do not be overpowered by them.
- Let them win (you win, too).
- Move faster than normal.
- Come on as strong as they are, but be friendly.
- Close sooner than usual.

Is Are Looking for
"The Experience"

- Allow them to talk, but keep your focus.
- Provide follow-up after the sale.
- Give recognition.
- Listen to their stories.
- Have fun with them.
- "Jump" to close when ready.

Ss Are Looking for
Security

- Give them the facts.
- Provide assurance.
- Be yourself.
- Close when you feel you have their trust.
- Assure them of the right decision.
- Introduce them to managers, service managers, and so on.
- Follow up after the sale.

Cs Are Looking for
More Information

- Answer questions with facts.
- Do not be too personal.
- Be direct and friendly.
- Do not touch.
- Give them their space.
- Do not fear their skeptical nature.
- Follow through with details.
- Give information, then close.

solve problems, but they may need help channeling their focus. They can get into long-winded discussions, so it's important to show them how they can transfer the talk into action.

When giving a compliment to Is, comment on their energy, enthusiasm, and social skills. Offer suggestions that make them look good. Remember their key psychological need is social recognition for their achievements, so you may wish to give praise in the presence of other people (the more, the merrier).

To help Is relive stress, ask how they "feel" about a given solution—they need time to talk about their feelings. Simply speaking out loud can sometimes resolve tension for them or create answers to problems in the process. For this reason, it is important to involve them in open and responsive conversations.

Steadiness

Ss are focused on relationships, so don't rush headlong into business or the agenda with them. Allow them time to get used to changes in people and processes. Don't be abrupt and rapid. Never force change on them or make decisions for them, since they may not say anything when they have objections. As they are not forthcoming with their feelings, you may not always know if you've done something wrong or offensive. You may have seriously hurt their feelings and never know about it. These considerations are particularly useful to keep in mind when you have clients whom you have identified as S types.

When giving Ss who are your employees new tasks, help them learn each step one at a time until they're comfortable. Remember to be persistent and to take your time. The S types will not enjoy a vague, haphazard approach such as "I don't really care what kind of decorations—just think of something." Instead, be sure to keep in mind that Ss need security and a proven model for getting things done. The approach should sound more like: "With the decorations, I'm thinking something modern and vibrant. We had an event last year in Fiji that Jane planned for us, so it would be a good idea to check with her first. She's always very helpful."

A harmonious team environment is important to the Ss, and loss of stability may cause them stress, sometimes even if the change has to do with someone else on the team, because Ss have a tendency to take on other people's problems and distress as their own.

When giving a compliment, be aware that they may not be comfortable in the spotlight. Compliments should be made in private and must be genuine and sincere. The S takes much longer than the I to completely trust others, so it may take more time and effort to work on building the foundation of a relationship with the S.

When giving correction to Ss, don't blame or judge, as they may take it personally. Be mindful of your tone of voice—never shout or yell at them or talk to them when you are extremely angry. Provide reassurance and emphasize what they are doing right. Help them learn how to improve, but always do so in a supportive way.

Sometimes Ss may seem like impenetrable vaults. You must be patient and willing to draw out their feelings: ask questions, wait, and then listen. Allow time to explore their thoughts and show them how changes will make their lives more stable. Remember that Ss need security: do not leave them without backup support; let them know who can help and what to do in case something doesn't go according to plan.

Compliance

To C types, any task is a task to be completed to the best of their ability, so it is important to give them sufficient or even extended time to complete a task. Even if the request is for a "thrown-together draft," it must be understood that a casual approach is not natural for meticulous Cs. They feel that substandard work would be viewed as a reflection on them personally. For this reason, it is especially important when giving Cs feedback to handle it with care, as any criticism of their work may be viewed by them as a personal attack.

When delegating to Cs, provide clear instructions with plenty of detail and with deadlines. Unlike Is, Cs have an inherent need to work within a structure governed by crystal-clear rules and regulations. They will do things by the book, so give them accurate information and logical steps to follow. Allow them to make rational choices based on facts, not opinions or gossip. The C does not like ambiguity or people who do things by approximate measures. If you wish to give Cs a good scare and see their eyes go wide, say to them: "Let's make it up on the fly!"

Cs appreciate having the opportunity for critical thinking and questioning. Critical thinking and skepticism are part of their natural language, and therefore their questions and observations may sound much harsher than intended. For instance, someone who says "It's quite a long distance" might be met by the C with "Well, how far is it? Do you mean 10 minutes or 10 hours?"

When giving a compliment to Cs who are your employees, offer them encouragement about the excellent standards of their work. Talk about the effort and organization that they put in. Try to give them your feedback in a clear, specific, and concise fashion. Remember, even the most intense Cs are not robots. Show genuine appreciation for the quality of their work.

When conveying criticism, keep in mind that the C has a strong fear of being wrong and a tendency to be their own worst critic. Be clear about the issues with the task being discussed. You may wish to include progress reports and deadlines so that Cs are able to avoid making similar errors in the future. Cs will be more relaxed in the presence of those who are willing to spend time investigating all possible options with them to ensure they can make better-quality decisions in the future. They will also appreciate it if you tell them they should not be so hard on themselves all the time.

Select Resources

Books

Bailey, Preston. *Design for Entertaining.* New York: Bulfinch Press, 2003.

Bailey, Preston. *Fantasy Weddings.* New York: Bulfinch Press, 2004.

Bailey, Preston. *Inspirations.* New York: Bulfinch Press, 2006.

Bayer, Patricia. *Art Deco Source Book.* London: Quantum Publishers, 1997.

Blanchard, Ken, and Sheldon Bowles. *Raving Fans.* New York: William Morrow and Co, Inc., 1993.

Boulanger, Norman C., and Warren C. Lounsbury. *Theatre Lighting from A to Z.* Seattle: University of Washington Press, 1992.

Buckingham, M., and C. Coffman. *First Break All the Rules.* London: Pocket Books, 1999.

Cunningham, Glenn. *Stage Lighting Revealed.* OH: Betterway Books, 1993.

Deal, Terrence, and M. K. Key. *Corporate Celebration.* San Francisco: Berrett-Koehler, 1998.

De Bono, Edward. *Serious Creativity.* New York: HarperCollins, 1992.

Goldblatt, Joe Jeff. *The International Dictionary of Event Management.* New York: John Wiley & Sons, 2000.

Goldblatt, Joe Jeff. *Special Events: Global Event Management in the 21st Century,* 3rd ed. New York: John Wiley & Sons, 2002.

Goldblatt, Joe Jeff. *Special Events: The Roots and Wings of Celebration,* 5th ed. New York: John Wiley & Sons, 2007.

Harvey Lawerence. *A Plaza Wedding.* New York: Random House, 1997.

Heute, I. *Ikebana Today.* Germany: Stichting Kunstboek, 2007.

Malouf, Doug. *How to Kiss and Keep Your Customers.* Amazon, 1997.

Malouf, Doug. *Power Up Your People Skills.* Amazon, 1990.

Malouf, Doug. *Selling Is a Cinch.* Amazon, Sydney, Business and Professional Publishing, 1990.

Malouf, Lena. *Behind the Scenes at Special Events: Flowers, Props, and Designs.* New York: John Wiley & Sons, 1999.

Malouf, Lena. *Parties and Special Events: Planning and Design.* Weimar, Texas: Chips Books, 2002.

McGartland, Grace. *Thunderbolt Thinking.* Toronto: Stoddart Publishing Company, 1994.

Michaels, Andrea. *Reflections of a Successful Wallflower.* Parker, Colorado: Outskirts Press, 2010.

Pierce, Heather. *Persuasive Proposals and Presentations: 24 Lessons to Understand and Evaluate Financial Health.* New York: McGraw Hill, 2005.

Price, Catherine H. *The Complete Guide to Professional Meeting and Event Coordination.* Washington, D.C.: George Washington University.

Raoul, Bill. *Stock Scenery Construction Handbook.* New York: Broadway Press, 1990.

Reynolds, Renny. *The Art of the Party.* New York: Viking Penguin, 1992.

Russell-Walling, Edward. *50 Management Ideas You Really Need to Know.* London: Quercus Books, 2007.

Smith, P. *Rules and Tools for Leaders.* New York: Avery Publishing Group, 1974.

Stewart, Martha. *Weddings.* New York: Clarkson N. Potter, 1987.

Turner, Kenneth. *The Floral Decorator.* New York: Weidenfeld and Nicolson, 1993.

Turner, Kenneth. *Kenneth Turner's Flower Style.* New York: Weidenfeld and Nicolson, 1989.

Watson, Linda. *Vogue Fashion: 100 Years of Style by Decade and Designer.* London: Carlton Books, 1999.

Wiersma, Elizabeth, and Kari E. Strolberg. *Exceptional Events: Concept to Completion.* Weimar, Texas: Chips Books, 2006

Winnert, Derek. *The Ultimate Encyclopedia of the Movies.* London: Carlton Books, 1995.

Zenger, John H., Ed Musselwhite, Kathleen Hurson, and Craig Perrin. *Leading Teams.* New York: McGraw-Hill, 1994.

Trade Magazines

BizBash (USA)
bizbash@bizbash.com

Convention and Incentive Marketing
  (Australia)
www.cimmagazine.com

Florists' Review (USA)
www.floristsreview.com

Live Design (USA)
www.livedesignonline.com

Special Events (USA)
www.specialevents.com

Spice (Australia)
www.spicemagazine.com.au

Industry Associations

**American Institute of Floral Designers
  (AIFD)**
720 Light Street
Baltimore, MD 21230
Phone: (410) 752-3318
E-mail: aifd@assnhqtrs.com
www.aifd.org

**International Festivals and Events
  Association**
Phone: (208) 433-0950 ext. 818
E-mail: schmader@ifea.com
www.ifea.com

**International Special Events Society
  (ISES)**
Chicago, IL
Phone: (800) 688-4737 or (312) 321-6853
Fax: (312) 673-6953
E-mail: info@ises.com
www.ises.com

Meeting and Events Australia (MEA)
Level 1, Suites 5 and 6
1 McLaren Street
North Sydney NSW 2060
Australia
Phone: +61 2 9929 5400
Fax: +61 2 9929 5600

E-mail: mea@mea.org.au
www.meetingsevents.com.au

**Meeting Professionals International
  (MPI)**
3030 Lyndon B. Johnson Freeway
Suite 1700
Dallas, TX 75234
Phone: (972) 702-3000
Fax: (972) 702-3070
www.mpiweb.org

**National Association of Catering
  Executives (NACE)**
9891 Broken Land Parkway
Suite 301
Columbia, MD 21046
Phone: (410) 290-5410
Fax: (410) 290-5460
www.nace.net

**Wedding Industry Professionals
  Association (WIPA)**
San Francisco, CA
Phone: (415) 751-0211
E-mail: info@wipausa.org
www.wipausa.org

Industry Contacts

Accent Décor, Inc
Margaret Hofland
Creative Director/Marketing Manager
E-mail: mhofland@accentdecor.com
www.accentdecor.com

Air Dimensional Design, Inc.
Hanna Melzer
Operations/Sales Director
E-mail: hanna@airdd.com
www.aridd.com

Ava Zhan
Book Developmental Editing and
    Copyediting
E-mail: ava.zhan@yahoo.com

BBJ Linen
Bill Pry
Vice President Sales
E-mail: BPry@bbjlinen.com
www.bbjlinen.com

CFP Studio
Craig Ferre
Professional Photographer
www.cfpstudio.com

Cheryl Fish and Associates
Cheryl Fish
Designer/Producer
E-mail: societycheryl@gmail.com
www.cfproposals.com

Designs by Sean
Sean DeFreitas
President
E-mail: sean@designsbysean.com
www.designsbysean.com

Distinctive Design Events
Tim Lundy, CSEP
Designer/Producer
E-mail: Tim@distinctiveevents.com
www.distinctiveevents.com
www.weddingdesign3.com

DTS International
Trevor O'Sullivan
General Manager
E-mail: info@dtssydney.com
www.dtssydney.com

Extraordinary Events
Andrea Michaels
President
E-mail: amichaels@extraordinaryevents.
    net
www.extraordinaryevents.net

Fancy Faces Special Events
Stephen Hamel
Principal
E-mail: shfaces@bellsouth.net
www.fancyfaces.com

Fortune Products, Inc.
Bob Kocher Jr.
President
E-mail: fpi@fortuneproducts.com
www.fortuneproducts.com

Four Seasons Hotel
George Merkouris
Catering Sales Manager
E-mail: george.merkouris@fourseasons.
    com
www.fourseasons.com/sydney

Get It Done!
Laura Ferre
Logistics Coordinator
E-mail: laura.ferre@verizon.net

Innovative Production Services
Jeremy Koch
Chief Executive Officer
E-mail: info@innovative.net.au
www.innovative.net.au

Joe Jeff Goldblatt, FRSA
Professor
Queen Margaret University, Edinburgh
E-mail: info@qmu.ac.uk

Kool Party Rentals
Jack Weiner
Chief Creative Officer
E-mail: jack@koolpartyrentals.com
www.koolpartyrentals.com

Lehman and Associates
Glen Lehman, CSEP
Chief Executive Officer
Special Events
E-mail: glen@lehman.com.au
www.lehman.com.au

Lion/Offray Ribbon
Randy Rice
Dallas Showroom Manager
E-mail: randy.rice@berwickoffray.com
www.lionribbon.com

Malouf Consultancy and Design
Sharon Malouf
Specialty Designer
E-mail: sharon.malouf@gmail.com
www.maloufconsultancy.com.au

The Meetinghouse Companies, Inc.
**Robert Sivek, CSEP, and Deborah
    Borsum, CSEP**
E-mail: info@meetinghouse.com
www.meetinghouse.com

Pages Hire Centre
Stephen Thatcher
Director, Sales and Marketing
E-mail: stephen@pages.id.au
www.pages.id.au

Platform XXIV Pty, Ltd.
Rick Williams
Director
E-mail: rick@platform24.com.au
www.platform24.net

Playbill Venue Management
Greg Pullen
Business Development Manager
E-mail: gregpullen@playbillvenues.com.au
www.playbillvenues.com

Smithers-Oasis Company
Kelly Mace
Marketing Programs/Communications
    Manager
E-mail: kmace@smithersoasis.com
www.oasisgrower.com

Special Events Magazine—Penton Media
Lisa Hurley
Editor
E-mail: lhurley@specialevents.com
www.SpecialEvents.com

The Special Event Trade Show/Conference
Kim Romano
Special Events Manager
E-mail: kim.romano@penton.com
Tara Melingonis
Conference Manager
E-mail: tara.melingonis@penton.com
www.TheSpecialEventShow.com

**Staging Rentals and Construction
    Services**
Meri Took
Chief Executive Officer
E-mail: meri.took@stagingrentals.com.au
www.stagingrentals.com.au

**Sydney Convention and Exhibition
    Centre**
Paul Davison
Audiovisual Services Manager
E-mail: pdavison@scec.com.au
www.scec.com.au

**Sydney Showground / Sydney Olympic
    Park**
Andrew Roberts
Business Development Manager
E-mail: sales@sydneyshowground.com.au
E-mail: enquiries@sopa.nsw.gov.au
www.sydneyshowground.com.au
www.sydneyolympicpark.com.au

Theme Travelers
Tina Sturchio
Chief Executive Officer
E-mail: tsturchio@themetravelers.com
www.themetravelers.com

USA Hosts
Holly Bethay
Director of Special Events
E-mail: holly.bethay@hosts-global.com
www.usahosts.com

Venables Creating Entertainment
Paul Venables
Creative Director
E-mail: wildflower1@hotkey.net.au
www.venablesentertainment.com

VenueCAD Pty. Ltd.
Wayne Elstub
Chief Executive Officer
E-mail: wayne@venue.cad.com
www.venuecad.com

Virgin Farms Inc
Peter Van Antwerpen
Director of Sales and Marketing
E-mail: sales@virginfarms.com
www.virginfarms.com

Wonderment
Andrew Cameron-Smith
Consultant Producer
E-mail: andrew@wonderment.com.au

Lena Malouf Consultancy
Lena Malouf, CSEP, AIFD
For training programs or presentations:
lena@bigpond.net.au

Index

F

G

H

I